PHILIP'S

ROME

ARCHITECTURE · HISTORY · ART

PHILIP'S

ROME

ARCHITECTURE · HISTORY · ART

JAMES BENTLEY

PHOTOGRAPHY BY JOHN HESELTINE

GEORGE PHILIP

The pictures on the following pages are reproduced by kind permission of
Scala, Milan: pp 50, 53, 68, 119, 120, 136, 168, 170, 173, 175.

TITLE PAGE *Looking down the
Spanish Steps from the Trinità
dei Monti, the Keats–Shelley
Museum appears on the left, and
the baroque dome of San Carlo
al Corso in the distance.*

First published by George Philip Limited,
59 Grosvenor Street, London W1X 9DA

Text © James Bentley 1991
Photographs © John Heseltine 1991
Maps © George Philip Limited 1991

British Library Cataloguing in Publication Data

Bentley, James *1937*—
  Rome.
  1. Rome (Italy)
  I. Title
  914.563204929

ISBN 0-540-01243-2

Maps John Gilkes
Page design Gwyn Lewis

Typeset by Keyspools Limited, Golborne, Lancashire
Printed in Hong Kong

Contents

....

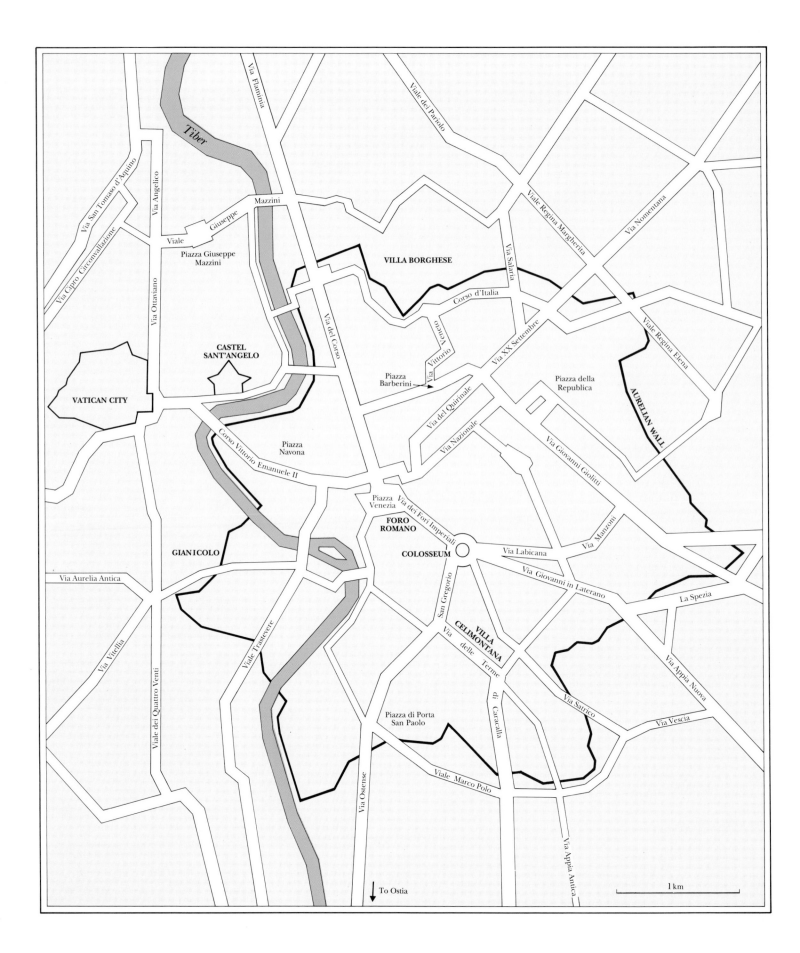

Preface

....

Rome is built up of mighty squares and dusty alleyways, of splendid palaces, churches both simple and opulent, huge ancient ruins and tiny workshops. Through it pulses the River Tiber. This book consists of six evocative walks through this city, almost all of them on foot (though the city has an excellent transport system, with rumbling tram cars, shuddering buses, fast trains and a modern metro system). All of these walks are tried and tested, so that if you followed them assiduously you would not go wrong. But they are primarily a device for displaying a city, and no device should become a strait-jacket.

Eating in Rome involves rich and sometimes heavy food, albeit washed down by the wines of the Castelli Roma (that is to say such outlying townships as Frascati, Rocca di Papa and Palestrina). For this reason alone I hesitate to say how long any of my six walks would take. It depends how much time you wish to spend in an art gallery, in a church, in a bar or over lunch. It also depends, as you explore, on whether you want to hop on and off buses or venture onto the metro.

I have some debts to acknowledge. I am particularly grateful to Mrs Pauline Young, PR director of Italiatour (241 Euston Road, London W1 2BT, telephone 071 373 3886). I must also express here my gratitude to Dr Emilio Tommasi, Director of the Italian State Tourist Office of Great Britain. Through Italiatour I stayed in the Albergo Quirinale, Via Nazionale 7, Rome, whose position and palatial warmth make it an exceptionally fine place from which to explore the city. I should like here also to express my thanks for the help given to me by the director of the hotel, Signora Johanna Fragano.

James Bentley
May 1991

OPPOSITE
ROME

Introduction

....

When the emperor Hadrian built his summer villa at Tivoli he could never have dreamed that he was laying the foundations for the modern Roman tourist industry. Villa Adriano, begun in AD 125, is today a rich honey-pot to swarms of travellers. Second only in interest is the villa transformed after 1550 from a Benedictine convent for the sophisticated cardinal Ippolito II d'Este.

The two of them, Hadrian and Ippolito, epitomize the rich diversity of individuals who have lived and worked in this remarkable city. Their villas, separated in time by 1500 years, call attention to the remarkable span of Roman history. That both buildings have preserved substantially their water-showered gardens bespeaks one of Rome's most notable features, for this is a city plentifully served by ancient aqueducts that still carry water to its gardens and from which its greatest architects have contrived fantastic and beautiful fountains. At Tivoli, too, Villa Gregoriana, with its spectacular waterfalls created for Pope Gregory XVI in 1835, displays another of Rome's unique advantages: the lavishness over the centuries of the popes, who were pre-eminent in the patronage of the arts, and who inspired others – princes of the church and state – to imitate them and to try to outdo each other. The genius of those they patronized has left a remarkable mark on the city. Henry James (1843–1916) spotted it in a Roman church on one of those afternoons when, as he put it:

> the glowing western light, entering the high windows of the tribune, kindles the scattered masses of colour into sombre brightness, scintillates on the great solemn mosaic of the vault, touches the porphyry columns of the superb baldacchino with ruby lights, and buries its shining shafts in the deep-toned shadows that hang about frescoes, sculptures and mouldings.

Nature, in Rome, conspires with human artifice.

OPPOSITE *In a city of fountains, that of the Villa Celimontana cools a shady corner of Rome with a glimpse of the Arch of Drusus through the trees, itself the remains of an ancient aqueduct. Emperors used the provision of aqueducts, public baths and fountains for propaganda purposes.*

Emperors, princes, cardinals and popes were men of action as well as patrons of the arts, and the background to their often harassed lives is also vital to an understanding of the city. A synopsis of Rome's origins and growth, beginning with the legendary twins Romulus and Remus, would gradually merge into history with the advent of the Etruscan kings. It would encompass the development of the Roman republic and the expansion of the Roman empire as well as its decline and fall. It would outline the ascendancy of the popes until their exile in Avignon, the coming of the Renaissance, and the efflorescence of baroque art and architecture. The story would continue with the creation of the kingdom of Italy and its uneasy truce with the papacy, culminating in the establishment in 1929 of a tiny Vatican state of immense cultural wealth and the foundation of the new Italian republic at the end of World War II.

As we know from the pottery excavated in the vicinity of the Capitoline Hill, the Romans arrived in the valley of the Tiber and on the neighbouring hills some thousand years before the birth of Christ, occupying sites peopled in the Bronze Age. They were primitive people, settling alongside Greeks and Etruscans, both nations possessed of a culture far in advance of their own. The Etruscans were civilized and warlike – a formidable enemy – and the Romans would eventually conquer them. The sheer energy involved in the Roman achievement of the next thousand years impresses historian and traveller alike. 'It is easy to speak of the Empire and to say that it established its order from the Tyne to the Euphrates,' wrote Hilaire Belloc (1870–1953), 'but when one has travelled alone and on foot up and down the world, and seen its vastness and its complexity, and yet everywhere the unity even of bricks in their courses, then one begins to understand the name of Rome.'

At the beginning of the Christian era this nation, which by now ruled the known world, began to invent for itself a legendary past. First the poet Virgil (70–19 BC), in the *Aeneid*, which he finished just before his death described how the Trojan Aeneas established a kingdom based at Rome. Next the historian Livy (64/59 BC–AD17) endowed the capital of their empire with a mythical foundation by Romulus, the son of Mars, and his twin brother, Remus. According to the legend, their uncle ordered the twins and their mother to be drowned. Miraculously rescued, they were reared by a she-wolf and then given protection by a shepherd named Faustulus and his wife.

Their grandfather Numitor, Livy declared, had been a king in Alba Longa, just outside present-day Rome, but had been expelled by their uncle Amulius. When they reached manhood, Romulus and Remus drove the usurper from his throne and restored Numitor. Gratefully Numitor granted them permission to build a city beside the River Tiber. Livy identified the year, in present-day usage, as 753 BC. The twins now began to quarrel about who should be king. When Remus mocked the walls that Romulus was constructing on the Palatine Hill, his brother slew him. Romulus decided that the Capitoline Hill should serve as an asylum for refugees.

So the extraordinary verve of the Romans was given a pseudo-historical basis. These wild ancestors needed wives and found them by stealing the women of the neighbouring Sabines. The inevitable war between the rival tribes ended in a compromise whereby Romulus and King Tatius of the Sabines jointly ruled Rome. After the death of Tatius, Romulus ruled alone, before his eventual deification as Quirinus. Curiously, Quirinus was not a Roman deity but the Sabine god of war, and consequently he and Romulus became equated with Mars, the third legendary founder of Rome.

The rule of Romulus was followed by that of some doubtless equally legendary kings. Authentic history intervenes with Lucius Tarquinius Priscus, an Etruscan who ruled from 616 BC until his murder in 578. His successor-but-one, Lucius Tarquinius Superbus, seventh and final king of Rome, came to the throne in 534. Ruthlessly he extended the power and colonies of Rome. But the city was outraged when his son, Sextus, violated

Seen from the Castel Sant'Angelo, a bend in the Tiber discloses the Ponte Sant'Angelo and in the distance the Ponte Vittorio Emanuele. The Ponte Sant'Angelo was originally erected for Hadrian in AD 134; the three centre arches are part of this structure. The arches at either end were enlarged and restored in the late nineteenth century when the Tiber was embanked.

Lucretia, the wife of a distinguished Roman patrician, Collatinus. Calling upon her husband and friends to take revenge, she stabbed herself to death.

Tarquinius Superbus had already made enemies, in particular Lucius Junius, the son of a rich Roman, whose property he had impounded and whose elder brother he had murdered. Junius escaped murder at the hands of the king only by feigning idiocy, which is why he was known by his family name of Brutus (which means stupid). In due course Brutus seized his chance to drive Tarquinius Superbus from Rome, the kingdom became a republic, and Brutus became one of the first of two consuls elected annually to rule Rome. The deposed monarch and his allies fought back, and some Romans would have welcomed their return – amongst them the two sons of Brutus, for which treachery their father put them to death. He himself was slain as his troops drove back an attack by Arruns, son of Tarquinius.

There was also dissension at home. Social and economic tensions had begun to appear under the Roman kings. Two classes, patricians and plebeians, emerged, competing for political power. Initially the patricians were dominant, for although both parties could participate in the election of the consuls, the plebeians had one vote and the patricians 192. So formidable became their rivalry that in 449 BC the citizens of Rome were obliged to seek a compromise by setting out the laws of the state in writing. The plebeians, although mollified by this *Lex Publilia* (Law of the Twelve Tables), appointed their own tribunes, whose task was to reject any arbitrary actions of the patricians. These political upheavals, which threatened to destroy the fabric of the state, did not prevent Rome's expansion, and by 396 BC the neighbouring Etruscan peoples had been subdued.

Other tribes also threatened the republic, among them the Samnites who were entrenched in the hills to the east of the city. In 390 BC bands of marauding Gauls would have taken the city had the Romans not been awakened by the cackling of the geese whom they had disturbed. Even so, the Gauls sacked Rome and exacted a ferocious tribute from the citizens before leaving. The Roman response was to erect a massive wall of tufa around their city, a barricade that was not breached for another eight hundred years. Eventually, internal disputes died down as the plebeians gained power and the deeds and rulings of their assembly were made legally binding on every Roman citizen.

Rome flourished. It controlled not just large parts of the Italian peninsula but also parcelled out the lands of its conquered territories among its citizens. By the mid third century BC the population of the capital had reached 100,000, with two aqueducts serving its baths and with roads and temples funded from the plunder of other nations. Increasingly, however, it envied the wealth and glamour of the Greek kingdoms, especially the states of southern Italy. Its chance to intervene came in 215 BC, when Philip V of Macedonia made an alliance with another traditional enemy, the Carthaginian soldier Hannibal. On the face of it, the alliance was shrewd.

Hannibal had already crossed the Pyrenees into Italy and in 217 BC slaughtered the Roman consul Gaius Flaminius and his army in a battle beside Lake Trasimene. The following spring he had taken on and completely routed a second Roman army. That was the summit of his military career. In the face of Rome's might Hannibal's allies wavered, and in 202 BC he was defeated at Zarna in North Africa. Six years later the Romans conquered Macedonia. The Hellenistic world fought back, to be finally destroyed in 31 BC, when Octavian defeated Antony and Cleopatra in the naval battle at Actium. Yet there was a paradox about this collapse of Hellenism. As the poet and satirist Horace (65–8 BC) put it: 'Captive Greece took captive its savage conqueror, introducing its own culture into rustic Italy.'

Although a republic, Rome, unlike some of the Greek city states, never became a democracy. Financially, its dependencies were bled to support the rulers of the capital. Revolts at home proved costly and futile, while the slaves (who finally and hopelessly rebelled in 73 BC under the leadership of the Thracian shepherd, Spartacus) were defeated by an army commanded by Crassus. Some 6000 slaves, seeking to escape, were savagely crucified by Crassus's fellow general Pompey alongside the Via Appia.

Pompey, Crassus and Julius Caesar formed a triumvirate to rule Rome, but the alliance soon broke up and Pompey fled to Egypt, where he was assassinated. Rome was continually at risk of civil war, and its rulers often suffered Pompey's fate. Two plebeian tribunes had been murdered for planning democratic reforms, Tiberius Gracchus in 132 BC and eleven years later, his brother Gaius. Another victim was to be the reformist soldier Julius Caesar – although his murderers claimed that he had been planning to restore the monarchy.

In 44 BC, the year of his assassination, Julius Caesar's adopted son and heir, his nineteen-year-old great nephew Octavian, was studying oratory at Apollonia in Illyricum. Returning to Rome, he was appointed consul and soon made a deal with the politicians Marcus Antonius and Marcus Aemilius Lepidus to divide the Roman empire into three, each one of them ruling as triumvir. But the days of the republic were numbered. Octavian, after defeating Marcus Antonius and Lepidus, became the sole ruler and first Roman emperor. Adopting the name Augustus, which means 'sacred', in 27 BC the new dictator proclaimed a regime of universal peace. True to his word, he ruled prudently, enhancing Rome itself. The Ara Pacis ('Altar of peace') built in his honour has been rebuilt on the banks of the Tiber.

The second emperor of Rome, the morbidly savage Tiberius, died in AD 37, to be succeeded by men of unparalleled brutality – the insane Caligula and the notorious Nero. Yet the glory that was Rome was not extinguished. At the mouth of the River Tiber, the emperor Claudius, Caligula's uncle and successor created a new port beside Ostia, through which shipments of grain reached the capital. When huge quarters of the city were devastated by the fire of AD 64, the emperor Nero not only built his own fabulous

Domus Aurea (Golden House) but also drove new streets through the city and persuaded the wealthier citizens to build better homes for themselves.

Later emperors included the civilized Trajan, Hadrian, the pious Antoninus, the Stoic philosopher Marcus Aurelius, Septimus Severus and his son Marcus Aurelius, nicknamed Caracalla after the long Gaulish tunic which he habitually wore. Trajan created a complex market with shops and a massive hall, while his forum remains one of the treasures of ancient Rome. Hadrian built the Pantheon and a mausoleum now transformed into the Castel Sant'Angelo. Another fire, in AD 191, enabled Septimus Severus to put through similar improvements to those achieved by Nero.

Save for Antoninus, all of these rulers faced opposition. The Spaniard Trajan faced and overcame the vicious hostility of the Dacians and celebrated his victories beyond the Danube on his vainglorious column. Hadrian had to put down a major revolt in Judaea. Marcus Aurelius was continually troubled by wars. Septimus Severus needed to crush two rivals before establishing himself as emperor. Caracalla, in an attempt to preserve his rule, reverted to savagery, and was assassinated in AD 217.

During these years the population of Rome reached perhaps a million, swollen by immigrants and captured slaves. By the time of Caracalla's death the city was again in decline. A plague during the reign of Marcus Aurelius (AD 161–80) had taken off 2000 a day. The new sect of Christians, persecuted even by Marcus Aurelius and particularly by the emperor Diocletian (284–305) in the early fourth century, had dug itself into catacombs. When Constantine the Great became emperor in AD 312 they were at last given a measure of tolerance; but although he gave Rome a great Christian basilica, he transferred his capital to Byzantium, which he renamed Constantinople.

Constantine died in 337. By the end of the century Rome was in disarray, virtually unable to defend herself. 'Upon the breaking and shivering of a great state and empire, you may be sure to have wars,' wrote Francis Bacon (1561–1616). 'So it was in the decay of the Roman empire.' So it remained for much of Rome's subsequent history. In AD 410, the troops of Alaric the Goth pillaged Rome for three days, and the city would have been sacked again in 452 by Attila the Hun had not Pope Leo I persuaded him to leave in peace. The Vandals arrived three years later to plunder the city for a full two weeks. Meanwhile, Attila's occasional ally, the Visigoth Theodoric I, was defeating Roman armies in Gaul. His successor-but-one, the Arian Christian Theodoric the Great (493–526), not only took over the whole of Italy but further contributed to Rome's decline by ruling from Ravenna.

Decline continued, although with the invasion of Italy in 536 by Belisarius, general of the Byzantine emperor Justinian, Rome was once again incorporated into the cultural life of the empire. In restoring his authority in the West Justinian's troops were obliged to besiege the city three times. Its defences were strengthened – to be severely tested when Totila besieged the city ten years later.

OPPOSITE *Much of the ancient statuary now in the Vatican museums used to be dotted around the gardens and courtyards, where renaissance artists could copy it, or take inspiration from it.*

Soon almost the sole authority in Rome was the church, and under Gregory I the Great (590–604), it consolidated both its secular and spiritual power. The population of Rome was starving when Gregory was elected. Vigorously he deployed the church and its estates to relieve the people's plight. Wherever possible, he made peace with Rome's enemies, and when they refused his entreaties he rallied the garrison of the city against them. By the end of his reign, the papacy ruled virtually the whole of Italy. The rulers of the West gradually recognized the spiritual primacy of Rome, a fact nowhere better displayed than when Charlemagne was crowned by Pope Leo III in the basilica of St Peter on Christmas Day, 800 – a coronation visibly recalled in the monuments of Rome today. Once again churches and public buildings were restored. Not that vicissitudes ceased. Saracens despoiled the city in 846. The nobility and the papacy were continually at odds. In 1084 the Norman allies of the papacy cruelly sacked the holy city. A revolution of 1143 attempted to wrest control from papal hands. In 1309 the French pope Clement V felt it prudent to move his entire court from Rome to Avignon. Not until 1377 did Pope Gregory XI restore his Curia to Rome. He found a city whose population, reduced to 30,000 at the start of the Avignon exile had been further cut down by the Black Death to 20,000. Wild animals roamed the streets at night.

Fortunately for posterity, the restored papacy – and especially the Colonna pope Martin V, who was elected in 1417 and entered Rome three years later – welcomed the architectural and intellectual stimulus of the Renaissance. Martin presided over a city of ruined churches and public buildings. At hand were architects and artists of genius, ready to restore them. Repeatedly as you walk through Rome you come upon buildings inspired by renaissance thought and ideals, and financed by successive popes and cardinals of the Catholic church. Under Nicholas V and Sixtus IV particularly, the city was transformed into a renaissance treasure-house.

With his passion for ancient manuscripts, the cultivated humanist Nicholas V (1447–55) virtually founded the Vatican library. He employed artists of the calibre of Fra Angelico and Benozzo Gozzoli. Three years after his election, he proclaimed a jubilee year which brought thousands of pilgrims to Rome and replenished the papal coffers. Nicholas was thus able to commission the restoration of the city's churches, palaces and fortifications. To him we owe the rebuilding of the Trevi Fountain – blocked up for some 1000 years – although its present late baroque splendour dates from an early eighteenth-century transformation by Nicolà Salvi.

The principal monument of Sixtus IV (1471–84) is the Sistine Chapel, but he also built the churches of Santa Maria del Popolo and Santa Maria della Pace as well as the hospital of Santo Spirito. His favoured artists included Botticelli, and his building projects were so lavish that he left the Vatican coffers empty. They were soon filled again. The Medici family began to produce popes, and Medici bankers supplied them with capital. By the time the first Medici pope, Leo X (1513–21), decided to transform St Peter's, his schemes had been matched by the creation of a new urban environment, with ecclesiastical palaces, sumptuous churches, spacious roads and fountain-cooled squares – many of them paid for by other scions of the church and their families. The second Medici pope, Clement VII (1523–34), was responsible for commissioning Michelangelo to paint the *Last Judgment* in the Sistine Chapel. The inspiration of antiquity was nowhere better displayed than in the piazza on the Capitoline Hill laid out by Michelangelo to display the equestrian statue of Marcus Aurelius – a statue which braved the pollution of Rome's atmosphere until the 1980s, when the sick horseman was finally protected behind glass.

Renaissance Rome blossomed. Yet there was a price to be paid for the involvement of the papacy in secular affairs. Religious reformers suffered at the hands of Counter-Reformation popes, or were put to death by the Inquisition simply for holding notions contrary to prevailing orthodoxy. In 1527 the city was once again sacked, this time by the enraged imperial army

Renaissance and seventeenth-century popes emulated emperors by providing fountains for the piazzas of the city.

of Charles V. For eight days the soldiers roamed the city like vandals. Among others Pope Sixtus V, in his short reign (1586–90), proved equal to the destruction. His prized architect was Domenico Fontana, and under his inspiration streets and squares were created, while new palaces, churches and aqueducts enhanced the life of the demoralized city. One of his peculiar fancies was the erection in Rome of Egyptian obelisks.

Soon the population had reached its former heights, rising to 100,000 in the mid seventeenth century. Palaces and parks were enriched. The baroque masters Bernini and Borromini left their mark on Rome. Then the city again sank into peaceful obscurity. 'I am very glad to see Rome while it yet exists', wrote Horace Walpole on his visit to the city in 1740. 'Before a great number of years have elapsed, I question whether it will be worth seeing.' He observed that its buildings 'are more demolished than any time or chance could have effected'. As for the temple of Minerva Medica, 'this glorious spot is neglected, and only serves for a small vineyard and kitchen garden,' he reported. Even so, by the end of the eighteenth century the population of the city had increased by another 65,000 and the architectural face of Rome had been enhanced by the late baroque façades of Santa Maria Maggiore and Santa Croce.

One of the many representations in Rome of the she-wolf suckling Romulus and Remus – this one by the steps to the Piazza del Campidoglio. The group is often used to symbolize the Tiber, as the twins were exposed on its banks.

Roman languor was rudely interrupted by Napoleon Bonaparte, who invaded the city in 1796, transporting many of its artistic treasures back to France. In 1798 his emissary proclaimed a Roman republic, deposing Pope Pius VI as head of the state and compelling him to depart for Tuscany. Pius was later forcibly transferred to France, where he died. His successor, Pius VII, suffered the further indignity of having to give his blessing to Napoleon's coronation as emperor, and when Pius refused to participate in the continental blockade of Britain Napoleon confiscated the papal states.

Pius VII returned to the Vatican only after the fall of Bonaparte in 1814. The rest of the century proved almost as traumatic for the papacy. The surge of revolutionary Italian nationalism was deplored by the reactionary Gregory XVI (1831–46), particularly since it encouraged disaffection in the papal states and the demand for a federal Italian republic. His successor, Pius IX, was more flexible, but not sufficiently so for the revolutionaries, and when a Roman republic was proclaimed in 1849, he saw his prime minister assassinated and ten days later fled from the city.

Although the forces of Austria, Spain, Naples and France hastened to overthrow the Roman republic, it was now to be defended by the brilliant soldier Giuseppe Garibaldi and his volunteer army. In the last days of April 1849, General Nicolas Charles Victor Oudinot, Duke of Regio and commander of the French forces, halted his troops outside Rome. 'Thus, with only the Gods on their side, the Romans armed for the fight,' wrote Garibaldi's biographer, the historian G. M. Trevelyan (1876–1962). 'Outside the city, friends and foes expected that they would surrender: "Italians do not fight," was the word passed round in the French camp, and even those who knew the North Italians had never heard of Roman valour in the history of the modern world.'

On 27 April, however, Garibaldi led his legionaries into Rome, riding on a white horse ahead of a column of sunburned men, their hair unkempt, black plumes waving from their conical hats, their beards shaggy, their legs bare. In the ensuing battle, wearing red blouses that fell almost to their knees, this motley force repulsed Oudinot, killing 500 French soldiers, taking 363 prisoners and driving the rest from the field.

It was a triumph that did not last. Reinforced, the French again besieged Rome and all Garibaldi's military skills could not this time repulse them. On 12 April 1850 the pope was restored to his secular throne. But Italian nationalism could not indefinitely be held back. Most of the papal states joined the kingdom of Italy that was established in 1861. Rome itself remained aloof, in spite of abortive attacks on the city by Garibaldi's army in 1862 and 1867.

Finally, in 1870, with the French allies of the papacy threatened by Bismarck, the nationalists once more occupied Rome, declaring it the capital of the newly united Italy. Pope Pius IX retreated to the Vatican, declared himself a prisoner there and never left it. Ten days earlier, mindful of the long papal tradition of enhancing the holy city with public works, he had inaugurated the gushing fountain in Piazza della Repubblica (though the nymphs riding the backs of sea-monsters were added only in 1901, 23 years after the pope's death).

After a plebiscite, Rome became the capital of the kingdom of Italy, ruled by King Vittorio Emanuele II. With the transfer from Florence of the Italian government, the city began to transform itself into a modern metropolis, with new and impressive thoroughfares: Corso Vittorio Emanuele, Via Nazionale, Via Vittorio Veneto, and Via del Tritone.

Religious and political passions could still run high. Pius IX excommunicated Vittorio Emanuele II. In 1881, as the pope's corpse was being transported from its provisional resting-place in St Peter's to San Lorenzo Fuori le Mura an anticlerical mob tried to throw it into the Tiber. The extreme clerical faction displayed a similar fanaticism in resisting the proposal, successful as it turned out, to set up a statue to the philosopher Giordano Bruno, burned at the stake in 1600, in the Campo dei Fiori. Vittorio Emanuele II's successor, Umberto I, was assassinated in 1900.

At the outbreak of World War I, 500,000 persons lived in Rome. Prime minister Giovanni Giolitti tried in vain to keep Italy neutral. The hardships endured by the city during the war, with the efforts of Pope Benedict XV to bring about a peaceful solution to the hostilities, led to partial reconciliation between the papacy and the civil authorities. In 1922, Pope Pius XI gave for the first time since 1870 the traditional blessing *Urbi et Orbi* from the balcony of St Peter's. Eight months later, 30,000 of Benito Mussolini's blackshirts marched on Rome and the way was paved for a fascist dictatorship.

The campanile of San Pietro in Montorio rises beside the Accademia Espagnole on the Janiculum. The rebuilding of the church was financed in the late fifteenth century by Isabella of Castile and Ferdinand of Aragon.

Mussolini loved Rome and had feeling for its history, naming his party after the bundles of rods (*fasces*) which the lictors of ancient Rome used to carry. Yet his megalomania led him to destroy some of its most fascinating medieval quarters to create new and monumental thoroughfares.

Towards the end of the eighteenth century archaeology had become a fashionable pursuit of the rich as well as the scholarly. In 1580 Michel de Montaigne had been distressed to find that ancient Rome was silted up under piles of earth. 'No Roman of the classical era would recognize this place', he complained. No longer: the new fashion gave a fresh impetus to the exploration of the Foro Romano, and archaeological digs proceeded more or less uninterruptedly until the late nineteenth century. In 1898 a professional archaeologist of genius, Giacomo Boni, took over the work. In the 1920s Mussolini's passion for ancient Rome, whose glories he longed to emulate, led his fascist government to support the task of further uncovering the treasures of the Foro Romano. The wattle-and-daub huts in which the seventh-century BC Romans lived were gradually revealed, along with basilicas, theatres and the sacred spot where the body of Julius Caesar was cremated.

By 1930 the population of Rome had exceeded one million. Fifty-nine years after the pope's self-exile in the Vatican a treaty between Pius XI and Benito Mussolini recognised papal sovereignty within the Vatican state. The Italian government compensated the papacy for the spoliation of the papal states. Although Pius XI had little sympathy for fascist ideals, condemning its racism in the encyclical *Non abbiamo bisogna*, he allowed his priests to bless Italian troops during Mussolini's Abyssinian adventure.

On Adolf Hitler's visit to Rome in May 1938, the pope departed speedily for his summer residence at Castel Gandolfo in order to avoid meeting the German Führer. During World War II, his successor, Pius XII, devoted his energies not only to the preservation of the Holy City but also to an often vain attempt to assert fundamental human rights. When Nazi troops occupied Rome in September 1943, Pius XII transformed the Vatican into an asylum for refugees, many of them Jewish. After the fall of Mussolini, Rome was occupied for six months by the Germans. Liberated on 4 June 1944, its citizens, along with the rest of the nation, were asked to decide between a republic or a constitutional monarchy. Almost 55 per cent of the population declared itself in favour of a republic, which was proclaimed on 2 June 1946.

Pope Pius XII was now acclaimed by the faithful as *defensor civitas* He died in 1958, to be succeeded by the son of a peasant family from Bergamo. To this fact as well as to John XXIII's own broad sympathies we owe a peculiar architectural feature of St Peter's, for the sculptor Giacomo Manzu had also been born in Bergamo and was a family friend. In spite of Manzu's widely known communist sympathies, the pope commissioned him in 1962 to create for St Peter's some monumental bronze 'doors of death'. Manzu had been horrified by the cruelties of World War II, and when the doors were inaugurated in 1964 the violence he had depicted created an enormous controversy, which has not yet entirely died down.

Rome has continued to improve its public face, with a variety of results. At the beginning of 1990, the city decided to restore the façades of some of its finest buildings, in preparation for hosting the competition for the football World Cup. Scaffolding and plastic sheets were erected in front of the Pantheon, the splendid church of Sant'Andrea della Valle and much else. By December the scaffolding was still in place, the restoration only half-finished. The World Cup was over and done with, but slowly new facets of exquisite buildings were revealed, as their faces were cleaned of the accumulated dust of centuries. Today, as you walk its streets, the stones of the city proclaim its history.

1
Classical and Renaissance

....

TRAJAN'S COLUMN *to* CAPITOLINE HILL

I n a celebrated aphorism, Augustus observed, 'I found Rome made of brick and I will leave it of marble.' Today some of the marble has disappeared; as Arthur Hugh Clough (1819–61) put it in his *Amours de Voyage*, 'Marble I thought thee, and brickwork I find thee!' But the vision of Augustus and of emperors imbued with similar genius still permeates the city. Their legacy repeatedly inspired the artists and particularly the architects who were to enrich the city in centuries to come.

There is a remarkable continuity in Roman history that reveals itself in the city's rich topography, and the first walk of this book explores it. Beginning at Trajan's Column, and proceeding to explore the Foro di Augusto and the Foro di Nerva, the walk burrows into Roman history and legend as it explores the evocative ruins of the immense Foro Romano. Although in a row of statues the Vestal Virgins still sit here beside the remains of their circular temple, in the Foro Romano you are also conscious of the eventual triumph of Christianity over paganism; but even now the monuments of Christianity continue to reflect the glories of the pagan past. And although the forum and its environs have been properly excavated only recently (and will remain in the process of excavation for many years), they too over the centuries have provided a source of inspiration for some of Rome's greatest artists, and as we walk, the cross-fertilisation of Roman art and architecture is increasingly revealed.

Our route climbs the Palatine Hill and remembers the remote origins of Rome, again both in legend and in history, before visiting a yet more awesome monument of ancient Rome, the Colosseum. An often neglected spot is the exquisite church of San Giorgio in Velabro, dedicated to a Roman soldier who had embraced the Christian faith and was martyred for it. The walk comes to an end on the Capitoline Hill, once the seat of ancient government, and now the epitome of renaissance architecture.

OPPOSITE *A romantic symbol of a long-dead religion: the Temple of Vesta in the Foro Romano was partially rebuilt in the 1930s by Alfonso Bartoli. The Vestals guarded the sacred flame which symbolized the everlasting nature of the Roman state.*

Monumental ancient Rome starts at **TRAJAN'S COLUMN** in the **FORO TRAIANO**. A spiral staircase of 185 steps winds inside it. One July evening in 1787 Goethe climbed them to the top of the column, recording that 'Seen from that height and at sunset, the Colosseum, with the Capitol hill close by, the Palatine behind it and the city all around, was a superb sight.'

Astonishingly well preserved, Trajan's Column was dedicated to the emperor in AD 113 to commemorate his conquest of the Dacians and is a perfect example of imperial arrogance. Eighteen drums of marble stand atop each other to reach a height of 33 metres. Its inscription declares that the Senate and the people of Rome determined that its height should equal that of the hill levelled to create this piazza, the Piazza del Foro Traiano. Around the shaft winds a frieze whose 2500 or so figures, sculpted in white Carrara marble, depict the glorious campaigns of the emperor, who appears in them no fewer than 60 times. (Since the frieze rises more than 30 metres above the ground one cannot of course properly follow these minutely detailed scenes, but casts of the 115 panels are on display in the Lateran Museum.) Trajan's ashes, in their golden urn, were stolen by the Goths, and his statue which topped the column was replaced in the sixteenth century by one of St Peter.

A pair of domed churches adorn the piazza. The older, **SANTA MARIA DI LORETO**, was commissioned by the bakers' company from Antonio da Sangallo the Younger in 1507 and finished in 1582 when Giacomo del Duca added the playful dome and yet more playful cupola. The statue of St Susanna inside was sculpted by François Duquesnoy in 1603. His contemporaries acclaimed it as a perfect blend of naturalism and antique symbolism. Next door rises the church of the **NOME DI MARIA**, built by the architect Derizet in 1738. Its dowdy exterior belies the glamorous baroque inside.

Beyond the column the steep steps of Via Magnanapoli rise to the monumental arches of **TRAJAN'S MARKET**. A huge three-storey covered market, almost certainly designed by the architect Apollodorus of Damascus, stands at the heart of this ancient supermarket. The whole is dominated by the **TORRE DELLE MILIZIE**, a fierce thirteenth-century relic of the days when the great Roman families were frequently at odds with one another. Today it leans slightly. Beyond the market rises the medieval house of the Knights of Rhodes, founded here in the twelfth century and rebuilt in 1470.

From the Piazza del Foro Traiano walk south-east along Via Alessandrina to the **FORO DI AUGUSTO**. Bronze statues of the emperors Trajan, Augustus and Nerva guard our route. The Foro di Augusto was built by the emperor Augustus in about 2 BC, to commemorate the Battle of Philippi of 42 BC. He envisaged a temple dedicated to Mars guarded by the triumphal arches of Drusus and Germanicus. What remain are entrancing fragments, set well below the present level of the street and most evocative when softly illuminated after dusk. (A spotlight plays on a marble fragment inscribed AVGVST ...) Two fluted columns, once part of the Temple of Mars, have preserved their delicate capitals. A stepped base and tumbledown columns

Sailors and horsemen, warriors and standard-bearers adorn Trajan's Column. The frieze is 200 metres long, and its 2500 figures tell the story of Trajan's campaigns against the Dacians, whom he finally conquered in AD 106.

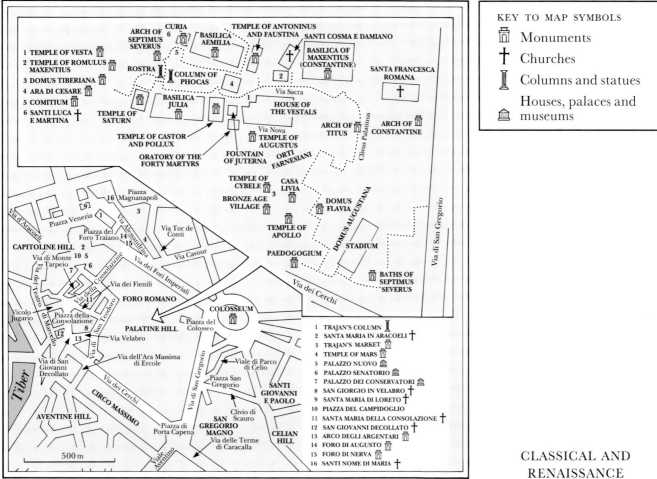

KEY TO MAP SYMBOLS

- 🏛 Monuments
- ✝ Churches
- Ⅱ Columns and statues
- 🏛 Houses, palaces and museums

1 TEMPLE OF VESTA
2 TEMPLE OF ROMULUS MAXENTIUS
3 DOMUS TIBERIANA
4 ARA DI CESARE
5 COMITIUM
6 SANTI LUCA E MARTINA ✝

CURIA
ARCH OF SEPTIMUS SEVERUS
ROSTRA
COLUMN OF PHOCAS
BASILICA AEMILIA
TEMPLE OF ANTONINUS AND FAUSTINA
SANTI COSMA E DAMIANO
BASILICA OF MAXENTIUS (CONSTANTINE)
SANTA FRANCESCA ROMANA
BASILICA JULIA
Via Sacra
HOUSE OF THE VESTALS
TEMPLE OF SATURN
TEMPLE OF CASTOR AND POLLUX
TEMPLE OF AUGUSTUS
Via Nova
ARCH OF TITUS
Clivus Palatinus
ARCH OF CONSTANTINE
ORATORY OF THE FORTY MARTYRS
FOUNTAIN OF JUTERNA
ORTI FARNESIANI
TEMPLE OF CYBELE
CASA LIVIA
BRONZE AGE VILLAGE
DOMUS FLAVIA
TEMPLE OF APOLLO
DOMUS AUGUSTANA
PAEDOGOGIUM
STADIUM
Via di San Gregorio
Piazza Magnanapoli
Piazza Venezia
Via d'Aracoeli
Piazza del Foro Traiano
Via Alessandrina
Via Tor de Conti
Via Cavour
CAPITOLINE HILL
Via di Monte Tarpeio
Via della Consolazione
Via dei Fori Imperiali
Via dei Fienili
FORO ROMANO
Vicolo Jugario
Via del Teatro di Marcello
Piazza della Consolazione
Via di San Teodoro
PALATINE HILL
Piazza del Colosseo
COLOSSEUM
Via Velabro
Via dell'Ara Massima di Ercole
Via di San Giovanni Decollato
Via dei Cerchi
Viale di Parco di Celio
Piazza San Gregorio
SANTI GIOVANNI E PAOLO
Tiber
CIRCO MASSIMO
AVENTINE HILL
Piazza di Porta Capena
SAN GREGORIO MAGNO
Clivio di Scauro
CELIAN HILL
Via delle Terme di Caracalla
Viale Aventino
500 m
BATHS OF SEPTIMUS SEVERUS
Via dei Cerchi

1 TRAJAN'S COLUMN Ⅱ
2 SANTA MARIA IN ARACOELI ✝
3 TRAJAN'S MARKET 🏛
4 TEMPLE OF MARS 🏛
5 PALAZZO NUOVO 🏛
6 PALAZZO SENATORIO 🏛
7 PALAZZO DEI CONSERVATORI 🏛
8 SAN GIORGIO IN VELABRO ✝
9 SANTA MARIA DI LORETO ✝
10 PIAZZA DEL CAMPIDOGLIO
11 SANTA MARIA DELLA CONSOLAZIONE ✝
12 SAN GIOVANNI DECOLLATO ✝
13 ARCO DEGLI ARGENTARI 🏛
14 FORO DI AUGUSTO 🏛
15 FORO DI NERVA 🏛
16 SANTI NOME DI MARIA ✝

CLASSICAL AND RENAISSANCE

face on to Via Alessandrina, as does the boundary wall of the forum. From a semicircular wall whose round-headed brick arches give way to a gallery, rise medieval houses and a renaissance loggia.

Beyond this forum is the **FORO DI NERVA**, its steps rising to impressive broken columns which are gracefully fluted. Two huge Corinthian columns remain from the massive entrance to the former Temple of Minerva. Between them is a bas-relief of the goddess Minerva, and in the frieze below she appears teaching, weaving and sewing. Arrogant Christians deliberately despoiled such spots. In the early seventeenth century Pope Paul V seized the marble stones of this temple to build a Roman fountain, the Acqua Paola in Via Garibaldi near the Porta San Pancrazio.

Via dei Fori Imperiali takes us from the Foro di Nerva to the magnificent ruins of the **FORO ROMANO**, its red brick contrasting with the white stone of the Colosseum which rises ahead. The Foro Romano was once merely a marshy hollow set among Rome's hills traversed by several streams. The city's main sewer, the Cloaca Maxima was traditionally begun in the sixth century BC, and as a consequence of this the surrounding land was drained.

This area evolved as the Roman republic's principal market (or *forum*); and here developed the legal and commercial hub of the nascent city. Protected by the citadel of the Capitol, public buildings and shops sprang up and moneychangers set up their stalls. Its main street, the Via Sacra, rose up to the Capitoline Hill. Above all, the Foro Romano became the heart of a network of sanctuaries and temples. Statues and triumphal arches glorified the deeds of the rulers of Rome; basilicas, or quadrangular, colonnaded halls, which functioned as law courts or business centres, sprang up around the area. The area was soon so crowded that Julius Caesar was obliged to extend the complex westward, just as his successors did to the north. Then, as Rome decayed, so did its proud forum despite an attempt by Diocletian to rebuild the complex after a fire in the third century AD. The sacred buildings were neglected. Both Christians and barbarians despoiled and robbed the buildings. Earthquakes ruined what remained. Soon the place was filled with rubbish, its superb monuments pillaged and crumbling.

Although a few medieval barons founded fortresses on the bases of ancient buildings and Pope Paul III in 1536 built a noble road through part of it, for the most part the Foro Romano was given over to cattle (and known to the Renaissance as the Campo Vaccino, or cow-field). When the archaeologist and engraver Giovanni Battista Piranesi (1720–78) published his magnificent copper engravings on the antiquities of Rome in 1764, he depicted the cattle still grazing at the foot of decaying ancient monuments. By now the stones of many of its great buildings had been re-used elsewhere and some of its pagan temples had been transformed into Christian churches. Even when artists such as Michelangelo (1475–1564) had part of the area dug up in the quest for the antique statues which they so much admired, the excavations were filled in again afterwards. Only in the late eighteenth and nineteenth centuries did archaeologists realize what a treasure store lay buried here. Since then the heart of ancient Rome has been increasingly unveiled, and each part of it is marked by a bronze statue of its founder.

This, then, is a complex ancient site, redolent with history and created over a thousand years. To savour it properly needs historical imagination, but walking through it you feel that you are unlocking the secrets of a long-dead civilization. As Henry James put it at the very moment when the Foro Romano was being seriously and systematically restored to the light of day:

> Nothing in Rome helps your fancy to a more vigorous backwards flight than to lounge on a sunny day over the railing which guards the great central researches. It 'says' more things to you than you can repeat to see the past, the ancient world, as you stand there, bodily turned up with the spade and transformed from an immaterial, inaccessible fact of time into a matter of soils and surfaces.

OPPOSITE *The baroque façade and the romanesque campanile of Santa Francesca Romana overlook the Foro Romano. On the left rises the Temple of Antoninus and Faustina, behind which looms the mighty Basilica of Maxentius. To the right of the Temple of Vesta stand the three remaining Corinthian columns of the Temple of Castor and Pollux.*

The Foro Romano, more than anywhere else in Rome, speaks of the grandeur of the past and its decay. The entrance from Via dei Fori Imperiali leads alongside the site of the **BASILICA AEMILIA**. Two censors, Marcus Aemilius Lepidus and Marcus Fulvius Nobilior built this huge assembly hall in 179 BC. Surrounded by porticoes, it was called the Basilica Aemilia after the censor Marcus Aemilius Paullus who paid for its restoration in 164 BC. Much was later destroyed by Christians who used its marble to build their own churches. Earthquakes shook it, the traces of Alaric's attempt to set it on fire in AD 410 mark its pavement, and the barbarians savaged the building; yet its remains are still awesome.

Its long rows of broken columns stretch to the **CURIA**, the forum's council hall and the seat of the Roman Senate. Beyond, you can see the domed church of **SANTI LUCA E MARTINA**, in front of which tourists, usually harangued by guides, lean over the wall for an overview of the whole forum. The original Curia was erected in the seventh century BC by the Sabine king Tullus Hostilius, and was first known as the Curia Hostilia.The present Curia, restored in 1937, dates from the time of the emperor Diocletian, being rebuilt on his orders after the fire of AD 283. Then the brick walls were clad with cool marble. Its square, austere façade is today pitted with cavities made to house medieval Christian tombs. Once it boasted bronze doors, but Francesco Borromini (1599–1667) appropriated them for the church of San Giovanni in Laterano, and today the building is closed by copies of the originals. Inside the floor is covered by marble tiles.

In AD 638 this venerable building was itself transformed into a Christian church, dedicated to Sant'Adriano. Where senators once reclined, the devout prayed; where the ruling consul presided, a priest preached the Gospel. The bas-reliefs of bulls, sheep and other animals carved inside, all of them undoubtedly destined for sacrifice, had become a shadow of the Christian sacrifice of the Mass.

In front of the Curia the citizens would gather in the narrow **COMITIUM** to debate the central concerns of the Roman Empire. This was a sacred spot, for steps nearby lead down to the black paving stone which covers the supposed burial place of Romulus, legendary founder of Rome. Although you cannot walk down to see it, an adjacent stele is carved with the oldest known Latin inscription. Its archaic letters, from the fourth century BC, run alternately from right to left, pronouncing a curse on anyone who should despoil the tomb.

Beyond the Comitium stands the triumphal **ARCH OF SEPTIMUS SEVERUS** erected in AD 203 to honour the tenth anniversary of the emperor's accession. The senate and people of Rome dedicated it to him and his sons Caracalla and Geta in tribute to their victories over the Parthians, Arabs and Assyrians. Because Geta was murdered by Caracalla nine years later, his name was expunged from the inscription on the arch, although the holes which were incised to hold the letters of his name are still visible. Four

Centuries divide the buildings in this corner of the Foro Romano: the Arch of Septimus Severus was erected in AD 203; the Column of Phocas in 608; the original Curia in 80 BC; and beyond, the domed church of Santi Luca e Martina was rebuilt in 1640 by Pietro da Cortona.

crumbling, but still powerful reliefs depict scenes from the three military campaigns, and as often occurs in triumphal Roman arches, the vanquished are depicted in their humiliation. Once the whole was topped by a bronze chariot, drawn by six horses, in which stood a statue of Septimus Severus himself, crowned with victory. The chariot, emperor and horses were melted down in the Middle Ages and the triumphal arch half silted up, to be excavated only in 1803 by Pope Pius VII.

In the church is another relic of pagan ways, a couple of sculpted balustrades (known as the **PLUTEI** or Anaglypha Traiani, '*anaglypha*' meaning reliefs) carved on one side with a pig, sheep and a bull destined for ritual sacrifice, and on the other the good deeds of the emperor Trajan. He is seen burning the records of outstanding debts, founding orphanages and receiving thanks. These are some of the most entrancing carvings in the whole Foro Romano and you can make out in the background some of the buildings that stood here in their original noble state.

Over the nearby wall orators would harangue the people from the imperial platform known as the **ROSTRA** (from the word for the ships' prows, captured at the Battle of Antium in 338 BC, which once stood here). Above the Rostra rise three elegant, white marble columns – the corner of the **TEMPLE OF VESPASIAN** erected at the end of the first century AD. Nearby stand nine white columns from the portico of a colonnade dedicated to twelve gods whom Jupiter was supposed to consult before launching his thunderbolt. Their statues were erected here in AD 367 by a prefect of the city named Vettius Agorius Praetextatus and this constitutes one of the last surviving relics of pagan religion in Rome. Back towards the Arch of Septimus Severus are the remains of the eight granite Ionic columns and crumbling brick arches from the **TEMPLE OF SATURN**, built in 498 BC and once the leading sanctuary of the Roman republic. Much rebuilt, this temple used to house the city's treasure, and on 17 December the end of the year was celebrated here with orgies and feasting.

East of the Rostra, the 13.8-metre **COLUMN OF PHOCAS** was erected in AD 608 in thanks to the Byzantine emperor for ceding the Pantheon to Pope Boniface IV, who wished to transform it into a church. The column was originally topped with a gilded statue of Phocas. Whether he deserved such a memorial is doubtful. A centurion elevated to emperor, he was, as Edward Gibbon (1737–94) commented in his *The History of the Decline and Fall of the Roman Empire*, a coward and a murderer, lustful, brutish and often drunk. He tortured and murdered his predecessor, along with most of his family, and delighted in having his subjects tortured to death *very* slowly. He did, however, come to a just end. Heraclius, exarch (governor of a Byzantine province) of Africa, for long refused to do the tyrant homage and finally dispatched his son and Nicetas the son of his friend and lieutenant, to terminate Phocas's savage rule. Reproached with the crimes of his abominable reign, he retorted, 'Will you govern better?' Then, wrote Gibbon, 'After suffering

every variety of insult and torture, his head was severed from his body, the mangled trunk was cast into the flames, and the same treatment was inflicted on the statues of the vain usurper.' His column in the Foro Romano survived, its identity forgotten, Byron (1788–1824) merely describing it as a 'nameless column with a buried base'.

South of this is the **BASILICA JULIA** built by Julius Caesar, restored by Augustus after a fire and rebuilt by Diocletian towards the end of the third century AD. Hardly anything remains of this once huge court-house, in which sat the four civil tribunes of Rome. Doric and Corinthian marble capitals lie on the ground; brick pillars have been rebuilt, using some of the original material, and you can still trace the scratchings on the marble pavement where people once played a game something like draughts. Every one of the beautifully carved capitals deserves a lingering glance. At the far end of the basilica, stand two of seven honorary columns, one still cloaked in marble, the other showing the fixing holes for the cladding.

With its central nave flanked by two aisles on either side, the Basilica Julia is 109 metres long and 40 metres wide. Imposing enough, it hardly matches in mute eloquence the remains of the **TEMPLE OF CASTOR AND POLLUX** next to it, set up in the forum in 484 BC after the Romans had successfully called upon help of the divine twins in their battle against the Tarquins and their allies at Lake Regillus. The emperor Augustus rebuilt this temple, reconsecrating it in AD 6. Only three of 38 slender Corinthian columns in Parian marble still stand, their capitals complex and incisive; but archaeologists have also discovered here some fragmentary ancient statues as well as the basin of a fountain, where, according to legend, Castor and Pollux watered their horses after the battle.

At the very centre of the Foro Romano is a podium, formerly part of a temple dedicated to Julius Caesar himself, for here his body was cremated on an altar after his assassination in 44 BC. Just beyond the Temple of Castor and Pollux and this **ARA DI CESARE** (Altar of Caesar) are the semi-circular remains of the **TEMPLE OF VESTA**, and the **HOUSE OF THE VESTALS**, the home of six daughters of patrician Romans dedicated, at the age of ten, to thirty years' virginity in order to guard the sacred fire of Vesta. For ten years they learned the secrets of their holy task; for the next ten they guarded the flame; for the final ten they taught newcomers to their order. Those who failed to remain pure were buried alive, and those with whom they had sinned were flogged to death.

The Vestals continued to guard the sacred fire until paganism was quenched by Christianity. Their temple was rebuilt at the beginning of the third century AD by Septimus Severus, and what remains today is an archaeologists' reconstruction. At the top of the temple there was probably a chimney to let out smoke from the sacred fire. The elegantly robed statues of the Vestals themselves, though most have lost limbs and heads, stand in what was once the atrium of the house, facing a rose garden.

To the west of the Temple of Vesta stands the restored **SHRINE OF JUTURNA**, goddess of healing waters, and beyond it a late imperial building which was transformed into the **ORATORY OF THE FORTY MARTYRS**. These were Armenian soldiers killed by Diocletian for embracing Christianity. Their deaths are depicted in some eighth- and ninth-century frescoes inside.

To the south stands the oldest church of the Foro Romano. **SANTA MARIA ANTIQUA** was once part of the Temple of Augustus, and was transformed into a church in the sixth century. Although this church was largely rebuilt in 1617, taking the name of Santa Maria Liberatrice, and then partly demolished in 1902, much of the original remains, including some sixth-, seventh- and eighth-century frescoes depicting, in half-Byzantine, half-Carolingian style, the Blessed Virgin Mary, the Annunciation and the Crucifixion. Three eighth-century popes are also portrayed here (St Zacharias, St Paul I and Adrian I). In the iconography of the time, their square haloes indicate that these portraits were painted while the men were alive. Next to Pope Zacharias is his secretary, Theodotus, who restored the church.

Look back across the Foro Romano to see the architectural triumph of Christianity over paganism. On the back of the **TEMPLE OF ANTONINUS AND FAUSTINA** sits the baroque façade of the eleventh-century church of **SAN LORENZO IN MIRANDA**. The temple, dedicated in AD 141 to the memory of the empress Faustina (and then to the memory of her husband Antonius Pius after his death twenty years later), survived intact only by being transformed into this Christian church. Its preservation is entirely justified, for Antoninus, though rich, was a gentle and temperate man who for the most part refused to persecute Christians. Pass through the baroque façade of 1602, which incorporates ten powerful columns from Faustina's temple, and you find inside more ancient Corinthian columns. On the entablature an inscription still dedicates the building to holy Faustina. A frieze of candelabra, vases and gryphons survives from early times.

Between this temple–church and the House of the Vestals has been excavated a necropolis which was in use from the tenth century BC. Walk gently uphill to reach on the left the circular remains of the **TEMPLE OF ROMULUS MAXENTIUS**, dedicated in AD 309 in memory of the son of the Maxentius who had served as consul in the preceding years. After his death he was declared a god. A couple of apses abut on to a circular building whose entrance is flanked by porphyry columns and guarded by ancient bronze doors with a delicately carved frieze.

Behind this temple rises more of the former Temple of Augustus, now incorporated into yet another Christian church. **SANTI COSMA E DAMIANO** also takes in a library, the Templum Sacrae Urbis which was built between AD 73 and 78 to house the plans, and street and house registers and other important documents of Rome.

The transformation of these two buildings was due to the initiative of Pope Felix IV (526–30). His was a revolutionary action, never before had a

Carlo Lombardi's splendid early seventeenth-century façade was attached to the much older foundation of Santa Maria Nova. The church was rededicated to St Francesca Maderna, and is known as Santa Francesca Romana.

pagan temple been used as a Christian church, and this paved the way for many more such rededications. Part of the building's complexity results from the dampness which affects the Foro Romano. In 1633 Pope Urban VIII tried to cope with this problem by having the floor raised. As a result of this the church is on two levels. In a translucent alabaster tomb in the lower church lie the bones of Cosmas and Damian, the patron saints of physicians, pharmacists, barbers and dentists. Martyred, like so many others, under Diocletian, the brothers were famed as doctors who treated the poor without payment.

Early sixth-century mosaics from the reign of Pope Felix decorate the upper church; still exquisite they retain their primitive vigour despite the effects of a restoration of 1660. The Lamb of God carries a book with seven seals, while Cosmas and Damian, two of the evangelists, several prophets, angels and Pope Felix himself (the earliest surviving portrait of a pope) worship him. Since Christ is depicted as a lamb, his twelve apostles appear as sheep, trotting out of Bethlehem and Jerusalem. The 24 elders of the

Apocalypse offer their crowns to the Saviour. The mosaic's dedicatory inscription declares that:

> The House of God shines in the splendour of glistening metal, but the light of faith remains bright. From the two martyr physicians mankind receives the wonderful hope of salvation, and this spot is made noble by their sacred glory. Felix has offered to God a worthy place, in order to dwell in the mansions of heaven.

Beyond this church rises the largest building on the Foro Romano. After a few days in Rome it is easy to see how the vaulted, three-aisled **BASILICA OF MAXENTIUS** with its massy piers, inspired many renaissance buildings (including St Peter's itself, where the vaults of the nave are exactly the same width). The three enormous coffered arches on the north side are awe-inspiring. Dominating the pavement of the Via Sacra, this basilica was started by Maxentius, but Constantine defeated him, finished the building and took credit for all of it, although now it is more usually known by the name of its founder.

The basilica dwarfs both the nearby church of Santa Francesca Romana and the triumphal Arch of Titus which stands to the south-west. Not surprisingly in this ancient part of the city, **SANTA FRANCESCA ROMANA** subsumes part of the site of the Temple of Venus and Rome. Hadrian is said to have designed this temple, which was restored in AD 307 under Maxentius. It rose from a vast terrace, the Temple of Venus abutting on to the temple of the goddess Rome. Around AD 850, when the church of Santa Maria Antiqua went out of use, Pope Leo IV decided that another church dedicated to the Virgin Mary was needed at the opposite side of the Foro Romano to replace it and this became known as Santa Maria Nova. Honorius III had it rebuilt in 1216. From this date comes the superb romanesque campanile with its majolica plaques, prototype of many in the surrounding areas of the Roman campagna.

In 1615 Carlo Lombardi gave the newly renamed church a new façade overlooking the forum, to coincide with its rededication to the recently canonized fifteenth-century saint, Francesca Maderna. She had devoted herself heroically to caring for the sick of the plague and founded an order of like-minded pious women named the 'Collatines'. Francesca's ordinary diet was hard and mouldy bread, and, according to the eighteenth-century hagiographer Alban Butler, 'she would procure secretly, out of the pouches of beggars, their dry crusts in exchange for better bread.' Her confessor made her lay aside her horse-hair girdle, but apparently allowed her to continue to drink only water, and that from a human skull. She combined her extreme piety with caring for her husband and children, and in 1608 Pope Paul V recognized her extraordinary virtues and canonized her. The church of Santa Maria Nova became the church of Santa Francesca Romana, and her relics now lie in its crypt.

The church houses some pleasing treasures, in particular a confessional by Gianlorenzo Bernini (1598–1680) and a tomb of 1585 designed by Pier Paolo Olivieri to house the bones of Pope Gregory XI who in 1377 had ended the papal exile in Avignon and brought the Curia back to Rome. The apse boasts thirteenth-century mosaics; there is a lovely fifteenth-century tabernacle by Mino da Fiesole or one of his pupils; and most extraordinary of all, Santa Francesca Romana treasures a couple of stones said to have been imprinted by the knees of St Peter himself, contrite because of his unkindness towards the wizard Simon Magus. (Simon had attempted to buy the power of the Holy Spirit, at which Peter had sharply retorted, 'Your money go with you to damnation.') St Luke is said to have painted the ancient Madonna over the high altar, but it actually dates from the sixth century. Next to the church is an early sixteenth-century cloister. The soldiers of Napoleon Bonaparte took a bronze statue of the patron saint, which was replaced in 1866 by a new marble one. To see all this, however, you must use the entrance to the building outside the Foro Romano.

The **ARCH OF TITUS** was set up in AD 81 to celebrate the victories of Titus and Vespasian in the Jewish war and the conquest and destruction of Jerusalem in AD 70. A single, beautifully proportioned arch with Composite columns bears inside a frieze displaying vanquished Jordan. Titus is borne to heaven by an eagle. One of the two finely preserved bas-reliefs depicts Titus and Victory, the other a triumphant procession bringing booty from Jerusalem, including the seven-branched candelabrum (*menorah*) and the altar of Solomon's Temple, which is decorated with trumpets.

According to the Jewish historian Josephus (AD 37/38–*c*.100), Titus himself had opposed the destruction of the temple at Jerusalem, but had been unable to restrain his soldiers. Josephus added that: 'while the holy house was on fire, everything was plundered that came to hand, and ten thousand of those that were caught were slain; nor was there a commiseration of any age, or any reverence of gravity; but children, and old men and profane persons, and priests, were all slain in the same manner.' The noise was unimaginable, he wrote: 'The flame was also carried a long way, and made an echo, together with the groans of those that were slain; and because the hill was very high, and the works of the temple were very great, one would have thought the whole city was one fire.'

To the south-west of the Foro Romano rises the **PALATINE HILL**, dotted with oaks and parasol pines, one of the city's seven hills, and Rome's oldest settlement. Happily, as in the Foro Romano, most of its buildings and ruins are identified with plaques, for the site is complex. You reach it by walking along the Clivus Palatinus, the stones of which were laid down by the early Romans themselves. Although the name 'Palatine' originally referred to the shepherd God Pales, so many imperial houses once graced this hill that its origin was forgotten and our word 'palace' derives from it. Among the distinguished residents of the past, the emperor Augustus was born here and

The work of restoring the temples of the Foro Romano is still in progress. These massive fragments lie just to one side of the Via Sacra – the processional way along which victorious general would parade up to the Capitol with plunder and captured slaves

the orator Cicero (106–43 BC) had a home on its slopes. Later the hill was colonized by medieval barons who built their fortresses here, and then in the sixteenth century rich merchant families planted vines and laid out gardens – their legacy the luxurious villa and gardens of the Farnese family, the Casino Farnesi and the Orti Farnesiani.

This is where in the ninth century BC Rome began. Legend has it that a follower of Pales, the shepherd Faustulus, discovered the twins Romulus and Remus near the Tiber being suckled by a wolf and took them into his home. Remus wanted to found the city on the Aventine Hill and decided to call it Rema. Romulus had fixed on the Palatine Hill and wanted it named Rome after himself. Remus claimed divine approval when six vultures flew over the Aventine, but then twelve flew over the Palatine. Romulus declared himself ruler of Rome and began laying the foundations of his settlement's walls, Remus leaped over them, and an enraged Romulus slew him.

The Clivus Palatinus rises beside the **CASINO FARNESE**, part of a sixteenth-century villa set amidst shady botanical gardens (the **ORTI FARNESIANI**). These gardens were laid out by the architect Giacomo Barozzi da Vignola at the behest of Cardinal Alessandro Farnese, a botanist himself, who was elected Pope Paul III in 1534. Carlo Rainaldi completed the work in the seventeenth century. Vignola also designed the portal through which you enter the gardens, an entrance incorporating an artificial grotto, where water drips down to a pool guarded by stone lions. The garden terrace rises 40 metres above the Foro Romano, affording a splendid view of its monuments and especially the three mighty arches of the Basilica of Maxentius. Nearly all of the rare plants planted here in Paul III's time have disappeared; but among these cypresses, oaks, palm trees and pines, across these lawns and beside these fountains, parterres and a little maze, the learned guests of the Cardinal discussed literature, politics and the gossip of the Roman Curia. Under some of the trees, benches have been provided for modern visitors.

Down steps from these gardens you reach the walls of the **DOMUS TIBERIANA**, or Palace of Tiberius, much of it still unexcavated under the Orti Farnesiani. The emperor Caligula rebuilt much of this palace, which became the chief residence of the emperors for most of the first century AD. It was near here on 24 January AD 41 that Caligula, the sadistic madman who had watched his victims being tortured and executed while he dined, and who had made his favourite horse, Porcellus, both a consul and a member of the college of priests, was himself assassinated. Eerie vaulted passages, once stuccoed, turn right and left to emerge at the remains of the **DOMUS FLAVIA** (Palace of the Flavians), the official residence of the imperial governor.

Built by the architect Rabirius in the late first century AD for the emperor Domitian, this huge complex embraces a courtyard which was surrounded by columns and reception rooms. Here the general public were admitted to treat with the emperor and his officials. Beside this palace are three imposing halls. On the left is a three-aisled basilica with an apse closed

The imperial family chose the Palatine Hill for their private homes. Originally the walls would have been frescoed or faced with marble, and the floors would have been covered with marble or mosaics.

by a marble balustrade, where the emperor's tribunal sat. Beneath it was built a chapel frescoed with scenes from the cult of Isis. In the centre is the former throne room, once adorned with massive statues.

To the right of the palace stands the **ANTIQUARIUM**, which was later used as a convent, and in which are displayed the treasures excavated from the Palatine Hill and in particular from its Bronze Age village. They include some of the stuccoes which once graced the Domus Tiberiana. The Antiquarium also contains the earliest representation of the Crucifixion, a celebrated piece of mockery which depicts Christ as a donkey. An inscription adds: 'Alexamenos worships his god'.

Just south of the Antiquarium is one of the granite porticoes of the school for imperial slaves, the **PAEDOGOGIUM**. One celebrated graffito on its marble walls, accompanying the drawing of an ass, reads *labora, aselle, quomodo ego laboravi et proderi tibi* (work, little donkey, as I have worked, and it will profit you). From other inscriptions scholars conjecture that part of the Paedogogium was used as a prison, which will not surprise many a child trudging unwillingly to school.

The Antiquarium gives directly onto an elliptical garden, 80 metres wide and 180 metres long, which was laid out by Domitian and served the Romans as a hippodrome and for military exercises. Looking down, you can still make out perfectly the plan of the stadium, set out in brick and stone. Here, during the reign of Diocletian, St Sebastian was clubbed to death, having survived the earlier attempt to execute him with arrows. Across it are the ruins of the mighty palace and extensive **BATHS OF SEPTIMUS SEVERUS**, their powerful substructure now open to the skies.

Behind the Domus Flavia are the remains of more intimate imperial quarters, such as the home in which Augustus and successive emperors lived, an aristocratic house built in the first century BC. Four rooms of the lower storey have been laid bare by archaeologists. The dining room and the little atrium are fascinating, decorated with refined *trompe-l'oeil* paintings of windows, landscapes and still lifes. Painted garlands of fruit, flowers and imitation marble enliven the side rooms. Among the mythological scenes decorating the centre room Acis and Galatea flee the wrath of Polyphemus, while on another wall Mercury comes to release Io from Argus. The upper storey is known as the **CASA LIVIA**, the house of Augustus's widow, and consisted of a central court surrounded by a dozen rooms.

A magnificent **TEMPLE OF APOLLO** formerly rose beside this house, but all that remains today is its impressive podium. Augustus himself restored the original **TEMPLE OF CYBELE**, dedicated to Magna Mater. Finished in 192 BC this earlier temple marked the first introduction into Rome of oriental religions, apparently at the command of the Sybilline prophetic books. Further excavations nearby have revealed a Bronze Age village with cabins dating from the ninth century BC. Such villagers hewed a large cavity in the rock, in which they apparently stored their food. In these scholarly times, it

The Domus Flavia was built for the emperor Domitian by the architect Rabirius at the end of the first century. It was used more for official functions than as a family home.

is disappointing to report that guides no longer identify one of the dwellings as the house of Romulus.

Leaving the Palatine Hill, you walk down a path leading to the **COLOSSEUM**, the massive amphitheatre which sums up ancient Rome better than anything else in the city. It is a staggering 186 metres long, 156 metres wide and 57 metres high, with an external circumference of 527 metres. No one is certain what its name signifies, although the best bet is that it derives from a colossal statue of the emperor Nero which stood near the start of today's Via dei Fori Imperiali until Pope Gregory the Great had it destroyed in the sixth century.

The emperor Vespasian began building this superb edifice in AD 72. His son, Titus, finished it eight years later, adding the fourth storey. For 80 days a festival inaugurating the arena entertained the citizens with the slaughter of 5000 beasts and anything up to 2000 gladiators. Clad in purple, the gladiators would greet the emperor with the words *Ave Caesar, morturi te salutant* ('Hail Caesar, we who are about to die salute you'). These were the first of many to perish here, their fates presaging those of countless Christians torn to shreds in front of often drunken spectators. (Although some scholars have hinted that these later martyrdoms took place elsewhere, I prefer to print the legend.) The Colosseum could even be flooded to provide a venue for naval spectacles and battles.

More civilized attitudes eventually prevailed. Gladiators were banned from the Colosseum in AD 405 and combats with wild animals in 523. Repeatedly damaged by earthquakes, this mighty pile was further humiliated by being used as a source of building materials throughout the Middle Ages. Palaces, churches, even the basilica of St Peter profited from the despoliation of one of Rome's finest relics. The plunder was halted in the mid eighteenth century by Pope Benedict XIV, who declared the Colosseum a holy site, sanctified by the blood of Christian martyrs. A wooden cross was erected in their honour at the heart of the elliptical arena (replaced by a bronze one in 1927). Inspired by this far-sighted pope, his successors, Pius VII, Leo XIII, Gregory XVI and Pius IX set about restoring the bruised monument.

The grandeur remains. Its north-eastern side is virtually intact, the arches of the three lower storeys displaying as they rise three orders of architecture (successively Doric, Ionic and Corinthian) while the upper storey is graced with slender, Corinthian pilasters. Eighty arches lead into vaulted concentric corridors, along which are the staircases which once conducted up to 50,000 spectators to their numbered seats – which were scrupulously allotted according to individual status. Members of the imperial court would sit in the finest seats, alongside important civil servants and the Vestal Virgins; patrician families occupied the next best rows; the third and fourth tiers were reserved for plebeians. Incredibly, you can still trace numbers XXIII to LIV. A labyrinth of underground passages led to the rooms in

OPPOSITE *The stadium built by Domitian near his palace on the Palatine Hill was the site of countless Christian martyrdoms: the most celebrated was that of St Sebastian.*

which wild beasts were caged, gladiators waited to die and stagehands toiled to raise scenery into the arena. In inclement weather, and still more in the blazing Roman sun, they were able to erect an awning to shelter the more important spectators.

In the Piazza del Colosseo is another Roman monument, the triumphal **ARCH OF CONSTANTINE**, some 230 years younger than the Colosseum. Erected in AD 315, it celebrates the victory three years earlier of the emperor Constantine over his rival, Maxentius, at the Battle of the Milvian Bridge. When Constantine's father died at York in AD 305, the soldiers proclaimed him emperor, but these were troubled times and for the next three years the Roman empire was cursed with no fewer than five emperors – three in the east, and two in the west: Constantine and Maximian. In AD 309 Maximian committed suicide, having been driven out of Rome by his own son, Maxentius who usurped the throne and began threatening Gaul.

Crossing the Alps, Constantine defeated him three times. At the final battle in AD 312, Maxentius foolishly emerged from Rome to fight with the River Tiber at his back. Retreating, he was drowned. Years later, Constantine told the historian Eusebius that before the battle he had a vision of the cross athwart the noonday sun, with the inscription 'In this sign conquer'. So he became a Christian – of sorts. As a modern historian (Henry Chadwick) has put it:

> If his conversion should not be interpreted as an inward experience of grace, neither was it a cynical act of Machiavellian cunning. It was a military matter. His comprehension of Christian doctrine was never very clear, but he was sure that victory in battle lay with the God of the Christians.

Soon Constantine was inscribing his coins and the shields of his warriors with the Chi-Rho symbol, a monogram of the name Christ.

This particular victory was thus of tremendous importance for the spread of Christianity. Embracing the teachings of the Prince of Peace because he believed his inferior forces had defeated his enemy only through the divine aid of Christ, Constantine, in 313, issued the Edict of Milan, granting tolerance to Christians throughout his realms. In 324 Christianity was raised to the status of a state religion.

Until the Battle of the Milvian Bridge, Constantine had worshipped the Unconquered Sun, and continued blithely to do so while also adhering to Christianity. He even postponed his baptism until he lay dying in AD 337, but this was no rare thing in the ancient world. Rulers often ordered the torture and execution of criminals and felt it wiser to delay until the last possible moment the total forgiveness which they believed came from being washed in the waters of the font.

All this is summed up on the Arch of Constantine – the best-preserved and largest in Rome – which the Senate and the people of Rome erected in

OPPOSITE *The Colosseum was started by Vespasian in AD 72, and a fourth storey was added by his son Titus before it was inaugurated in AD 80. The rooms which were originally under the floor of the amphitheatre held cages for animals and changing rooms for the gladiators.*

the emperor's honour beside the Colosseum. It depicts the drowning of Maxentius and his troops in the Tiber, and the inscription proclaims that Constantine's victory came 'by the prompting of the deity' (INSTINCTV DIVINITATIS, three lines down on the Colosseum side of the arch). Which deity: divine Constantine; the sun-god; or Christ? The arch keeps its counsel, although one of its medallions depicts the moon sinking in its chariot, while the sun rises.

We are not even certain which of these lovely medallions graced the original arch, for in later years many were taken from other buildings and brought here to link Constantine's name with the glories of ancient Rome. As a result an arch designed to honour Constantine is plastered with medallions glorifying other great Romans; some of these, including those above the entablature, are earlier than the arch itself, dating from the second century AD. Two reliefs on the inside of the central arch and two more on the sides depict Trajan's victories over the Dacians. The statues on the arch represent barbarians he had conquered. Eight others are said to derive from a monument to Marcus Aurelius (though some scholars think this is Trajan again), showing him sacrificing, addressing the army and the people and making a triumphal entry into Rome. Other charming reliefs depict a boar hunt and a ceremony in honour of Apollo.

Walking from the triumphal arch along Via di San Gregorio you pass under a huge three-arched viaduct to see rising on the left the baroque façade of the church of **SAN GREGORIO MAGNO**. This façade, created by Giovanni Battista Soria around 1630 surprisingly leads not into the church but to an arcaded renaissance courtyard, frescoed with scenes from the life of St Gregory the Great. Here amongst other tombs are those of two English Catholics (Sir Robert Peckham and Sir Edward Carne) who sought refuge in Rome at the time of the Reformation.

The finest work of art inside the church is a tabernacle created by Andrea Bregno in 1469 for the chapel of St Gregory. Four ancient columns rise from a mosaic pavement, all strangely at odds with the early eighteenth-century interior. Three cypress-shaded chapels are reached from the courtyard. The one on the right dates from 1603 and is dedicated to Gregory's mother St Sylvia, and rises over her grave. The other two are older. That dedicated to St Andrew, houses Domenichino's (1581–1641) painting of the apostle's flagellation and a recently discovered eleventh-century mural. In the third, dedicated to St Barbara, is a third-century table from which the founder is said to have served twelve paupers each day. One day a thirteenth pauper appeared who turned out to be an angel in disguise, hence the popular name of the chapel, the Triclinium Pauperum.

It was here that Gregory commissioned St Augustine of Canterbury to evangelize the English, and a fresco painted in the church by Antonio Viviani in 1602 illustrates one of the pope's most delightful remarks. As the Venerable Bede tells the tale: 'One day some recently arrived merchants

OPPOSITE *The Arch of Constantine, built by the Senate to celebrate his victory over Maxentius at the Battle of the Milvian Bridge, was successively embellished with medallions and carvings from other ancient Roman buildings.*

displayed their wares in the crowded Roman market-place. Gregory saw that amongst the goods some boys were exhibited for sale.' Looking with interest at their fair complexions, finely cut features and fair hair, Gregory asked where they came from and received the answer 'From Britain'. What, then, was their race? he asked. Told the boys were English, he replied, 'Not Angles but Angels' (*non Angli sed Angeli*).

High to the left of San Gregorio Magno, you can see through the trees the eighteenth-century dome and the pillars which circle the apse of the romanesque basilica of **SANTI GIOVANNI E PAOLO**, one of the oldest churches on the **CELIAN HILL**. Pagan survivals have embedded themselves in this Christian church, and as you pass under the ancient buttresses supporting its north wall, you can still trace the complex patterns of successive rebuilding and what may well have been a pre-Christian house.

A rich convert named Pammachius built it in around AD 370 on the site of a house where two imperial officials named John and Paul were executed in private for their faith and refusal to serve him by Constantine's successor, Julian the Apostate, who feared their deaths might provoke a revolt. Remains of this house evoke those perilous times. Excavated since 1887, they consist of twenty or so rooms which you can visit by descending the staircase at the end of the south aisle of the church. Many other martyred corpses were discovered as the excavations continued, while the bathrooms, cellars, storehouses and reception rooms, frescoed from the second to the fourth centuries AD with birds, cupids and vines, speak of the sophisticated civilization which these men and women were willing to forsake in favour of their newly discovered faith. The fresco of the bathroom is especially charming, probably dating from the third century and depicting Proserpine returning to the earth's surface from Hades.

The church itself was restored during the reign of Pope Paschal II (1099–1118). Adrian IV (the sole English pope) added a portico of eight Ionic columns in 1158, as well as the apse and the complex romanesque campanile with its coloured tiles. In his reign was laid down the Cosmatesque pavement (named after the twelfth-century family of mosaicists) and around the same time the apse was frescoed with portraits of Christ and six of his apostles.

A much-loved church risks being continually rebuilt. The restoration of 1454 was paid for by Cardinal Latino Orsini, and another, in 1575, by Cardinal Niccolò de Pelleve. Cardinal Antonio Carafa of Naples employed Niccolò Circignani to fresco the apse and the walls of the nave. Finally, in 1718 Antonio Canevari was commissioned by Cardinal Fabrizio Paolucci to transform the interior with granite columns, and chandeliers. Happily, the portico, with its columns, early romanesque lions and narrow twelfth-century mosaic around its main door still beckons you inside. In a little chapel fourth-century frescoes portray the martyrdom of saints Crispin, Crispinius and Benedicta under Julian the Apostate.

To the north-east of this church are the vestiges of the **TEMPLE OF CLAUDIUS**, erected by Agrippina, niece and wife of the emperor she had assassinated so that her son Nero (by a previous husband) might succeed him.

Walking back to San Gregorio Magno and then along Via dei Cerchi, you pass what was undoubtedly the greatest circus of ancient Rome. Laid out in around 600 BC in the hollow that separates the Aventine and Palatine Hills, the wooden seats of the **CIRCO MASSIMO** (Circus Maximus) initially catered for something like 260,000 spectators. Julius Caesar substituted stone seats, and the circus was subsequently enlarged to accommodate 385,000. Its race-track was an ellipse 550 metres long and 80 metres wide. As at the Colosseum, the various orders of society were segregated, but here men and women mingled together – offering, according to Ovid (43 BC–AD 17) scope for dalliance and prostitution. Horse-drawn chariots continued racing here until AD 549, when the city lay in ruins and Totila the Ostrogoth witnessed the last contest. Today, although you can trace the lines of the circus, scarcely a stone remains. The obelisks which once marked the course now stand elsewhere, one in the Piazza del Popolo, the other in the Piazza San Giovanni in Laterano. The racetrack now is the road itself, along which hurtles the Roman traffic.

Turn right along Via di San Teodoro. Climbing up the street you spot to the left, along Via del Velabro, the squat brick campanile of the romanesque

The Circo Massimo was almost half a kilometre long, and although it is supposed to have been founded in the sixth century BC, the enclosures were probably not completed for some 400 years. The final games were held here in AD 549 by Totila the Ostrogoth.

church of **SAN GIORGIO IN VELABRO**. The Velabrum was the marsh which once separated the Palatine Hill from the Capitoline Hill. At times the Tiber flooded and the Velabrum was passable only by boat. Floods are still a hazard, and you discover inside the porch of the church a mark indicating the height reached by the last one.

A church has stood here probably since the fourth century. Pope Leo II restored it in the seventh century and dedicated it to St Sebastian. In the 740s Pope Zacharius made St George its co-patron. The extraordinary renown of this saint in both eastern and western Christendom is all the more remarkable since next to nothing historically reliable is known about him. Having enlisted as a Roman soldier in the age of Diocletian, he is said to have resigned his commission when the emperor turned against the Christians. In consequence he was tortured and then beheaded. Later tradition added the tale of George rescuing a maiden from a dragon, a feat which supposedly persuaded thousands to convert to Christianity. Pope Zacharius somehow obtained what he believed to be the saint's severed head, his spear and a part of his standard, and gave them to this church. Another reason for rededicating San Giorgio in Velabro to a saint revered in the east was that in the eighth century the Byzantine militia of Rome had its headquarters in this part of the city.

Entering the church through a thirteenth-century portico, you step back into antiquity. Twenty-four ancient grey columns, four of the veined marble pavonazzo, the rest of granite are, like so many features of Roman churches, reused from an older, pre-Christian building and divide the starkly simple building into three aisles. Irregular arcading rises from their Ionic and Corinthian capitals. Whoever built this church was skilled enough to arrange for the columns to converge as they near the apse, giving an illusion of greater length. Above the twelfth-century ciborium, which rises from the altar on marble Corinthian columns, are frescoes by the painter and mosaicist Pietro Cavallini who spent most of his time in Rome from around 1280 until his death in 1330. Greens and reds contrast sharply with St George's white charger. Christ blesses us, surrounded by the Virgin Mary and Saints Peter and Sebastian. Selenite instead of glass fills the windows, darkening the church but protecting its precious frescoes from harmful sunlight. The baldacchino over the high altar dates from the eighth century, and under the altar are the relics of St George presented to the church by Pope Zacharius over 1200 years ago.

Abutting on to the church is the **ARCO DEGLI ARGENTARI** built in AD 204 by Rome's moneychangers in honour of Septimus Severus. On it a sculpted Hercules leans on his tree-like club and carries a lion-skin. Continuing between the Foro Romano and the renaissance palaces of Via di San Teodoro along Via dei Fienili you reach the Via della Consolazione and the apse of **SANTA MARIA DELLA CONSOLAZIONE**, the white baroque façade of which is by Martino Longhi the Elder (d. 1591) while the mannerist frescoes inside were painted by Taddeo Zuccaro (1629–66). Pause now for a drink and a green salad in the excellent self-service bar in Via San Giovanni Decollato above the piazza.

The church of **SAN GIOVANNI DECOLLATO** was built in 1535 by the Confraternità della Misericordia, a charitable brotherhood to which Michelangelo belonged, whose aim was to succour those condemned to execution. Visiting the condemned in gaol, members of the confraternity would accompany them to the gallows and after their execution bury their corpses and say masses for their pardon. Thus the dedication of this church to St John the Baptist, whose severed head was brought to King Herod Antipas on a platter, is apposite.

San Giovanni Decollato was severely restored in the early eighteenth century, though the interior is lavish. In its oratory are frescoes, including scenes from the life of John the Baptist, by Jacopino del Conte (1510–98), and a portrait of Jacopino by Michelangelo. The grisliest sights are reserved for those who are brave enough to visit the museum. Here are displayed the knives which sliced through the ropes of those who had been hanged, the baskets in which were caught the heads of those who had been decapitated, the inkwells and pens offered to men and women needing to write out their wills, and the lanterns which would burn throughout the final night on earth of a doomed criminal.

Walk back to the church of Santa Maria della Consolazione, to climb Via di Monte Tarpeo, up the **CAPITOLINE HILL**. The steep cliff above which it rises may well be the Tarpeian Rock over which criminals were thrown to their deaths. It takes its name from a woman called Tarpeia, who betrayed the Romans to the Sabines. Her reward, she said, should be what they wore on their left arms, meaning their costly bracelets. The Sabines also carried their shields on this arm, and with them they crushed Tarpeia to death. Via di Monte Tarpeo ziz-zags up from the church of Santa Maria della Consolazione to the Capitoline, Rome's smallest, but most important, hill.

On the Capitol Tarquinius Superbus built a magnificent temple in 509 BC, dedicated to Jupiter Optimus Maximus, to Minerva and to Juno. The Capitol was where the people would meet to debate important issues, but it has also seen bloodier events. Here in 390 BC, when the Gauls attempted to take the city by stealth at night, the sacred geese dedicated to Juno set up such a cackling that the citizens were roused and repulsed their enemies. In 133 BC the tribune Tiberius Sempronius Gracchus was murdered and 300 of his followers clubbed to death here in the ensuing civil war between those for and against reform. Razed to the ground in 83 BC during another civil war, the temple was restored by Domitian (AD 81–96) and finally plundered and destroyed by the Vandals in AD 455.

For much of the Dark Ages the Capitol was deserted, save by goats and those who herded them. The prefect and senators of Rome moved back here in the eleventh century, building themselves a palace which Boniface IX

In front of the double staircase that Michelangelo designed for the Palazzo Senatorio he placed ancient statues of the gods of the Nile and the Tiber flanking the goddess Minerva.

converted into a fortress in the late fourteenth century. But the Capitoline today breathes not medievalism but the High Renaissance. Pope Paul III vigorously set about its restoration in 1537 to welcome the Holy Roman Emperor Charles V, decreeing that the then concave centre of the Capitol should be filled in to create a piazza, the **PIAZZA DEL CAMPIDOGLIO**. This beautifully proportioned, mathematically rational trapezoid, its buildings exquisitely illuminated at dusk, was designed by Michelangelo and finished in the seventeenth century. For many years it was the showcase of a bronze statue of the stoic philosopher and emperor Marcus Aurelius, dating from the second century AD and one of the rare equestrian statues of that era. Michelangelo designed a base for it. This representation of a pagan emperor survived intact because Christians supposed it to represent their liberator Constantine. The depradations of twentieth-century pollution have proved deadlier, and today the statue, restored and polished, is hidden behind glass in the Cortile di Marforio of the Palazzo Nuovo.

The **PALAZZO SENATORIO** on the right as we turn into the piazza, now serves as Rome's city hall. Michelangelo drew up plans for its façade but in 1592 these were modified by Giacomo della Porta and Girolamo Rainaldi. Below it is a fountain on which sits a little statue of the goddess Minerva, and its double staircase, again the work of Michelangelo, is graced by rather less elegant Roman statues of the Nile (in the form of a Sphinx) and the Tiber (Romulus and Remus). A sixteenth-century statue of Rome by Martino Longhi the Elder rises from the tower which he also designed. From the balcony of this palace in 1849 a free and united Roman Republic was proclaimed by Giuseppe Mazzini. 'I entered the city one evening with a deep sense of wonder, even of worship', Mazzini wrote. 'Rome to me was then as now, in spite of her degradation, the temple of humanity. From Rome will one day spring the religious transformation which is destined to bestow a moral unity on Europe.' Was his prophecy in part fulfilled in 1957 when the same building saw the signing of the Treaty of Rome which set up the European Economic Community?

The best place to see the coherence of the design of the piazza is from the top of the ramp opposite the Palazzo Senatorio. The buildings to either side make up what is known as the Capitoline Museum. The **PALAZZO DEI CONSERVATORI**, on the right of the piazza was built in around 1450, but remodelled in the 1560s by Giacomo della Porta and Guidetto Guidetti, again to plans by Michelangelo. This houses the Sale dei Conservatori, the Museo del Palazzo dei Conservatori, and the Pinacotheca. The **PALAZZO NUOVO**, to the left of the piazza, is more properly known as the **PALAZZO DEL MUSEO CAPITOLINO** and contains the Museo Capitolino itself. This building was designed by Michelangelo, but not completed until the middle of the seventeenth century.

In the Palazzo Nuovo, whose courtyard is dominated by a colossal second-century statue of a river god, dubbed 'Marforio', is a collection of antique sculptures, including it has to be said a good number of replicas rather than originals. The Emperors' Room contains the busts of 64 emperors as well as several remarkably realistic sculpted heads of other members of imperial families and famous philosophers. In Room 7 stands a stunning *Venus*, sculpted in Asia Minor in the second century BC, and a copy of the *Aphrodite of Cnidos* by Praxiteles (*fl.* 370–30 BC). But the most famous work here is undoubtedly the *Dying Gaul* in Room 1. This sculpture probably is part of a series commissioned by Attalus I Sotor, King of Pergamum, after he had defeated the Gauls in 239 BC. The warrior sits on his shield, blood seeping from a self-inflicted wound, for he evidently prefers death to the ignominy of capture.

Relics of a massive statue of Constantine which once stood in the Basilica of Maxentius adorn the courtyard of the Palazzo dei Conservatori. With its monumental staircase and splendidly sculpted ceilings, this palace houses a collection celebrated for a delicate first-century BC bronze of a boy pulling a thorn from his foot, the *Spinario*, and above all for a late sixth- or early

Michelangelo designed the Piazza del Campidoglio and its three palaces in 1546. The massive colonnade of the Palazzo del Museo Capitolino echoes the giant order he used for St Peter's.

fifth-century BC statue of the she-wolf which suckled Romulus and Remus. To this Etruscan masterpiece Antonio del Pollaiuolo added the statues of the twins in 1509. Another masterpiece is Bernini's statue of an inscrutable Pope Urban VIII. On the upper floor, works by Titian, Tintoretto, Giovanni Bellini, Lorenzo Lotto and Caravaggio vie with masterpieces by Velazquez, Rubens and Van Dyck. Two of my favourites in this gallery are Pietro da Cortona's baroque *Rape of the Sabine Women*, and the sole copy of a brooding portrait of Michelangelo by Jacopino del Conte.

One side of the Piazza del Campidoglio is open, with a staircase and ramp leading down flanked by balustrades, on which are the Trophies of Marius – two sets of barbarian weapons – followed by statues of the emperor Constantine and his son Constantine II. Then come two colossal statues of Castor and Pollux as horse-tamers, and finally a couple of granite Egyptian lions. In a little garden on the right is a nineteenth-century bronze statue of Cola di Rienzo, the self-styled tribune who in the fourteenth century tried to reintroduce the old forms of government and sweep away the decadence and corruption of his own day. The bronze marks the spot where he was killed by the mob in October 1354.

In around 1550 Giacomo Barozzi da Vignola designed the steps and colonnades which lead from this piazza (and from a little statue of the wolf suckling Romulus and Remus) up to the church of **SANTA MARIA IN ARACOELI**, which stands at the highest point of the Capitol on the site of the Temple of Juno Moneta. The name derives from a legend of Augustus. In AD 14, conscious that his life was drawing to a close, the emperor asked the sibyl who lived on the Capitol to prophesy his successor. She replied that a Jewish child, born of a virgin, would destroy the altars of false gods and bring the whole world under his sway. In response Augustus built an altar here which he inscribed HAEC EST ARA PRIMOGENITI DEI,

One of the most celebrated of ancient statues, the Dying Gaul in the Palazzo Nuovo.

In spite of the wear and tear of centuries, this horse-tamer in the Piazza del Campidoglio presents a noble figure.

'This is the altar of God's first-born'. So the church is dedicated to the 'Ara Coeli', the altar of heaven.

Above it rose a basilica which the Franciscans remodelled and partially rebuilt in the thirteenth century, never managing to cover its brick façade with marble (although a classical doorway was added in the Renaissance). Over the entrance is a thirteenth-century mosaic of the Madonna and Child. The massive romanesque church retains 22 ancient columns, eighteen of Egyptian marble, two of apollino and two of white marble. Look at the third column on the left, where the inscription A CUBICULO AUGUSTORYM indicate that it derives from a building of Rome's imperial age.

Porphyry, serpentine and coloured marble pave the floor of the nave. In 1571 the Roman Senate paid for a new, sumptuously gilded ceiling, to commemorate the victory of the Christians over the Turks at the Battle of

Lepanto, and from it hang splendid chandeliers. A couple of mosaic-encrusted *ambones* (pulpits) in the crossing were made by Lorenzo and Giacomo di Cosma at the end of the twelfth century. As in many other Roman churches, the painting over the high altar is said to be by St Luke.

Other paintings here are superb. In the 1480s Pinturicchio decorated the first chapel on the right with frescoes colourfully depicting the life of St Bernardino of Siena, who had been canonized in 1450. This was among the first works in Rome of the Perugian master who was to decorate the splendid Borgia apartments in the Vatican. Benozzo Gozzoli painted a portrait of St Antony of Padua in a chapel in the right aisle. The tombs in this church are equally remarkable. That of Pope Honorius IV, who died in 1287, was brought here when the old basilica of St Peter's was demolished to build the present one. Honorius's father, Luca Savelli, his mother and one of his family named Pandolfo also lie in fine tombs (Pandolfo's designed by Giotto, Savelli's perhaps by Arnolfo di Cambio). The earthly remains of Cardinal d'Albret lie in a tomb of 1465 by Andrea Bregno; and in 1432 Donatello designed the now much-mutilated tomb of Archdeacon Giovanni Crivelli. On the tomb of the astronomer Lodovico Grato Margani who died in 1531 is a statue of Christ by Andrea Sansovino. Just beside the sacristy is the tomb of Cardinal Matteo d'Acquasparta, created in 1302, and above it is a fresco of the Virgin Mary, carrying her divine child and supported by saints, which was done by the painter and mosaicist Pietro Cavallini.

Two other religious treasures add lustre to Santa Maria in Aracoeli. In the third chapel on the right of the high altar a chapel of 1602 contains an urn reputed to shelter the bones of St Helena, mother of the emperor Constantine. Here Augustus is said to have set up his altar. And in the Sacristy you can see the bejewelled and richly clothed Santo Bambino, an image of the infant Jesus carved out of olive wood in the sixteenth century. This statue is credited with miraculous powers, and around Christmas the children of Rome sing its praises with poems and little speeches.

Taken to the houses of the sick, the Bambino is still reputed efficacious at curing them, and letters are written to him from all over the world, by or on behalf of sick children. They are placed near the statue for some days and then burned, unopened.

Until recently it was believed that the church of Santa Maria in Aracoeli had risen on the site of the Temple of Jupiter. Gibbon thought so, and sitting in this church conceived the notion of writing what became an historical masterpiece of sustained satire and invective. He wrote in his *Autobiography*,

> It was at Rome, on the fifteenth of October, 1764, as I sat musing amidst the ruins of the Capitol, while the barefooted friars were singing Vespers in the temple of Jupiter, that the idea of writing the decline and fall of the City first started to my mind.

The very plain façade and sides of Santa Maria in Aracoeli dominate the capital. The name is derived from Augustus's Altar of Heaven which stood here.

Not everyone would agree that the church of Santa Maria in Aracoeli represents any sort of decline from the ancient splendours which once rose on the Capitoline Hill.

Pinturicchio's skill at blending pathos and religious fervour is masterfully displayed in the Death of St Bernardino of Siena, *as is the artist's evident delight in architectural perspective.*

2
Fountains and baroque façades

....

PIAZZA NAVONA *to* SANTA MARIA DEL POPOLO

Throughout the age of the Renaissance and the baroque era, Rome was blessed with popes, cardinals and princes who devoted themselves to enriching the urban landscape of the city. In exploring what these princes of church and state have left us, this tour principally devotes itself to baroque Rome. It takes us through piazzas watered by ornate fountains and flanked by equally sumptuous façades. It explores a Rome in which two artists especially flourished, the Rome of the sculptor and architect Gianlorenzo Bernini, and his rival Francesco Borromini. Our walk encounters the legacy of such powerful families as the Barberini, a Tuscan dynasty which had become rich on trade in the sixteenth century and in the next became one of the most powerful in Rome when Maffeo Barberini was elected Pope Urban VIII in 1623.

The legacy of such men is delightful, especially for those who do not have to pay for it. Ancient buildings were cleared away to make space for sumptuous palaces and squares (giving rise to the pun *Quod non fecerunt barbari, fecerunt Barberini*: 'what the barbarians failed to do, the Barberini did'). Amongst the luxurious buildings explored on the tour are the Palazzo Doria Pamphilj and the Villa Borghese.

Baroque architects loved the play of sumptuous fountains, and this walk starts with three of them and visits more. Even the Pantheon is fronted by a rippling fountain. Few of these architects could resist a visual conceit, and amongst the stunning squares they enhanced we visit the often neglected piazza in which Bernini set an obelisk on the back of an elephant. In addition superb churches are visited, amongst them the ornate Jesuit church of the Gesù, sinuous Sant'Ignazio and the swaggering Sant'Andrea della Valle, whose dome is second in size in Rome only to that of St Peter's.

Rome's most harmonious piazza, the traffic-free **PIAZZA NAVONA**, derives its name from *agone*, the Italian word for contest, for it occupies the site and

OPPOSITE *The ubiquitous Romulus and Remus, and their friendly she-wolf, here seen amid the statuary of the Porta del Popolo.*

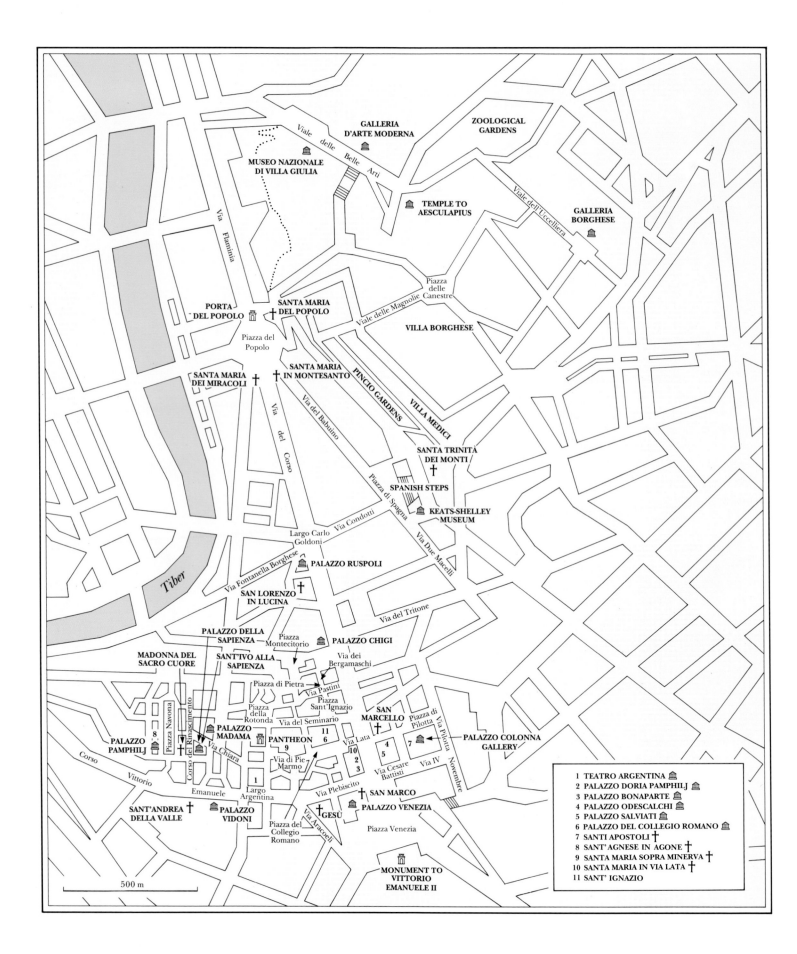

GALLERIA
D'ARTE MODERNA

ZOOLOGICAL
GARDENS

Viale delle Belle Arti

MUSEO NAZIONALE
DI VILLA GIULIA

TEMPLE TO
AESCULAPIUS

Viale dell'Uccelliera

GALLERIA
BORGHESE

Via Flaminia

Piazza delle Canestre

PORTA
DEL POPOLO

SANTA MARIA
DEL POPOLO

Viale delle Magnolie

VILLA BORGHESE

Piazza del Popolo

SANTA MARIA
DEI MIRACOLI

SANTA MARIA
IN MONTESANTO

PINCIO GARDENS

VILLA MEDICI

Via del Babuino

Via del Corso

SANTA TRINITÀ
DEI MONTI

SPANISH STEPS

Piazza di Spagna

KEATS-SHELLEY
MUSEUM

Via Condotti

*Largo Carlo
Goldoni*

Via Due Macelli

Via Fontanella Borghese

PALAZZO RUSPOLI

Tiber

SAN LORENZO
IN LUCINA

Via del Tritone

PALAZZO DELLA
SAPIENZA

*Piazza
Montecitorio*

PALAZZO CHIGI

MADONNA DEL
SACRO CUORE

SANT'IVO ALLA
SAPIENZA

*Via dei
Bergamaschi*

Piazza di Pietra

Via Pastini

*Piazza
Sant'Ignazio*

SAN
MARCELLO

*Piazza di
Pilotta*

PALAZZO COLONNA
GALLERY

*Piazza della
Rotonda*

Via del Seminario

11

Via Lata

PALAZZO
PAMPHILJ

8

Piazza Navona

Corso del Rinascimento

PALAZZO
MADAMA

PANTHEON

9

6

4

7

Via Pilotta

Corso Vittorio

Via Chiara

*Via di Pie
Marmo*

10

2

5

Via IV Novembre

1

3

*Via Cesare
Battisti*

SANT'ANDREA
DELLA VALLE

PALAZZO
VIDONI

*Largo
Argentina*

Via Plebiscito

SAN MARCO

Emanuele

*Piazza del
Collegio
Romano*

GESÙ

Via Aracoeli

PALAZZO VENEZIA

Piazza Venezia

MONUMENT TO
VITTORIO
EMANUELE II

500 m

1	TEATRO ARGENTINA
2	PALAZZO DORIA PAMPHILJ
3	PALAZZO BONAPARTE
4	PALAZZO ODESCALCHI
5	PALAZZO SALVIATI
6	PALAZZO DEL COLLEGIO ROMANO
7	SANTI APOSTOLI
8	SANT'AGNESE IN AGONE
9	SANTA MARIA SOPRA MINERVA
10	SANTA MARIA IN VIA LATA
11	SANT'IGNAZIO

follows the pattern of a stadium built by Domitian and long used for festivals, races and jousts. Today three fountains adorn the spot, always surrounded with animated crowds and illuminated in the evenings to glamorize the cafés and restaurants whose tables spill out into the open air. And from early December to 6 January the piazza is filled with a children's market, selling sweets, Christmas decorations, toys and Neapolitan crèches. These are made out of twigs, broken-off branches and deftly arranged bark.

Gianlorenzo Bernini created masks and mermen for the southernmost Fountain, the **FONTANA DEL MORO**. The Moor bestrides a spurting dolphin. At the northern end of the piazza, amid nereids and sea-horses, Neptune wrestles with a monster from the deep, in the **FONTANA DEL NETTUNO** created in 1878 by Leone della Bitta and Gregorio Zappalà. The sea-god plunges his spear into an octopus which grasps his legs; and the watery scene is further enlivened by mermaids, fish, dolphins and foaming sea-horses.

The central fountain, the **FONTANA DEI FIUMI**, is the most entrancing of the three. In 1648 Pope Innocent X commissioned Bernini to design a fountain representing rivers from the four corners of the world. Bernini's pupils sculpted the four massive figures of the Ganges, the Nile, the Danube and the Plate, each bearing Innocent's coat of arms, displaying fleurs-de-lys and a dove with an olive branch. The Nile is blindfolded, for at the time no one knew its source. From the centre of the simulated grottoes rises an obelisk which once stood in the Circus of Maxentius. Its hieroglyphics spell out the names of the emperors Vespasian, Titus and Domitian. Perching on top of it is the pope's family symbol, the dove of peace.

Bernini's great rival Francesco Borromini designed the baroque façade of the church of **SANT'AGNESE IN AGONE** on the west side of the piazza. The story runs that the statue of the Nile was deliberately depicted covering his eyes so that he might not see Borromini's work, whereas the Plate raises his hand to curse the building. In fact, Borromini began work only when the fountain had been finished. His façade is a triumph of convex and concave curves, of windows, columns and busy little pillars. Innocent X's coat of arms appears once more over the door.

Sant'Agnese in Agone stands on the reputed site of a fourth-century brothel, and its foundation springs from the inspiring tale of St Agnes. Agnes was a girl of such beauty that countless rich noblemen sought her hand in marriage, but she steadfastly refused, declaring that she was the spouse of Jesus. Enraged, some of these suitors betrayed her faith to one of Diocletian's magistrates. Threatened with torture, she was dragged before idols and commanded to burn incense to them. The great doctor of the church, St Ambrose of Milan (334/340–397) recorded that 'she could be compelled by no means even to move her hand, save to make the sign of the cross'.

In an attempt to break her resolve, the magistrate decided to send her to the brothel, to be humiliated and debauched. Agnes calmly told him that Jesus Christ was too jealous of her purity to allow it to be violated.

OPPOSITE

FOUNTAINS AND
BAROQUE FAÇADES

According to one account, when she was exposed naked in the house of ill repute, a speedy growth of hair miraculously covered her entire body. Another version (quoted by the hagiographer Alban Butler) declares that: 'Many young profligates ran thither, full of the wicked desire of gratifying their lust, but were seized with such awe at the sight of the saint, that they durst not approach her – one only excepted, who, attempting to be rude to her, was that very instant, by a flash, as it were, of lightning from heaven, struck blind, and fell trembling to the ground.' Agnes charitably broke off hymn-singing to restore him to health. Then she was led away to be beheaded, according to St Ambrose 'going to the place of execution more cheerfully than others go to their wedding'.

Borromini's façade was added to the seventh-century church rebuilt by Girolamo Rainaldi (1570–1655) and completed in the 1650s by the latter's son Carlo, to whom we owe the dome and towers. The interior is glamorous with gilding, its cupola frescoed by Ciro Ferri (1634–89) and Sebastiano Corbellini (*fl.* 1689–95) its consoles designed by Giovanni Battista Gaulli (Baciccia: 1639–1709). Although Pope Innocent X (who commissioned this rebuilding and whose monument, by Giovanni Battista Maini, is over the main door of the church) gave many commissions to Bernini, he did not patronize him to the same extent as had Urban VIII, and in the crypt is a work by an even deadlier rival than Borromini. The Bolognese Alessandro Algardi can certainly claim to be the second finest sculptor to work in Rome during the seventeenth century. For Sant'Agnese in Agone he depicted the saint with her miraculous growth of hair.

To the left of the church is the **PALAZZO PAMPHILJ** which Carlo Rainaldi built in 1650, and which now serves as the Brazilian Embassy. Across the piazza from its elegant long façade and magnificent porch stands the church of the **MADONNA DEL SACRO CUORE**, formerly dedicated to St James of Compostela (San Giacomo degli Spagnoli), patron saint of Spain. Built in the twelfth century by the Infante Don Enrique, son of King Ferdinand III of Spain, it was once crammed with Spanish works of art. Then the Issoudun Order of the Sacred Heart took over the church, and the Spaniards were given in exchange the church of Santa Maria di Monserrato, which stands to the south-west in Via Monserrato. This was designed by Antonio da Sangallo the Elder in 1495 and shelters the tombs of two Spanish popes, Calixtus III and his nephew Alexander VI, as well as that of King Alfonso XIII of Spain, who was deposed in 1931 and died at Rome ten years later. A museum next door houses the treasures from San Giacomo.

Corso del Rinascimento, behind the church of the Madonna del Sacro Cuore leads south directly to Piazza Sant'Andrea della Valle. But first turn left to discover across the street the elegant seventeenth-century **PALAZZO MADAMA**, the home of the Italian Senate since 1871. The Medici were responsible for enlarging an earlier palace which they had inherited, adding its powerful baroque façade. Atlantes and caryatids flank the first-storey

OPPOSITE *Antonio della Bitta and Gregorio Zappalà's Fontana del Nettuno at the northern end of the Piazza Navona was completed in 1878. The god is shown struggling with a sea-monster, surrounded by nereids and sea-horses.*

windows, and a delightful frieze of cherubs and lions runs under the cornice. The palace's name comes from one of its former residents, Madama Margaret of Parma, illegitimate daughter of the emperor Charles V, a remarkable woman who married first Alessandro de'Medici, then Ottavio Farnese and, at the request of her half-brother, Philip II of Spain, was Regent of the Netherlands from 1559 to 1567.

On the way to Piazza Sant'Andrea della Valle you pass on the left the **PALAZZO DELLA SAPIENZA** (palace of learning), aptly named since it served as Rome's university from the fifteenth century until 1935. Its magnificent two-storeyed courtyard was designed by Borromini in the mid seventeenth century as was the superb chapel of **SANT'IVO**, which opens only for an hour on Sunday mornings unless you can persuade the concierge to let you in.

In 1614 Carlo Maderno designed the fountain which cools the Piazza Sant'Andrea della Valle at the end of Corso del Rinascimento. In 1622-5, he worked on the dome of the church of **SANT'ANDREA DELLA VALLE**. Built for the Theatine Order, one of the most vigorous of the Counter-Reformation, its splendid façade is by Carlo Rainaldi. For the lavish, barrel-vaulted interior Michelangelo designed the second chapel on the right, the Strozzi Chapel in which are found bronze reproductions of his *Pietà* and his statues of *Leah* and *Rachel*. The first chapel on the right, built by Carlo Maderno, inspired the first act of Puccini's *Tosca*, where an escaped political prisoner hides in a church and is helped by an artist who is painting there.

In front of the apse of this church are the tombs of two Piccolomini Popes. Aeneas Silvius Piccolomini, who was elected as Pius II in 1458, was the more scandalous of the two. Having put off ordination for several years in order to continue enjoying a dissolute life, he was celebrated for writing a lecherous love-story called *Euralus and Lucretia*. The future pope fathered numerous bastards before a serious illness led him to change his ways. A brilliant orator, he rose rapidly in the church after his ordination as priest in 1446 and was elected pope when he was only 53 years old. Even now his humanist leanings came to the fore, for he chose the name Pius from the legendary 'Pious Aeneas'. As a resolute enemy of the Turks, he was leading a crusade against them when he died at Ancona in 1463.

His heart is buried there, but the rest of his corpse was brought back to Rome to lie in a tomb by Niccolò da Guardiagrele and Pier Paolo da Todi, while on the other side of the nave another pope, Francesco Todeschini Piccolomini, occupies a tomb by Francesco di Giovanni and Sebastiano di Francesco Ferrucci. A nephew of Pius II, he was created Archbishop of Siena at the tender age of 21; he, however, was a man of integrity, sternly refusing bribes when he was voting to choose his uncle's successor. His was the shortest papacy on record. Elected as Pius III on 22 September 1503 to succeed the Borgia pope Alexander VI, he died ten days later.

The magnificent frescoes of this church were done by two rival artists, both of whom had been pupils of members of the Carracci family. In the

1620s, Annibale Carracci's favourite, Domenico Zampieri, nicknamed Domenichino, painted with classical verve the four evangelists in the pendentives, as well as six virtues and scenes from the life of St Andrew in the apse. The commission to fresco the dome went to Domenichino's archenemy Giovanni Lanfranco, a pupil of Agostino Carracci. His *Assumption of the Blessed Virgin*, painted between 1625 and 1627, with its brilliant foreshortening and masterly deployment of figures, marks the triumph of Baroque over classicism in Roman church art. It depicts Jesus descending from heaven to welcome his mother, while the whole scene is contemplated by the heavenly throng of saints, cherubs and angels. After Lanfranco's death in 1647 his follower Mattia Preti (who was nicknamed Il Cavaliere Calabrese since he came from Calabria) began painting in Sant'Andrea della Valle, contributing the huge frescoes in the tribune.

From Piazza Sant'Andrea della Valle walk east along Corso Vittorio Emanuele, passing the **PALAZZO VIDONI**, whose south façade was designed by Raphael in 1515 (although, alas, you cannot see it) to reach the Piazza del Gesù. On the way you pass the square known as Largo di Argentina, containing not only a medieval tower and loggia but also the excavated remains of four temples. A little raised altar and some frescoes are open to the skies. Across the square stands the early eighteenth-century **TEATRO ARGENTINA** (with an early nineteenth-century façade) where Rossini's *Barber of Seville* was booed off the stage at its first performance in 1816.

In the Piazza del Gesù stands a building that marked in its time a revolutionary advance in religious architecture. The church of the **GESU**, built for the new Jesuit order, is the prototype of a sumptuous style that was to become the hallmark of all subsequent Jesuit churches. Paid for by Cardinal Alessandro Farnese (whose fleurs-de-lys dot the church) and built between 1566 and 1575, its architects were Vignola and Giacomo della Porta, who was responsible only for the façade. Designed to emphasize the play of light and shade, the facade's central section and doorway are accentuated, a device which, with the motifs of the double pediment and a tall, balconied window, would be increasingly deployed in the future. The arms of Cardinal Farnese and the Holy Cross added decoration peculiar to this church.

Vignola's long interior, a huge open space with side chapels, gleams with multicoloured marble, statuary, bronze and gilt, much of this being added later so that the church only gradually assumed its resplendent baroque aspect. Adopting the plan of an ancient basilica, the architect added a transept, and topped the crossing with a dome. This open plan was specifically designed for the passionate preaching enjoined by the Council of Trent (1545–63), so that all could comprehend the Catholic faith and be protected from the inroads of Protestantism, and for liturgical drama that would move the hearts of communicants. The Genoese Baciccia decorated the vault and the cupola with *trompe-l'oeil* frescoes of the *Adoration of the Name of Jesus*, at the end of the seventeenth century.

In the north transept is the dazzling tomb of the founder of the Jesuit order, St Ignatius Loyola, a masterpiece by Andrea Pozzo (1642–1709). Ignatius (*c.* 1491–1556) lived nearby, in a house across Via Aracoeli at 45 Via del Gesù, its corridor decorated with *trompe-l'oeil* paintings by Pozzo and his followers. Once a solid silver statue of the saint graced the high altar of the church, but Pope Pius VI melted it down in 1797 to rid himself of the indemnity demanded by Napoleon Bonaparte, so the present statue is merely silver-plated. A second great Jesuit saint, Francis Xavier (1506–52), missionary to Japan and China, is represented here by his uncorrupted right arm. It is housed in a shrine in the south transept, in a chapel designed by Pietro da Cortona.

In front of the church the seventeenth-century Palazzo Cenci Bolognette, with its balustrades and broken pediments, is the headquarters of one of the two branches of Italian freemasonry. Take Via del Plebiscito from the Piazza del Gesù to reach another hub of the city, the Piazza Venezia. From here Via Nazionale runs east to the main railway station, Via del Corso leads north, the road we have just walked along runs westwards in the direction of the Vatican, Via del Teatro di Marcello leads south-west towards the Tiber and the Isola Tiberina, and Via dei Fori Imperiali runs south-east towards the Colosseum.

Ahead of us Via Cesare Battisti (named after an Italian patriot hanged by the Austrians in 1916) joins Via Quattro Novembre, on the left of which stands the magnificent **PALAZZO COLONNA**. Signifying a gentler phase of Roman history after its earlier turbulent days, this palace was rebuilt in the fifteenth century on the site of a medieval fortress (by the Colonna pope Martin V) and again in the eighteenth century. On 4 June 1802, King Carlo Emanuele IV of Savoy and Sardinia abdicated here and spent the rest of his life as a Jesuit.

The palace houses another private art gallery, open to the public only on Saturday mornings. (You have to walk round to 17 Via della Pilotta to get in through the back door.) The finest room is the gilded Festival Hall, its ceiling frescoed with a scene depicting the defeat of the Turks at the battle of Lepanto in 1571 and the apotheosis of Marcantonio Colonna, who took part in the conflict. The painter was Sebastiano Ricci, who also frescoed the walls with moody landscapes. The gallery's other treasures include works by Annibale Carracci and Guercino, as well as works by the Florentine mannerist painter Domenico Ghirlandaio. Set against these Italian master-pieces are a sumptuous and mysterious *Assumption of the Blessed Virgin Mary* by Rubens and eleven evocative watercolours by the French landscape artist Gaspard Dughet, who in 1639 married a daughter of Nicolas Poussin and thereafter found it more profitable to call himself Gaspard Poussin.

These works of art are less well frequented than the waxworks museum in the corner of the palace. Its founder was inspired by a visit to Madame Tussauds in London. You can view Snow White with her seven dwarfs, Pope

OPPOSITE *Sumptuous, dazzling* trompe-l'oeil *frescoes, including* Baciccia's Triumph of the name of Jesus, *adorn the church of the Gesù, the prototype of Jesuit churches throughout the world.*

John XXIII appointing a new cardinal, Madame de Pompadour, and Abraham Lincoln in that fatal theatre box. Here, too, models of Winston Churchill, Joseph Stalin and Franklin Delano Roosevelt eternally confer at Yalta. And, on a local note, a group of waxy blackshirts represent the Italian fascists conferring in 1943. They are about to betray Mussolini.

Return to the Piazza Venezia, which is dominated by the **MONUMENT OF KING VITTORIO EMANUELE II**. 'He hunted women with as little rest or scruple as he hunted game,' G. M. Trevelyan noted of the man who was proclaimed king of Italy in 1861. At that time the capital of his kingdom was Turin, for Rome was occupied by the French. Soon Florence succeeded Turin as the Italian capital, and only in 1870 was Vittorio Emanuele able to enter Rome.

On his death in 1878, the Romans wished to raise a suitable memorial to this popular king and in celebration of their unity. To make way for it they demolished countless medieval gems, including a Franciscan monastery, the palace of Pope Paul II and the house in which Michelangelo died. The monument to Vittorio Emanuele in Piazza Venezia is grandiose, pretentious and impressive. Designed by Giuseppe Sacconi (who defeated 97 fellow-architects in the competition for the commission), it took nearly 30 years to complete, and was dedicated in 1911, six years after the architect's death. Writing in 1926, Gabriel Fauré hoped that one day the passing of the years and 'incrustation' would soften the glaring white of the monument. We are still waiting for it to be toned down.

In seeking a new national style, Rome oddly decided to ape the columns and steps of ancient Greek temples. Towering some 70 metres high and stretching for 135 metres, the Vittoriano was built out of white marble from Brescia. The whole, startling monument drips symbolism. The fountains which flank it represent, on the left, the Adriatic (with a shell on his head like a baby's bonnet), and on the right, the Tyrrhenian Sea. Above them on pedestals rise four carved groups signifying from left to right Law, Sacrifice, Concord and Strength. Winged lions, colossal bronze statues representing Action and Thought, a monumental figure of Rome herself, more sculptures signifying Patriotism, Labour, War, Revolution, Politics and Philosophy surround the gilt bronze equestrian statue of Vittorio Emanuele himself – the suitably pompous work of a sculptor named Enrico Chiaradia. Around its base are the symbolic statues of the major Italian cities and towns.

This is by no means all. Sixteen other sculptures celebrate the provinces of Italy. On the propylaea a couple of charioteers stand for civil liberty and the unity of the *Patria* (Fatherland). Their horses are arguably the finest statues of the whole monument, ready to leap off into the square ahead.

The Romans have dubbed this ice-cold, megalomaniac monument the 'wedding cake' and 'Mussolini's typewriter'. Today it houses the tomb of Italy's unknown soldier, a maritime museum and a museum of that series of stirring events which led to Italian unity – the Risorgimento. From its upper

The Monument to Vittorio Emanuele II, a symbol of Italian unity, was completed in 1911 and has become a Roman landmark in spite of its megalomanic grandeur.

terrace – on the rare occasions when you are allowed to climb it – you have a magnificent view of the Foro Romano and the Colosseum.

A superb early renaissance palace rises in Piazza Venezia north of the Vittorio Emanuele II monument. The **PALAZZO VENEZIA** was designed in the mid fifteenth century by Leon Battista Alberti, who was one of the most important architectural theoreticians of the Italian Renaissance. In 1435 he had published a work in Latin (*Della Pittura*) which contains the first description of the theory of perspective. (He decided to translate it into the vernacular when he discovered that his friend, the architect Brunelleschi, did not read Latin.) Other works – on statuary and architecture – followed and consolidated his reputation, although the last was published only in 1485, thirteen years after his death.

Alberti deeply admired the works of classical antiquity. He also influenced his fellow humanist artists by defining great art and architecture not in terms of their religious functions but in the light of their graceful and carefully calculated proportions. Although other architects had already used antique architectural elements, Alberti was among the first to try to understand the rules of proportion and the different orders: Doric, Tuscan, Ionic, Corinthian and Composite, as they had been used in ancient Rome. In his view the painter, sculptor and architect needed to seek inspiration not just from poetry and history but also from mathematics. In this way he was a leading light of the Renaissance, the rebirth of art, literature and philosophy which swept Europe from the second quarter of the fifteenth century.

Alberti held a secretarial post in the papal court, and his design for the Palazzo Venezia was commissioned in 1455 by the Venetian cardinal Pietro Barbo who, eleven years later, became Pope Paul II. Paul made the palace his Roman home, and it remained the principal residence of the popes until 1564, when the Venetian ambassador moved in (hence its name). Today it houses the Institute of Archaeology and the History of Art, has its own permanent collection of decorative arts and is often the venue of special exhibitions. Thirty rooms of masterpieces begin with medieval art and end with the works of Antonia Canova and his contemporaries. Room 16 displays some marvellous little bronzes by Giambologna and in Room 18 you can see a couple of terracotta models of St Mark by Jacopo Sansovino. A particular treat are the geographical and architectural frescoes on the walls of the Sala del Mappamondo, painted probably by Andrea Mantegna in around 1490.

In spite of the renaissance details of its architecture, the Palazzo Venezia, with its powerful crenellated tower and its narrow windows, retains a medieval defensive air; but its position in the centre of the city and next to a church indicates a new spirit of openness, even friendliness displayed towards the lower orders by the princes of the church at this time. The apparent simplicity of the lines of this three-storey building is deceptive. An illusion of greater height is given by the device of reducing the size of the windows in each storey, and the mathematical regularity of the pattern of the façade is subtly lightened by Alberti's casual expedient of placing the entrance slightly off-centre. The interior, palm shaded courtyard was delicately handled by Alberti, with its two-storeyed loggia supported on Doric columns below and Ionic ones above.

This palace took on a more sinister role in the twentieth century, when Mussolini made it his headquarters and would frequently harangue the crowds from the balcony. The church of SAN MARCO, incorporated in the building, has an even longer history. The bones of a fourth-century pope named Mark lie under its high altar, although the present church was rebuilt by Gregory IV in the ninth century. Sicilian jasper pillars divide its aisles, and baroque stucco adorns its walls. An early ninth-century Byzantine mosaic glitters in the apse. Its figures are stiff, isolated and immobile, save for that of St Paul, who places a hand on the shoulder of Pope Gregory (still in this world, as his square nimbus indicates) to present him, proudly carrying a model of his church, to Christ. Christ himself bestows a blessing in the Greek and not the Latin fashion. His twelve apostles are depicted not as shepherds but as sheep.

The romanesque belfry was added a couple of centuries after this mosaic. Pope Paul II paid for the splendid renaissance ceiling inside. Joining the church to his palace, he also added the three-arched portico, designed by Alberti and Giuliano da Maiano, to glorify (and shelter) himself whenever he made a public appearance outside the church. From its upper balcony he would bless the people. Over the main door is a fifteenth-century statue of St Mark the Evangelist by Antonio Filarete, his gospel in hand. The portico now shelters the tomb of Vanozza Cattanei, mistress of the Borgia pope, Alexander VI, and mother of his children, Lucrezia and Cesare (You can make out the word LVCRETIA on the right-hand wall). Lucrezia has given her name to the huge statue of the goddess Isis at the corner of the piazza. This is one of those sculptures which the Romans dub 'talking statues', since in the past poets would hang satirical or love verses around its neck.

Opposite the Palazzo Venezia is a building of 1907, the **PALAZZO DELLE ASSICURAZIONE GENERALE**, with a sixteenth-century winged lion on its façade, brought here from Padua. This palace courteously mimics the battlements and tower of the Palazzo Venezia. The equestrian statue of Vittorio Emanuele II seems ready at any moment to leap off the monument and canter up Via del Corso, which runs north from the piazza. The ancient Romans called this street Via Lata, which means broad street. It leads directly to the Via Flaminia outside the city.

Today a fashionable shopping street, Via Lata became Via del Corso when it began to be used for horse racing (and it is said that Paul II built his Palazzo Venezia where he did to be able to watch the end of these races). The street seems far too narrow for races, but engravings show horses and riders careering down it, with the crowds of onlookers pressing against the buildings on either side. At carnival time rich and eminent Romans and visitors would parade up and down the Corso in their carriages in the late afternoon. The sides of the street were filled with a crush of bystanders, and it is amazing that no disaster seems to have occurred. The Corso is roughly like this today, although theoretically it is traffic-free, save for buses. Its one-and-a-half kilometres stretch as far as the Piazza del Popolo, lined with bars, banks and boutiques.

At the corner of Via del Corso and Via del Plebiscito is a café which is emblazoned, above the window over its entrance, with the French imperial eagle and turns out to be the **PALAZZO BONAPARTE** which Mattia dei Rossi built in the seventeenth century and where Napoleon's mother, Letizia Ramolino, lived from 1815 until her death in 1836. Beyond it, a few yards up Via del Corso, rises the **PALAZZO DORIA PAMPHILJ**, still the home of this Genoese family. Its rococo façade faces the **PALAZZO DEL COLLEGIO ROMANO**, which was where the crusty, suspicious Pope Innocent X (who was born Giambattista Pamphilj) studied as a young man, and it was he who opened

In his portrait of Pope Innocent X, which hangs in the Galleria Doria Pamphilj, Velazquez has portrayed the inscrutable character of a man who was both a prince of the church and a man of the world.

up the palace opposite as an art gallery. Fittingly, then, one of its masterpieces is his portrait, painted by Velazquez in 1650.

Gabriele Valvassori designed the main façade of the Palazzo Doria Pamphilj in the early 1730s, Paolo Ameli the mid eighteenth-century south façade, and Antonio del Grande the north one dating from the 1660s. The interior is far more complex than those façades might indicate. Today its five courtyards (the main one exquisitely late renaissance in style) and four great staircases lead to the private family apartments.

The apartments also house a collection of Italian and foreign paintings and sculpture dating from the fifteenth to the seventeenth centuries, based on works acquired by Donna Olimpia Maidalchini, who was sister-in-law to

Innocent X. (She was also maliciously libelled as his mistress, but it is true that the vacillating pontiff could take no decision without consulting her.) Although this is a private home, it is open four days a week. Here hang works by Giovanni Bellini, Caravaggio, Titian and Filippo Lippi among the Italians, while Claude Lorraine, Jan Breughel the Elder and Velazquez represent the finest of the foreigners. The collection also includes a dazzling bust of Innocent X by Bernini, imaginatively displayed in the same room as the pope's portrait by Velazquez.

At the other side of the Via del Corso stands the **PALAZZO SALVIATI**, designed in the seventeenth century by Carlo Rainaldi. Next to it runs the façade of **PALAZZO ODESCALCHI**, which appears to be a fifteenth-century Florentine palace, but is a pastiche by its owner Don Baldassare, in 1888.

Take Via dei Santi Apostoli beside the palace to find the basilica of the **SANTI APOSTOLI**. The Byzantine general Narses, who in AD 552 had defeated the Ostrogoths, driving the Goths out of Italy and taking possession of Rome, built a church (or restored an older one) here to celebrate his victory. In AD 565 Pope John III added to its renown by placing inside what he took to be the bones of the apostles Philip and James the Less, rededicating the building to all twelve apostles. Several times restored, the church was so much damaged by an earthquake in 1346 that for 80 years it stood ruined and abandoned.

Fortunately it stands next door to the Palazzo Colonna, and after a member of the family was elected as Pope Martin V in 1417 he set about rebuilding the damaged house of God. Soon the Franciscans were in charge of Santi Apostoli and the church flourished, although this prosperity preserved all too little of the building, for in 1702 a complete restoration was entrusted to Carlo Fontana, and in 1827 the church was given a neo-classical façade by the architect Giuseppe Valadier.

You enter by a huge late fifteenth-century portico built by Baccio Pontelli and surmounted by baroque windows and statues of the twelve apostles added by Carlo Rainaldi in the 1680s. The bas-reliefs of an oak leaf and the imperial Roman eagle to the right of this portico come from the Foro Traiano and date from the second century AD. In the vestibule look out for the memorial created in 1807 by Antonio Canova to honour his tutor, the engraver Giovanni Volpati. Baciccia in 1702 was commissioned to decorate the vault of the central nave with a painting depicting *The Triumph of the Franciscan Order*. Two years later Giovanni Adoazzi painted the choir vault with a splendid *Fall from Grace of the Rebel Angels*. The tombs inside this church are also remarkable, particularly the tomb of Cardinal Pietro Riario, in part the late fifteenth- century work of Mino da Fiesole, and (towards the end of the left aisle) that of Pope Clement XIV, sculpted in 1769 and the first monument executed by Canova in Rome.

Michelangelo was temporarily buried in this church in February 1564, before his body was exhumed and taken to Florence. A monument marks

Even the robes of Carlo Fontana's statues of the church of San Marcello swirl in baroque ecstasy. Fontana added this façade to a much older church in the 1680s.

the spot where he lay. The bones of St James the Less and St Philip had long been lost, but during yet another restoration in 1872 their alleged bodies were discovered in a marble sarcophagus. These relics now lie in the crypt immediately under the high altar. Apart from these remains, the oldest part of the church is a lovely chapel at the east end of the right-hand nave, its spiral columns chiselled in the fourth century.

Walk beside the Palazzo Colonna back to the Corso. A few paces to the right stands the church of **SAN MARCELLO**, rebuilt by Jacopo Sansovino after a fire in 1519 and graced in the 1680s with a baroque façade by Carlo Fontana. Sansovino also created the tombs of two bishops which lie to the left of the entrance, and the rich frescoes include work by Pellegrino da Modena (1483–1523) and Daniele da Volterra (1509–66).

Crossing the Corso from Via di Santi Apostoli and entering Via Lata, you pass the ancient church of **SANTA MARIA IN VIA LATA**, rebuilt twice after the flooding Tiber made its foundations unsafe. The first rebuilding under Pope Leo IX in the mid eleventh century has left us the oratory, the second under Pope Innocent VIII in the 1480s the upper church. Via Lata leads into the Piazza del Collegio Romano, a college long run by the Jesuits and built by Bartolomeo Ammanati in 1582.

Running west from this piazza, Via del Piè Marmo winds quietly on to Piazza Minerva. The black walls and façade of the church of Santa Maria sopra Minerva appear first. The square in front of the church centres on a quaint work by Bernini, a marble elephant carrying on its back an obelisk from the Temple of Isis which once stood nearby. Its hieroglyphs mention Apries, the last independent Egyptian Pharaoh, who in the sixth century BC joined forces with King Zedekiah of Judah to make war against King Nebuchadnezzar of Babylon. The alliance did Zedekiah no good, since Nebuchadnezzar defeated him, slew his sons, knocked down the walls of Jerusalem, burned down the royal palaces and Solomon's Temple, and finally put out Zedekiah's eyes, bringing him to Babylon in fetters of bronze.

As its name implies, **SANTA MARIA SOPRA MINERVA** rises on the site of the former Temple of Minerva. The only medieval gothic church in Rome, it was begun around 1285 by Fra Sisto and Fra Ristoro who were responsible for the church of Santa Maria Novella in Florence. Finished in 1370, it was handed over to the Dominicans by the Senate and people of Rome. Little plaques on the church indicate the height reached by the flooding Tiber before it was properly canalized.

Through an almost blank façade, which was in 1453 by Meo del Caprina and scarcely prepares you for the lovely interior, you enter a building which contains the tombs of five popes and sixty cardinals. Its most venerated bones are those of St Catherine of Siena and the painter Fra Angelico. St Catherine lived in a cell of a convent in the Via Chiara, which runs off the piazza, but after her death in 1280 the walls were brought to this church, rebuilt as a room off the sacristy and frescoed by Pietro Perugino

One of Bernini's characteristic jokes; an elephant carrying an Egyptian obelisk in Piazza Minerva. The obelisk was found in the remains of the Temple of Isis which used to stand nearby and erected here in 1667.

(1446–1523). Her body, under the high altar, remains wholly uncorrupted.

Fra Angelico lived here having been summoned to Rome by Pope Nicholas V to decorate a chapel in the Vatican. Either he or Benozzo Gozzoli frescoed an Annunciation in the fourth chapel of the right aisle. Fra Angelico died in 1453 and his body lies in a tomb on the left of the sanctuary. In front of this is Michelangelo's *Christ carrying the Cross*, for which he was paid 200 ducats in 1521. The curiously nonchalant Jesus seems to lean on the cross as if it were a walking stick. Behind the high altar lie the Medici popes Leo X (1513–21) and Clement VII (1523–34), both in tombs by Baccio Bandinelli. Raffaello da Montelupo sculpted Clement's statue and Nanni di Baccio Bigio Leo's. The artist Andrea Bregno lies at the corner of the nave and the north transept. In 1477 he had sculpted the tomb of Diego de Coco for the seventh chapel of the south aisle.

The fifth chapel in the same aisle has a pleasing Annunciation over the altar, painted in around 1500. In it a kneeling Cardinal Juan de Torque·mada presents three poor girls to the Virgin Mary. This altarpiece commemorates a confraternity in aid of penniless girls, which the cardinal founded in 1460. The nephew of this charitable man was the inquisitor Tomas de Torquemada. Two cupids painted by Andrea del Verrocchio flank the arch of the Carafa Chapel in the south transept, which was frescoed in 1489 by Filippino Lippi. Over the altar he painted an Annunciation and the scene of St Thomas Aquinas presenting Cardinal Olivieri Carafa to the Blessed Virgin Mary. On the right-hand wall Thomas Aquinas confounds the heretics, including Arius and Sabellius, watched by the group on his right among whom are two youths depicting the future Medici popes already mentioned – Leo X and Clement VII. Above them are more scenes from the life of St Thomas.

From the corner of the square you can see the dome of the **PANTHEON**. Via Minerva runs north alongside the Pantheon to the Piazza della Rotonda. A renaissance fountain of 1575 gushes from the centre of the square and carries an obelisk from the time of Rameses the Great. Argentine wood once paved the square, so that no noise might disturb the dead inside the Pantheon itself. Today the wooden pavement has gone, and noisy children play football in front of the monument.

Built of travertine (the tufa from around Tivoli) in 27 BC during the third consulate of Augustus's son-in-law Agrippa to commemorate the victory at Actium over Antony and Cleopatra, the Pantheon is the best preserved and (along with the Colosseum) the finest ancient monument in Rome. Despite its inscription declaring 'M AGRIPPAM L. F. COS. TERTIUM FECIT' the Pantheon was rebuilt on a much larger scale by Hadrian, after a fire of AD 80, and both Septimus Severus and Caracalla restored it.

The early Christians hated it, and the barbarians pillaged it. Then, oddly enough, the Christians helped to preserve it when Pope Boniface III consecrated it as the church of Santa Maria ad Martyres in AD 609, since he believed that 28 wagon-loads of martyrs' bones had been brought here from the catacombs.

Sixteen Corinthian columns, rising from white marble and bearing marble capitals, form the porch in front of the sanctuary. Since popes Urban VIII and Alexander VII restored the three on the east side, their coats of arms also adorn the capitals. You enter through a bronze door repaired by Pope Pius IV in 1563.

The interior walls were once lined with marble and the coffering of the dome in bronze, but the present bare brick of the Pantheon remains tremendously impressive, its diameter of around 50 metres roughly equal to the height of its dome. The walls are pierced with seven alternately rectangular and semicircular niches, the middle one embellished with fluted Corinthian columns. They formerly contained statues of the seven ancient deities of the city. Here today are the tombs of Italian monarchs, including Vittorio Emanuele II and Umberto I, assassinated at Monza in 1900, and who lies in a tomb designed by Giuseppe Sacconi, architect of the Vittorio Emanuele

OPPOSITE *The portico of the Pantheon seen across the fountain in the Piazza della Rotonda, with the first letters of its misleading inscription. One of the most complete of ancient Roman temples, it owes its preservation to its adoption as a Christian church in the early seventh century.*

monument. Next to Umberto's tomb is the humble one of Raphael. Its inscription was translated by Pope (1688–1744):

Living, great Nature feared he might outvie Her works,
And dying, fears Herself may die.

Other artists buried here include Annibale Carracci and Baldassare Peruzzi.

Tall palaces shade the narrow Via del Seminario, which leads from the eastern corner of the Piazza della Rotonda as far as the Piazza Sant'Ignazio. Here stands the Jesuit church of **SANT'IGNAZIO**, almost as magnificent as the Gesù, dedicated to St Ignatius Loyola in honour of his canonization and built between 1626 and 1685. In the 1720s the architect Raguzzini re-designed the piazza as a series of enthralling curves which inexorably draw your eye to the façade of this church, in part the work of the Jesuit Fra Orazio Grassi, in part that of Algardi. Inside, in 1694 the vault of the nave was covered by Andrea Pozzo with a brilliantly theatrical *trompe-l'oeil* fresco representing the four corners of the earth and the entry of St Ignatius into heaven. Pozzo even managed to create the illusion of a cupola and in the apse he painted the saint descending from heaven, accompanied by angels, to heal the sick. St Aloysius (Luigi) Gonzaga (1568–91) lies in a chapel of the right transept, his bones in a lapis-lazuli urn, his glorification celebrated by a splendid marble relief sculpted by Pierre Legros at the end of the seventeenth century. Another lapis-lazuli urn, flanked by twisting baroque columns in a chapel of the north transept, contains the earthly remains of another Jesuit saint, John Berchmans, whose relics were brought here in 1893.

Walk from the far side of the piazza along the Via del Burro to reach the Piazza di Pietra, where once stood an imposing temple in honour of the emperor Hadrian. All that remains is an entablature borne by eleven stupendous Corinthian columns, made of white marble. They rise from a podium which was itself once covered with marble. Take the narrow Via dei Bergamaschi which runs north from this piazza to the Piazza Colonna. This is an exceedingly handsome square. Its glory is the **PALAZZO CHIGI**, which was begun in 1562 by Matteo di Castello and finished by Felice della Greca in the early seventeenth century. In the square stands the **COLUMN OF MARCUS AURELIUS**. Obviously inspired by Trajan's monument and set here only 80 years later, its reliefs, rising around the column, illustrate the emperor's victories over the Germans and the Sarmatians. In 1559, when Pope Sixtus V commissioned Domenico Fontana to restore the column, he ordered him to replace the statue of Marcus Aurelius standing on it with one of St Paul. The vigorous can climb to the top up 190 steps inside the column.

Further north along Via del Corso, Piazza San Lorenzo to the left is guarded by the church of **SAN LORENZO IN LUCINA**, founded in the fourth century, whose twelfth-century romanesque campanile is all that remains of the first rebuilding. The present interior was reshaped in 1650 by the

ABOVE *White marble Corinthian columns support the entablature of the Temple of Hadrian in the Piazza di Pietra. Antoninus Pius erected this temple in 145 in honour of his father.*

OPPOSITE *Not to be outdone by his predecessor Trajan, the emperor Marcus Aurelius set up his own column in the Piazza Colonna. It was erected between 180 and 196, and is made of 27 blocks of marble from Luni.*

Neapolitan baroque architect Cosimo Fanzago. Two monuments are worth a moment's pause. By the second pillar on the right is the monument of Nicolas Poussin. Although he died in 1665, this was the gift in 1803 of the writer and critic Chateaubriand. The other treasure in this church is a bust of Innocent X's physician Gabriele Fonseca, one of Bernini's last works. The doctor peers vigorously from the wall of the fifth chapel on the right.

Across the piazza stands Ammanati's **PALAZZO RUSPOLI**, and then the luxurious shops of the Via Condotti run north-east as far as the 137 famous **SPANISH STEPS** which rise from the romantic Piazza di Spagna up to the church of the Trinità dei Monti. The piazza takes its name from the palace of the Spanish ambassador on the right. Gianlorenzo Bernini's father Pietro designed the fountain in the piazza at the foot of the steps. Palm trees shade the piazza to the left, with a column rising on the right.

In a house to the right of the steps, the poet John Keats died in 1821, aged only 25. He had come to Rome, mortally ill with consumption, in the previous September. From here he wrote to his friend Charles Brown that: 'My stomach continues so bad, that I feel it worse on opening my book.' He ended his letter: 'I can scarcely bid you goodbye. I always made an awkward bow.' In view of this melancholy, it is pleasing that Keats's last written words were about Roman food, observing that he 'fell to with an appetite'. The house has been transformed into a **KEATS–SHELLEY MUSEUM**, displaying watercolours by Joseph Severn, who was with Keats during his final days, as well as manuscripts of the two poets, of Byron and Leigh Hunt, books on the English Romantics and a death mask of Keats himself.

The church of the **TRINITA DEI MONTI** at the top of the steps was built in 1495 for King Charles VIII of France and is one of five French churches in Rome. Carlo Maderno added its mannerist façade. Michelangelo's pupil Daniele da Volterra painted a superb Deposition for this church (in the third chapel on the left) as well as an Assumption for the chapel opposite. The piazza in which it rises offers superb views of the domes and roofs of the city, as well as the parasol pines, oaks, ilexes and exotic vegetation of the surrounding gardens. Adding to the charm of this spot is the fact that both the obelisk (a second-century relic brought here by Pius VI in 1788) and the church itself are slightly offset from the piazza.

Of the surrounding gardens, the terraces of the Pincio immediately beckon. As Stendhal (1783–1842) ironically remarked, it was the French, who in his view had done so many ridiculous things to their own capital, who created these admirable terraces. On the way we pass the **VILLA MEDICI**, built in around 1540 by Ammanti for Cardinal Ricci di Montepulciano and rebuilt in the 1570s for Ferdinando de'Medici. Its gardens retain the basic pattern laid out in the sixteenth century. Cypress trees line a spiral walk to the summit of a recreated Mount Parnassus.

Henry James considered the garden of the Villa Medici almost 'the most enchanting place in Rome'. Beyond it the fountains, statues, avenues and

OPPOSITE *The Spanish Steps rise to an obelisk in front of the façade of the church of the Trinità dei Monti. The 137 steps were built in the early 1720s by Francesco de Sanctis to provide a better approach to the church.*

A mute bust shelters beneath the trees of the Pincio terraces. Although the present gardens were laid out only early in the nineteenth century, they follow a tradition of formal gardens here dating back to the imperial age.

shady alleyways of the **PINCIO GARDENS** were created by Giuseppe Valadier during the Napoleonic occupation of Rome between 1809 and 1814. Behind us is Rome's favourite public park. The gardens of the **VILLA BORGHESE** were first laid out in the seventeenth century for Cardinal Scipione Borghese and extended in the next two centuries. A late eighteenth-century lake garden includes, in the middle of the lake itself, a copy of a Greek Temple to Aesculapius. Horses race in the Piazza di Siena. The park now embraces Rome's zoological garden, as well as several museums and galleries: the Galleria Borghese; the Galleria Nazionale d'Arte Moderna and the Etruscan collection of the Museo Nazionale di Villa Giulia.

The **GALLERIA BORGHESE** is housed in a villa built in the early seventeenth century by Flaminio Ponzio and Giovanni Vasanzio. Its treasures include a Deposition by Raphael in which the body of the dead Christ seems almost too heavy for the two who carry it. Here, too, is Canova's sensuous, semi-nude *Pauline Bonaparte*. **VILLA GIULIA** is about 50 years older, fronted by a façade created by Vignola and boasting both a loggia and a nymphaeum by Ammanati. The **GALLERIA NAZIONALE D'ARTE MODERNA** contains an

One of the four lionesses guarding the obelisk in the Piazza del Popolo. Like many of the other obelisks dotted about Rome, this was brought from Heliopolis by Augustus, and re-erected here by Sixtus V in the 1580s.

international collection, but most visitors come to see Italy's masters, especially Giorgio de' Chirico (1888–1974). A road, flanked since 1825 with Ionic columns carrying the Borghese eagle, reaches the Piazzale Flaminio. The piazza stands at the beginning of the Via Flaminia, which runs from Rome to Rimini and was built by the censor Caius Flaminius, who met his death at the battle of Lake Trasimene in 217 BC.

On our left is the superb **PORTA DEL POPOLO**, built at the behest of Pope Pius IV with the intention of impressing pilgrims as they arrived at the Holy City. Nanni di Baccio Bigio designed its east façade in the 1560s. The yet more resplendent west façade was added by Bernini to mark the occasion of the visit to Rome of Queen Christina of Sweden in 1655. An obelisk rises in the centre of the piazza between four lion fountains. Its hieroglyphs speak of the triumphs of the kings Seti and Rameses the Great, who lived in the thirteenth and twelfth centuries BC. Augustus brought this obelisk from Heliopolis, after his conquest of Egypt, and it was set here by Pope Sixtus V in 1589. The piazza is also decorated with fountains whose allegorical statues were designed by Giuseppe Valadier between 1816 and 1824. Those on the left represent Neptune and a couple of tritons. On the right stands Rome between the Tiber and the Aniene (the ancient Anio).

Twin baroque churches flank the piazza. Built to designs of Carlo Rainaldi by Bernini and Carlo Fontana, **SANTA MARIA DEI MIRACOLI** stands to the west of Corso, with **SANTA MARIA IN MONTESANTO** to the east. And across the piazza is the majestic church which bears its name, **SANTA MARIA DEL POPOLO**. It stands on a Roman graveyard which contained the bodies of the Domitians and, since one of them was Nero, was considered to be haunted. Before the building of the church commenced in 1099, Paschal II cut down a walnut tree which, it was believed, protected them. Rebuilt in the 1220s and 1470s, this church has an early renaissance façade, but much of the interior has been altered. Bramante lengthened the apse, and Raphael designed the octagonal Chigi Chapel, which was later enriched, along with much of the rest of the church, by Bernini.

Walk up to the apse, one of Bramante's very first works in Rome. Built at the beginning of the sixteenth century, its vault was frescoed in the same decade by Pinturicchio, who depicted here the *Coronation of the Virgin*, the *Four Evangelists*, the *Four Sibyls* and the *Four Fathers of the Church*. The stained glass, virtually unique in Rome, was made by the Marseilles glazier Guillaume Marcillat and paid for by Pope Julius II.

On the left just before the apse, is the Cerasi Chapel with two noted paintings by Caravaggio (1571– 1610), one of the *Conversion of St Paul*, the other of the *Crucifixion of St Peter*. Unfortunately for Annibale Carracci, his own *Assumption* on the altar has to compete with these two masterpieces. At the other side of the church are a couple of magnificent tombs, made by Andrea Sansovino in around 1505 for cardinals Basso della Rovere and Ascanio Sforza.

The other chapels of Santa Maria del Popolo are sumptuous and many of them were decorated by the finest artists of the fifteenth, sixteenth and seventeenth centuries. The second chapel west of the Sansovino tombs was frescoed by Pinturicchio's pupils with *Scenes from the life of the Virgin Mary*. Next to it is the richly marbled baroque Cybo Chapel, designed by Carlo Fontana in the 1680s, its altar bearing a painting of *The Assumption* by Carlo Maratta. The last of the south aisle, the della Rovere Chapel, was frescoed by Pinturicchio himself in the 1480s, with *Scenes from the Life of St Jerome* in the lunettes and a *Madonna and Child* over the altar. Cardinal Cristofero della Rovere lies on the left in a tomb designed by Mino da Fiesole and Andrea Bregno. On the right Cardinal de Castro lies in a tomb by Antonio da Sangallo the Younger.

Opposite is the chapel which Raphael designed for the Sienese banker Agostino Chigi. The mosaics in the dome of this chapel were done to Raphael's designs, under the inspiration of Dante's vision of the Creation – each of the planets guided by an angel. Raphael also designed the statues of Jonah and Elijah which, sculpted by Lorenzetto Lotti (1490–1541) guard

Jonah standing on his whale, by Lorenzetto Lotti to Raphael's designs, in the Chigi Chapel of Santa Maria del Popolo. Raphael laid out the whole chapel for his friend the Sienese banker Agostino Chigi. Lorenzetto also sculpted Elias, but the other Old Testament figures of Daniel and Habbakuk were done by Bernini in the next century.

St Ann proudly holds her daughter in Sebastiano del Piombo's Birth of the Virgin Mary *in the Chigi chapel. Although the altarpiece is different to anything that Raphael would have produced, it is nevertheless a stunning example of high renaissance painting.*

respectively the left-hand side of the altar and the right-hand side of the entrance. Bernini's contributions to the Chigi Chapel include the statues of Habakkuk and the angel, who help to guard the altar, and of Daniel and his very friendly lion who overlook the entrance. He also altered the pyramidal tombs of Agostino and Sigismondo Chigi from Raphael's original design, while Sebastiano del Piombo in the 1530s painted *the Birth of the Virgin Mary* for the altar.

The plethora of tombs in this splendid church ends with a mad baroque monument on the right of the exit which an architect named Chisleni made for himself in 1672. Blessed are the dead which die in the Lord, but not those who design for themselves such a pompous memorial.

3
Peaceful corners
and parks

....

THE ARA PACIS *to* THE JANICULUM

Rome has such a wealth of culture and so many superb buildings, not to speak of the delights of its restaurants, the liveliness of its people and the countless curiosities that continually entertain the visitor, that some entrancing parts of the city are often neglected. This tour is designed to explore them. It begins with the Ara Pacis Augustae, a monument neglected even by the Romans themselves, yet one filled with symbolism and redolent of antiquity. Fittingly this altar, which has been almost completely reconstructed by archaeologists, stands next to another overlooked monument of ancient Rome, the Mausoleum of Augustus. From here we find ourselves in medieval streets, animated, narrow and filled with shops, little boutiques, cafés, and trattorias. Our passage is frequently enlivened with delightfully pungent smells. It opens out into sudden piazzas and comes upon unexpected palaces, such as the Palazzo Borghese and the complex Camera dei Deputati, built over centuries and sadly rarely lingered over by tourists.

Among the unusual nooks and crannies of this tour are some better-known corners, such as the Campo dei Fiori, notorious for the burning by the Inquisition of the brilliant philosopher Giordano Bruno in 1600 and today the home of one of Rome's liveliest markets. The tour ends at one of the most entrancing complexes in Rome, the group of buildings comprising the Teatro di Marcello, the church of San Nicola in Carcere, the so-called Temple of Fortuna Virilis and the fascinating church of Santa Maria in Cosmedin and crosses the Tiber to the Trastevere.

The Romans occasionally build monuments to celebrate peace as well as war. Just before the outbreak of World War II, between the Via di Ripetta (a street of modest little shops) and a bend of the Tiber above the Ponte Cavour, Roman archaeologists were patiently putting together an exquisite white marble altar erected by the Roman Senate between the years 13 and

OPPOSITE *Baldassare Peruzzi designed for Agostino Chigi the villa now known as the Farnesina in the first years of the sixteenth century. The loggias shelter sumptuous frescoes by Peruzzi himself, Sebastiano del Piombo and Raphael.*

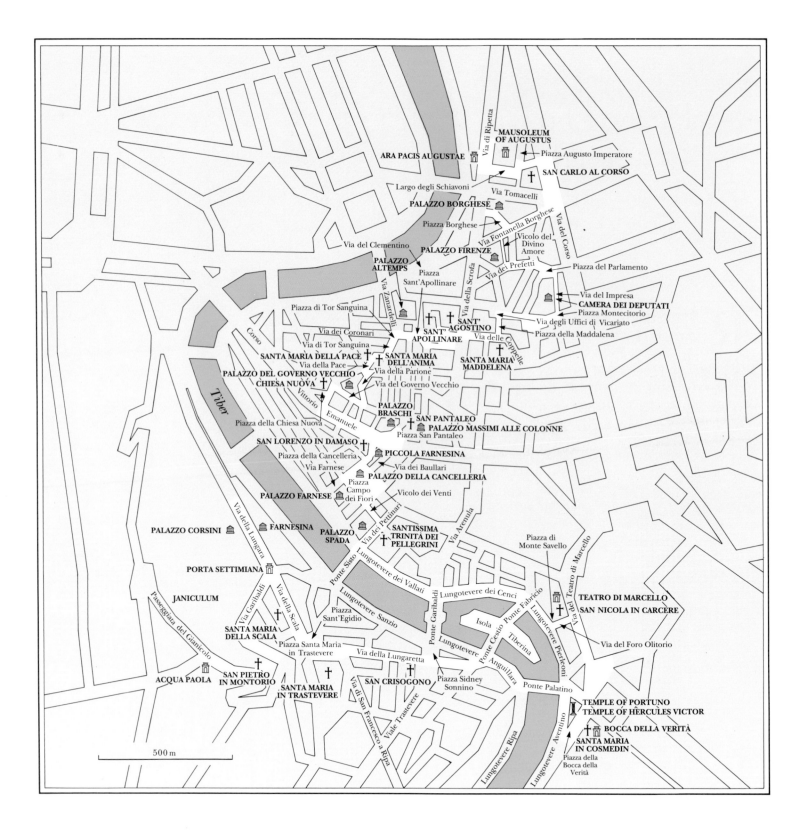

MAUSOLEUM OF AUGUSTUS

Via di Ripetta

ARA PACIS AUGUSTAE

Piazza Augusto Imperatore

SAN CARLO AL CORSO

Largo degli Schiavoni

Via Tomacelli

PALAZZO BORGHESE

Piazza Borghese

Via Fontanella Borghese

Via del Corso

Vicolo del Divino Amore

Via del Clementino

PALAZZO FIRENZE

Piazza del Parlamento

PALAZZO ALTEMPS

Piazza Sant'Apollinare

Via dei Prefetti

Via della Scrofa

Via del Impresa

CAMERA DEI DEPUTATI

Piazza Montecitorio

Via del Zanardelli

Piazza di Tor Sanguina

Via degli Uffici di Vicariato

SANT' AGOSTINO

Via delle Coppelle

Piazza della Maddalena

Via dei Coronari

SANT' APOLLINARE

Via di Tor Sanguina

Corso

SANTA MARIA DELLA PACE

SANTA MARIA DELL'ANIMA

SANTA MARIA MADDELENA

Via della Pace

Via della Parione

PALAZZO DEL GOVERNO VECCHIO

CHIESA NUOVA

Via del Governo Vecchio

Vittorio

Emanuele

PALAZZO BRASCHI

SAN PANTALEO

Tiber

Piazza della Chiesa Nuova

PALAZZO MASSIMI ALLE COLONNE

Piazza San Pantaleo

SAN LORENZO IN DAMASO

PICCOLA FARNESINA

Piazza della Cancelleria

Via dei Baullari

Via Farnese

PALAZZO DELLA CANCELLERIA

PALAZZO FARNESE

Piazza Campo dei Fiori

Vicolo dei Venti

Via Avenula

PALAZZO CORSINI

FARNESINA

Via della Lungara

Via dei Pettinari

SANTISSIMA TRINITÀ DEI PELLEGRINI

Piazza di Monte Savello

Via del Teatro di Marcello

PALAZZO SPADA

PORTA SETTIMIANA

Via Garibaldi

Ponte Sisto

Lungotevere dei Vallati

Lungotevere dei Cenci

TEATRO DI MARCELLO

SAN NICOLA IN CARCERE

JANICULUM

Passeggiata del Gianicolo

Via della Scala

Piazza Sant'Egidio

Lungotevere Sanzio

Ponte Garibaldi

Lungotevere Pierleoni

Via del Foro Olitorio

Isola

Ponte Fabricio

Ponte Cestio

Tiberina

SANTA MARIA DELLA SCALA

Piazza Santa Maria in Trastevere

Via della Lungaretta

Ponte Anguillara

Ponte Palatino

ACQUA PAOLA

SAN PIETRO IN MONTORIO

SAN CRISOGONO

Piazza Sidney Sonnino

TEMPLE OF PORTUNO

TEMPLE OF HERCULES VICTOR

SANTA MARIA IN TRASTEVERE

Via di San Francesco a Ripa

Viale Trastevere

BOCCA DELLA VERITÀ

SANTA MARIA IN COSMEDIN

Lungotevere Ripa

Lungotevere Aventino

Piazza della Bocca della Verità

500 m

9 BC in honour of the emperor Augustus, who by conquering the Gauls and the Spaniards had brought a period of temporary prosperity and quiet to the empire. Fragments of the **ARA PACIS AUGUSTAE** ('Altar of Augustan Peace') had been discovered underneath the foundations of Palazzo Fiano in 1568, and between then and 1937 the rest had been unearthed piece by piece.

Today the restored altar is protected from the savage Roman environment by a shelter of concrete and glass. Inside a surround of Carrara marble, which is decorated with garlands of fruit, acanthus leaves and flowers, and supported on the heads of oxen, stands the altar itself rising on ten steps and guarded by sphinxes. Among the acanthus plants a serpent robs the nest of a lark.

Here is symbolized the ancient Roman concept of the state. The reliefs of the altar tell the legendary history of Rome (and where the sculptures have still to be uncovered, archaeologists have thoughtfully scratched in the bits we cannot yet see). On the left Faustulus discovers Romulus and Remus being sucked by the she-wolf. On the right, Aeneas sacrifices to the household gods. Augustus's sacred pedigree is thus proclaimed. On one side are represented the emperor, his family and his court in solemn procession for the dedication of the altar. You can still make out the rods carried by the lictors. No one can be sure, but the women in the party are probably the emperor's wife Livia, his daughter Julia and his niece Antonia. The children are portraits of Germanicus and the future emperor Claudius. And on the far face of the altar are carved allegorical figures representing the goddess of Rome, along with Earth, who protects two of her children, Air, riding on a swan, and Water, riding a sea-monster.

In 1937 the authorities chose this spot wisely to re-erect the ancient altar, for it stands next to one of ancient Rome's sacred sites. Chunks of marble stick out from the brick wall of the **MAUSOLEUM OF AUGUSTUS**, which was built in 28 BC. The emperor commissioned it on his return from Egypt to serve as his own burial place and that of his imperial dynasty. His architectural model was the tombs of the Etruscans, although at Alexandria he had seen the tomb of Alexander the Great, which also must have influenced the circular pattern of his own mausoleum. At one time cypresses grew inside, surrounding a huge statue of the emperor. Concentric walls spread out from the centre to reach a diameter of 87 metres, and two granite obelisks (one now in the Piazza del'Esquilino, the other on the Quirinal) guarded its entrance – another Egyptian trait. From this entrance a corridor ran to the burial chamber. The ashes of the emperor's nephew Marcellus were the first to be placed here, to be followed in due course by all the imperial family. Nerva was the last emperor to be laid to rest here in AD 98.

By the Middle Ages the mausoleum was in ruins. The urn which once housed the ashes of Agrippina and is now displayed in the Capitoline Museum was used for measuring corn. The Colonna family transformed the place into a fortress. Travertine was taken away to be used elsewhere. Then

OPPOSITE
PEACEFUL CORNERS
AND PARKS

the fortress itself collapsed, and the area of the mausoleum was planted with vines and a garden. Transformed into an amphitheatre in 1780, Augustus's burial place was used for public entertainment. Seven years later, Goethe recorded that the great building, now empty inside and open above, was being used for baiting animals, a spectacle he described as far from edifying. In the nineteenth century the building became a concert hall, famous for the orchestras which performed there during the winter season. Its reconstruction was due to Mussolini, who planned in vain to be buried here himself.

Today, in spite of the roses which surround it, the mausoleum stands forlorn and slightly neglected. A more cheerful building is the church of **SAN CARLO AL CORSO** whose dome rises beyond the Piazza Augusto Imperatore. It was begun in 1612 by Onorio Longhi to replace an older church dedicated to St Ambrose of Milan, and finished in 1668 by Pietro da Cortona. Two years after building had started, Cardinal Federico Borromeo gave the church the heart of St Charles Borromeo, whom Pope Paul V had canonized two years earlier, and it received its present name (although it is still also called Santi Ambrogio e Carlo). Borromeo was such a rigorous reformer that some lax opponents tried to assassinate him. What killed him in 1584 at the age of 46 was the medicine he took for a fever, which was too strong for a body accustomed only to bread and water.

Carlo Maratta painted the scene over the high altar of the Virgin Mary presenting the patron saint to Jesus. Borromeo's heart rests in an ornate urn behind it. The façade of 1684, which by Roman standards is cool and unassertive, is by a third architect, Giambattista Menicucci. As if to emphasize this homeliness, a house has been let into the side of the church.

The narrow passageway to the right of the apse suddenly opens out into the animated Via del Corso, with its shops and hotels. A tablet on the wall informs you where the composer Pietro Mascagni lived, and died. He is remembered today only for the opera *Cavalleria Rusticana*, which he wrote at the age of 26. Mascagni succeeded Arturo Toscanini as musical director of La Scala, Milan, in 1929, but because of his support for the Italian fascists, died here dishonoured in 1945.

Pushing your way southwards through the crowds which invariably throng this part of the Corso, you can escape to the right into Via Fontanella Borghese through the market in Piazza della Fontanella Borghese, which sells bric-a-brac, rare books and prints, and so to the Piazza Borghese and the austere, late sixteenth-century **PALAZZO BORGHESE**, nowadays the home of the Spanish Ambassador, and nicknamed 'the Roman harpsichord' (*Il Cembalo romano*) – because of its shape. It was bought in the 1600s by Cardinal Camillo Borghese, recently elected Pope Paul V, who entrusted further work to Flaminio Ponzio. Cardinal Scipione Borghese, who moved into the palace after the death of his uncle Camillo in 1621, next employed Giovanni Vasanzio and Carlo Maderno to finish the building. The great courtyard, with its double loggia supported on paired Doric and Ionic

OPPOSITE *Air rides on a swan and the goddess of Rome suckles two of her children, white Water is borne on a sea-monster, on the Ara Pacis.*

OPPOSITE *The Mausoleum of Augustus with the late seventeenth-century dome and apse of San Carlo al Corso. The mausoleum is now laid bare to its classical foundations and is of a traditional Etruscan type, but on a massive scale.*

LEFT *The Vicolo del Divino Amore is typical of many small streets in the area which follow their medieval line and runs along the side of the Palazzo Firenze, once the home of Medici cardinals.*

columns, is rendered all the more exquisite by the pool from which gush three early rococo fountains, the so-called Nymphaeum of Venus, designed by Carlo Rainaldi in the 1660s. Although the palace is private property, you can walk through the massive doors to a gateway and peer into this courtyard. At the opposite end is an arcade decked with pots of flowers and small trees. Two mighty statues guard an arch at the far end of the courtyard, beyond which is another garden enhanced with statuary.

This ancient quarter of Rome is crammed with exquisite buildings and entrancing squares. The narrow Vicolo del Divino Amore, suddenly quiet again, curves gently south from the Palazzo Borghese into Piazza Firenze where the early sixteenth-century **PALAZZO FIRENZE** (so-named because it used to be the Florentine Embassy) boasts another ravishing courtyard, this one with a little formal garden. Go the other way along Via dei Prefetti and the quiet street opens out to discover the yet more monumental architecture of the Piazza del Parlamento, which is bounded on its southern side by the **CAMERA DEI DEPUTATI** (Chamber of Deputies).

The early twentieth-century extension and façade of the chamber are by Ernesto Basile. This is art nouveau Rome (a facet of the city not much explored, but treasured by architects and buffs of the style, who adore above all the newly restored Perugia Savings Bank of 1902 in Via Ferdinando di Savoia near the Piazza del Popolo). Inside the chamber are art nouveau frescoes by Giulio Aristide Sartorio, and a splendid multicoloured skylight.

Walk south alongside the Camera dei Deputati and baroque Rome appears again in the shape of the old **PALAZZO DI MONTECITORIO** into which the deputies moved in 1871. Bernini began building this palace in 1650 at the command of Pope Innocent X who wanted it as a present for the Ludovisi family. When the pope fell out with Cardinal Ludovisi, work stopped, so the palace was only finished by Carlo Fontana in 1694. Its convex, shallow polygonal façade, rising from massive blocks of travertine, follows Bernini's design and overlooks the Piazza di Montecitorio and a fourth-century BC Egyptian obelisk – yet another brought from Heliopolis by Augustus, and erected here in 1792.

Our route now takes us on a narrow zig-zag walk west from the left-hand corner of the palace along Via degli Uffici del Vicario, whose shops sell sticky toffees and irresistible cakes. Gently curving Via della Maddalena reaches the piazza of the same name, shaded by the convex rococo façade which Giuseppe Sardi designed for the church of **SANTA MARIA MADDALENA** in 1735. This façade hides a seventeenth-century church, frescoed by such masters as Carlo Fontana and abutting onto a sacristy of 1741.

To find Rome's earliest renaissance church, take Via delle Coppelle, once the street in which barrel-makers (coopers) lived, passing Palazzo Baldassini, designed by Antonio da Sangallo the Younger in the early sixteenth century, and thus to the Piazza Sant'Agostino, where, from 1479 to 1483 the church of **SANT'AGOSTINO** was built.

Cardinal d'Estouteville, who was Archbishop of Rouen and protector of the Augustinian Order, wanted a suitable shrine for the remains of St Augustine's mother, St Monica. Giacomo da Pietrasanta built it in the form of a Latin cross, using travertine cannibalized from the Colosseum. Sansovino and Luigi Vanvitelli restored Sant'Agostino in 1750, but they did so sensitively, preserving his façade with its rose window and wide arches. St Monica lies under the altar of the Blessed Sacrament, at the end of the north aisle, her fifteenth-century statue by Isaia da Pisa.

The finest work of art in Sant'Agostino, on the third pillar on the north side, is a fresco of Isaah between two putti which Raphael painted in 1512 (although it was later restored by Daniele da Volterra, known as the 'breeches painter' because he was employed to fresco breeches on the nudes in the Sistine Chapel). Underneath it, Andrea Sansovino added a statue of the Madonna with St Anne.

Bernini built the lavishly marbled high altar (which, contrary to tradition, is at the north end of the building) in 1627. Over it is a Byzantine

painting of the *Madonna del Parto* with an inscription declaring, 'Your glory, O Virgin, is your motherhood'. Since it was brought from the church of Santa Sophia in Constantinople after the Turkish invasion of 1453, it was inevitably attributed to the evangelist St Luke.

Sansovino's sculpted version of the same subject, dated to 1521, stands in a niche to the right of the main doorway, surrounded by many ex-voto plaques from those who have sought its blessing and have worn down the Madonna's right foot with kisses. The divine infant stands sturdily (and improbably) on her knee, and our Lady holds open a book with her finger, as if longing to read more about the mystery of the immaculate conception of her child. The other frescoes inside the church are mainly by Pietro Gagliardi, painted in 1855. Far more entrancing are the seventeenth-century altarpiece and panels by Guercino in the chapel of Sant'Agostino, and the superb *Madonna di Loreto* in the first chapel on the left, painted by Caravaggio

Sant'Agostino can claim to be Rome's earliest remaining renaissance church, built between 1479 and 1483, with travertine taken from the Colosseum. St Augustine's mother, St Monica, is buried in a chapel to the left of the altar, in a tomb by Isaia da Pisa.

in 1605 after he had paid a visit to the Holy House of Loreto. If you put a coin in the device which illuminates this chapel, you see that the bare soles of the pilgrims' feet are dirty, for they have walked a long way. Before leaving Sant'Agostino, do not miss a fifteenth-century crucifix which hangs inconspicuously in the last chapel on the right.

Through an arch in the Piazza Sant'Agostino, walk west and turn right to find the church of **SANT'APOLLINARE**, which is dedicated to the first Bishop of Ravenna, martyred in the reign of Vespasian. The church was completely rebuilt in the mid eighteenth century by Ferdinando Fuga.

Across the Piazza Sant'Apollinare is the turreted **PALAZZO ALTEMPS**, which Baldassare Peruzzi began for Girolamo Riario and which was finished by Martino Longhi the Elder. Its courtyard is filled with ancient statues, including a resting Hercules sculpted in the fifth century BC. Altemps is an odd-sounding name for a Roman palace, but represents the attempted transcription of the owners' family name – Von Hohenems – into Italian.

South-west from the Palazzo Altemps, in Piazza di Tor Sanguina, is displayed a massive Roman arch excavated in the stadium of Domitian. The bloody tower, after which the square is named, is the sole remnant of a medieval fortress belonging to the powerful Sanguini family. Perhaps their most famous coup was to have one of their members elected Pope Leo VI while his predecessor was still alive (for Pope John X was deposed and then imprisoned in Castel Sant'Angelo, where he was later murdered by being suffocated with a pillow).

Via di Tor Sanguina takes us south-west from here to the church of **SANTA MARIA DELL'ANIMA**. Although the façade is attributed to the Italian Giuliano da Sangallo, this church was built by Flemish and German architects to cater for their countrymen on pilgrimage to Rome. A Flemish resident named Jan Peeters left cash to start the church in 1400. German Catholics finished the building in 1514. The church derives its name from a statue formerly on the tympanum of the entrance which showed a pair of souls in purgatory supplicating the Madonna. Today you enter Santa Maria dell'Anima by the back door, to find yourself in a church more reminiscent of the hall churches of Germany or the Low Countries. In the north German style, it boasts two naves divided by pillars. Since its building spanned 114 years, Santa Maria dell'Anima is a mixture of gothic and renaissance elements. Adorning the high altar is a Madonna painted by Giulio Romano (c. 1492–1546) for the high altar.

Pope Adrian VI, who came from Utrecht (and was the last non-Italian pope until the election of John Paul II in 1978), died in 1523 after a short, unhappy reign, during which the cardinals treated him as an uncouth northerner, the Lutherans refused to come to heel and his plans to repulse the Turks from Christendom failed. He lies here in a tomb designed by Baldassare Peruzzi, embellished by four statues representing the cardinal virtues of Courage, Justice, Prudence and Temperance. Another foreign notable lying here in a tomb by Gilles de Rivière and Nicolas d'Arras is the Duke of Cleves, father of Henry VIII's fourth wife.

On the other side of the Via della Pace is the church of **SANTA MARIA DELLA PACE**. Built in 1482 by Baccio Pontelli on behalf of Pope Sixtus V as a thank-offering for the restoration of peace between Naples, Florence and Milan, it was restored by Pope Alexander VII in the mid seventeenth century, this time in gratitude for the peace which had prevailed during his pontificate. This period saw the addition of the semi-circular Doric portico, by Pietro da Cortona. Commissioned by Cardinal Oliviero Carafa, Donato Bramante produced for this church his first Roman building, the renaissance cloisters with their double loggias, in 1504. Its design was the fruit of four years which Bramante had devoted to the study of classical ruins.

Inside the church (which opens these days only for Mass) a short nave leads to an octagon with an imposing dome. Chapels surround the octagon, each dedicated to an episode in the life of the Blessed Virgin. Carlo Maderno created statues of Peace and Justice to adorn the high altar, which also incorporates a miraculous painting of the Virgin Mary. (When a madman threw a knife at it, the Virgin's face bled.)

Even more fascinating is the decoration of the first chapel on the right, which was frescoed by Raphael in 1514. His theme is *Sibyls inspired by Angels*. Four pagan holy women, the Cumaean, Persian and Phrygian Sibyls, and the exceedingly old Sibyl of Tibur, have learned of the resurrection of Jesus. Over them an angel holds a flaming torch, a sign that the Sibyls must carry the light of the gospel to the pagan world. Above these figures Raphael's pupils, including the skilful Timoteo Viti, painted Old Testament worthies (Daniel, David, Habakkuk and Jonah). In the first decade of the sixteenth century the Sienese master Baldassare Peruzzi frescoed the first chapel on the left with portraits of the Virgin Mary, St Bridget and St Catherine as well as the donor, the Sienese banker Agostino Chigi. Another enthralling corner of this church is the Cesi Chapel, built by Antonio da Sangallo the Younger (1483–1546) with high renaissance sculpture by Simone Mosca.

This part of Rome is a city of old, deliciously smelly streets. Across from the portico of Santa Maria della Pace is Via di Torre Millina, named after a towered fifteenth-century palace, of which only the tower remains at number 25. Via della Parione runs from here past the fifteenth-century **PALAZZO DEL GOVERNO VECCHIO** (once the home of the papal governors of Rome) into the picturesque and narrow Via del Governo Vecchio. Formerly papal processions would wind along this street on their way from the Vatican to the cathedral church of Rome, San Giovanni in Laterano. Today it is lined with antique shops. Turn right and walk along it to Via della Chiesa Nuova, alongside the church of **SANTA MARIA IN VALLICELLA**, known to everyone as the **CHIESA NUOVA**.

This monument to the Counter-Reformation, built between 1580 and 1605 by Martino Longhi the Elder and Giovanni Matteo di Città di

Castello, has a baroque façade by Faustolo Rughese and an interior designed by Borromini. It shelters three paintings by the young Rubens, who had come to Italy in 1600. That over the high altar already reveals the master's liking for chubby cherubs. Since Counter-Reformation churches are filled with light, Rubens took the precaution of painting the pictures which flank the altar on slate, to counteract reflection.

This church was a gift of 1575 from Pope Gregory XIII to St Philip Neri as a way of thanking the saint for founding a group of fervent Catholics known as the Confraternity of the Oratory. The saint used to pray in ecstasy at the altar of the Visitation which Federico Barocci painted in 1594 for the first chapel on the left. (Barocci also painted the Presentation in the left transept.) Although he loved music and relished jokes, St Philip Neri hated ostentation and wanted his church simply to be plain.

To the right of the apse is another gilded chapel, designed by Carlo Rainaldi with an altarpiece by Carlo Maratta. The whole church was sumptuously frescoed by Pietro da Cortona (who began work in 1647 and finished the paintings twenty years later). The swagger of these frescoes is probably in complete contrast to the founder's wishes but they are nevertheless delightful, depicting virtually the whole Bible story from the creation of the world to the resurrection of Christ.

Some 50 years after the death of St Philip Neri, Alessandro Algardi sculpted a group depicting the saint and an angel, which now stands in the sacristy of the church. Philip lived and died in the adjoining oratory, where he organised concerts of sacred music from which is derived the term 'oratorio'. The present huge oratory, with its seductively curving façade, was built by Borromini between 1637 and 1652.

South-west of the church is a mid nineteenth-century statue of the bewigged Pietro Metastasio. Court poet at Vienna for half a century until his death in 1782, Metastasio had an extraordinarily successful career as an opera librettist; his work influenced Mozart himself. Walk south-east along Corso Vittorio Emanuele to discover a series of extremely elegant palaces. PALAZZO SORA, at 217 on the left, was built in the first decade of the sixteenth century. Then comes Piazza San Pantaleo, with the late seventeenth-century church of SAN PANTALEO, the façade of which was added by Giuseppe Valadier in 1806. The vault was frescoed towards the end of the seventeenth century by Filippo Gherardi. Martyred in AD 303 under Diocletian, Pantaleo is second only to St Luke as the patron saint of doctors, possibly because a relic of his blood at Ravello liquifies miraculously each year on his feast day, 27 July. This church's major relic is the saint's head.

Also in the piazza is one corner of the gracious triangular PALAZZO BRASCHI, built by Cosimo Morelli in the 1790s for Pope Pius VI (born Giovanni Angelo Braschi). Rustic stonework in the lower storeys gives way to three storeys faced with brick and enlivened by windows topped by alternately triangular and segmental pediments.

Pietro Metastasio contemplates one of his works. The poet's talent was discovered by the eighteenth-century philosopher, Gian Vincenzo Gravina, who heard him as a boy improvising verses in the Piazza Sant'Andrea della Valle.

Palazzo Braschi now serves as the Museum of Rome. The 51 exhibition halls behind its classical façade retrace the history of the city from the Middle Ages until today. At the corner of its north façade is a fragmentary marble group depicting Menelaus supporting Patroclus. The Romans have forgotten this and dub the statue Pasquino, from the habit of a sixteenth-century tailor of that name who lived close by and used to hang on the statue caustic squibs or 'pasquinades' against the public authorities.

Farther east across the piazza, at 141 Corso Vittorio Emanuele, admire the convex façade and the elegant inner courtyard of the **PALAZZO MASSIMO ALLE COLONNE**. Baldassare Peruzzi designed it in 1532 to replace a palace destroyed when Rome was sacked five years earlier. You can visit this palace with its beautifully stuccoed portico annually on 16 March, the day when St Philip Neri in 1587 healed a mortally sick son of the house.

Slightly further to the west, on the opposite side of the Corso Vittorio Emanuele, at number 168, is a palace known as the **PICCOLA FARNESINA**. Two offset loggias sweeten its façade, the lower one supported by Doric columns, while the upper one rises on Corinthian columns. As you might guess from its frieze of fleurs-de-lys, the palace was built in 1525 for a French prelate, probably by Antonio da Sangallo the Younger. The Piccola Farnesina houses the Museo Barracco, a collection of antique sculpture bequeathed to Rome in 1902 by Baron Giovanni Barracco. It includes several superb pieces, in particular a head of Rameses II and a pensive head of Alexander the Great. It is easy not to spot this lovely palace, since Enrico Gui gave it a new façade in 1901.

Across the Piazza della Cancelleria is the magnificent early renaissance **PALAZZO DELLA CANCELLERIA**. The architect of this long and imposing palace, which was raised between 1483 and 1517 was possibly Andrea Bregno, possibly Bramante. Stones were plundered from the Colosseum to build it. Its geometric forms and austerely regular design were interrupted and enlivened in 1589 when Domenico Fontana added a baroque entrance. In the so-called hall of the hundred days is a huge fresco which Giorgio Vasari (with many assistants, some of them inferior) did for Cardinal Alessandro Farnese in 1546, taking only that short period to complete the task. After viewing the painting, Michelangelo sarcastically remarked that one could see readily that this was so. When he was restoring the nearby church of San Lorenzo in Damaso. Bramante took away some of its ancient granite columns and used them to create a superb arcaded, two-storeyed courtyard for the Palazzo della Cancelleria. The roses on the capitals, the windows and the pavement of the courtyard come from the coat of arms of the wealthy Cardinal Raffaele Riario, for whom the palace was built. Part of the cost was borne by Franceschetto Cybo, a nephew of Pope Innocent VIII, from whom Riario won 60,000 scudi at the gaming table. Riario joined the abortive conspiracy of 1517 against Pope Leo X, and as a punishment had his goods and his palace seized.

In a corner of the palace is the fifteenth-century church of **SAN LORENZO IN DAMASO**. From its two rich aisles, from its gilded, coffered ceiling (incorporating the Riario roses), from the late sixteenth-century Coronation of the Virgin by Federigo Zuccaro over the high altar and from the marble Corinthian columns which support its baldacchino one would never guess that this church is based on a basilica built here in the fourth century. An indication of its antiquity is a twelfth-century icon in the Chapel of the Holy Sacrament, though this particular treasure was housed elsewhere till 1465. A genuine survival from the earlier church is the tomb of Cardinal Scarampo in the south aisle. Here, too, is buried Count Pellegrini Rossi. He died in 1848, assassinated in the Palazzo della Cancelleria as he set out to inaugurate the new Chamber of Deputies instituted by Pope Pius IX.

Walk south through the Piazza della Cancelleria, glancing at the papal coat of arms on the corner of the palace (its oak tree identifying the pope as Julius II) to the **CAMPO DEI FIORI**. On weekdays mornings and Saturdays there is a busy market here. Parasols cover stalls selling clothing, flowers, vegetables, fish, fruit and meat. In this pleasant square the magistrates used to execute malefactors and heretics, the most illustrious of the latter being the philosopher, astronomer and monk Giordano Bruno, one of whose alleged errors was to argue that the earth circled the sun, and not vice versa. A late nineteenth-century monument by Ettore Ferrari marks the spot where the heretic was burned alive three centuries earlier. Bruno broods in his cowl. The side panels depict him teaching, defying his judges, and burning to death.

There is nothing grand about this square. Indeed, its crumbling houses, with little balconies and washing hanging out of windows, belong not to a capital city but to a small town. Three small streets lead from it to the **PALAZZO FARNESE**, the finest renaissance palace in Rome. (Alas you can visit it only on written application.) Antonio da Sangallo the Younger began it in 1514 on behalf of the humanist cardinal Alessandro Farnese, who a year before had abandoned his mistress to seek ordination and would be elected Pope Paul III in 1534. His façade, the longest of all the private palaces of Rome, stretched the length of the Piazza.

The future pope, however, was ill-pleased with Sangallo's work and opened the project to competition. Michelangelo won, and his is the splendid mannerist entablature, with the Farnese fleurs-de-lys underneath. Michelangelo was also responsible for the upper storey of the courtyard, whose windows have a remarkable architectural liveliness not previously seen in Rome. Vignola and Giacomo della Porta designed the late sixteenth-century façade which overlooks the Via Giulia, while Annibale Carracci and his pupils frescoed the main gallery with a painting depicting the *Triumph of Love*.

In front of the main façade a couple of fountains spout from granite basins taken from the Baths of Caracalla. Turn south-east from here along

*Ettore Ferrari's statue of the monk
Giordano Bruno in the Piazza Campo
dei Fiori stands beside the spot where
he was burned to death in 1600.*

Vicolo dei Venti as far as another renaissance palace, the **PALAZZO SPADA**. The architect Giulio Mazzoni completed the building in 1540 for Pope Paul III's protégé Cardinal Girolamo Capo di Ferro. Borromini, employed in the 1650s, remodelled the palace for Cardinal Bernardino Spada, and was also responsible for the inner staircase, and for a famous colonnade between the two inner courtyards, the clever use of perspective in which makes it seem four times longer than its mere 9 metres. (Some art historians dispute Borromini's hand in this colonnade, attributing it to an Augustinian monk named Giovanni Maria da Bitonto.)

The main courtyard is exquisite. Statues of gods and goddesses surmount a frieze of sea monsters and ships. Below them another delicate frieze depicts men fighting centaurs, satyrs chasing terrified women, bull fights, hunting scenes and a lion getting its own back on a hunter.

Today part of this palace houses the art collection of Cardinal Bernardino Spada and his family. Its masterpieces include a *Visitation* by Andrea del Sarto and a *Landscape with Windmills* by Jan Breughel the Elder.

ABOVE *One of the twin fountains in the Piazza Farnese. These are made of Egyptian granite and were brought here from the Baths of Caracalla.*

OPPOSITE *Rome's oldest surviving bridge, the Ponte Fabricio, was built in 62 BC. The name of the consul Fabricius who paid for it is inscribed on the far arch.*

Also on display is a statue of Pompey before which, it is claimed, Julius Caesar was murdered. Here, too, are two portraits of the cardinal, the more exuberant by Guercino, the more subdued by Guido Reni.

Opposite this palace is the church of **SANTISSIMA TRINITÀ DEI PELLEGRINI**. Although its façade (by Francesco de Sanctis) dates from 1723, the rest of the church was built in 1614 by Paolo Maggi. It is worth a visit just to see the altarpiece by Guido Reni depicting the Holy Trinity. This pilgrim church is attached to a hospice founded by St Philip Neri.

Walk between the church and the Palazzo Spada to reach the River Tiber. On the way you pass the minuscule church of **SAN SALVATORE IN ONDA**. The late eleventh-century Corinthian columns (which do not quite match one another) reveal the antiquity of this church, which was remodelled in the seventeenth century. At this spot on the Tiber, Pope Sixtus III built a narrow, still-surviving bridge, the Ponte Sisto, for pilgrims to the Holy City.

Stroll south-east alongside the gently curving river, which is overhung with trees. Shortly the Tiber is divided by the **ISOLA TIBERINA**. Ahead appear the three marble arches of the **PONTE FABRICIO** (its central arch much smaller), supporting a brick superstructure. This is the oldest surviving bridge in Rome, built in 62 BC and named after the Roman consul who paid for it (and had inscribed on it the words L FABRICIUS CURATOR VIARUM). Other consuls embellished the bridge in 21 BC and also inscribed their names (Q LELLIUS AND M LOLLIUS) on the arch nearest to the left bank of the river. Modern Romans dub it the Ponte dei Quattro Capi, on account of the four crumbling Janus heads that adorn it.

On the island you can see the medieval **TORRE DEI PIERLEONI-CAETANI** as well as the twelfth-century campanile and the romanesque church of **SAN BARTOLOMEO**. The tower, which rises from **PALAZZO PIERLEONI-CAETANI**, is a reminder that Rome long hosted a substantial Jewish community, sometimes treating the Jews with honour and sometimes shamefully. About 500 Jewish families still live in the city, their handsome synagogue of 1904, situated just behind us on Lungotevere dei Cenci. (John Paul II visited it on 13 April 1986, probably the first time a pope had set foot in a synagogue since the days of St Peter.)

The Pierleoni family was rich enough to control much of Rome in the eleventh and twelfth centuries. One of their members, Baruch-Benedict, converted to Christianity, and his great grandson, Cardinal Pietro da Santa Maria in Trastevere, was elected pope in 1130, taking the name Anacletus II. Unfortunately a rival conclave elected a rival pope, who took the name Innocent II. Even though most of Christendom sided with Innocent, Anacletus held out in Rome, but these days he is generally described not as pope but as anti-pope.

The façade of San Bartolomeo was added by Martino Longhi the Younger in 1625, but the pillars inside come from an ancient temple and the fresco of the Madonna and Child in the chapel on the south side was painted

in the tenth century. As the pillars indicate, this church is built on the site of a temple dedicated in the third century BC to Aesculapius, the Roman god of healing, and the waters of the well set in the steps of the chancel were once considered efficacious in curing all manner of diseases. The saint carved alongside Christ on this well is St Adalbert of Prague, the patron saint of Bohemia, to whom the emperor Otto III dedicated the church when he paid for its construction in the tenth century. Adalbert usurped Aesculapius and in turn has been usurped by Bartholomew. No one can be certain that St Bartholomew, one of Christ's apostles, actually lies here. His remains were allegedly brought to Rome from Benevento, but the Christians of Benevento denied this. In 1740 the authorities decided that Bartholomew must have been cut in two, so that both cities could share title to his earthly remains.

Aesculapius was honoured here because in 293 BC one of his symbols, a snake, was brought from Epidaurus to Rome and put an end to a fearsome plague which had carried off thousands of citizens. Not only did the grateful Romans build him a temple here; they also reconstructed Isola Tiberina in the form of a ship, to commemorate the snake's journey from Epidaurus. Somehow the statue of Aesculapius which stood in the temple has found its way to the Museo Nazionale in Naples. To the east of the church he is still honoured beside the Tiber with blocks of travertine in the shape of a boat and carved with his snake. Fittingly, too, to the west of the church is a hospital, founded in 1548 by the order of friars known as the Fatebenefratelli (i.e. 'Brothers, do good'). But the influence of Aesculapius has spread even further afield. In the early twelfth century, Rahere, variously described as a courtier, a prebendary at St Paul's, a monk or a court jester to King Henry II of England made a pilgrimage to Rome, where he fell fell sick of malaria. He was nursed on the island and vowed that should he recover he would build a hospital when he reached London again. Granted land at Smithfield, he founded both the church and hospital of St Bartholomew.

Near the **HOSPITAL OF THE FATEBENEFRATELLI** stands their pharmacy. On its ceiling is their symbol, a split pomegranate topped with a cross. And on the far side of the island is yet another church based on a pagan foundation. **SAN GIOVANNI CALABITA**, which in spite of its eighteenth-century interior (with a ceiling by Corrado Giaquinto), was founded in the eleventh century. A mosaic discovered inside depicts Jupiter Jurarius, the god of oaths.

Walk back to the left bank of the Tiber, to approach one of the most evocative spots in Rome. Across the road stands the **TEATRO DI MARCELLO** (Theatre of Marcellus), which Julius Caesar planned and Augustus completed in AD 13. Augustus dedicated it to Marcellus, the son of his sister Octavia, who had died in 23 BC. Here the Romans leaned heavily on the Greek trick of using a slope as the natural basis for seating spectators. Semicircular and open towards the river, the Teatro di Marcello boasts two superimposed rows of 52 arches, the lower one carried on Doric colums, the upper on Ionic. Once there were three tiers, the topmost one Corinthian,

OPPOSITE *The hospital of the Fatebenefratelli rises in the Piazza San Bartolomeo. The Isola Tiberina has long been associated with healing: a temple was dedicated to Aesculapius here in 293 BC.*

The ancient drain cover known as the Bocca della Verità glowers in the portico of Santa Maria in Cosmedin.

but this disappeared in the Middle Ages when the theatre was for a time transformed into a fortress. In its heyday the theatre, which is 120 metres in diameter, could hold 15,000 spectators. In front of the theatre are the remains of an even more ancient building: three columns of a **TEMPLE OF APOLLO** built in the fifth century BC and restored by C. Sosius in 32 BC.

Close by stands the little church of **SAN NICOLA IN CARCERE**. Its name is derived from a prison which once stood nearby, and it stands on the site of three temples once dedicated to Juno Sospita, Spes (Hope) and Janus. It resembles an old temple, and so it once was, as is evident from columns that survive, some fluted, some with Corinthian capitals. The church was erected here in the eleventh century and two of the bells in its campanile were cast in 1286. Giacomo della Porta gave it a new façade in 1599, and although it breathes antiquity, the upper storey dates only from 1865.

Ancient Rome and medieval Christianity are marvellously set against each other in this corner of Rome. From San Nicola in Carcere, Via del Teatro di Marcello leads to the ruins of two temples. The rectangular **TEMPLE OF PORTUNUS** (still better known as the Temple of Fortuna Virilis), dating from the second century BC, was saved from destruction when it was turned into a church, and some fine ninth-century frescoes remain. Its original god, Portunus, was protector of sailors and tutelory god of ports – and Rome's first harbour, created by the Etruscan kings, stretched from the site of San Nicola in Carcere to this temple. The ancient called the spot the 'Forum Boarium' (or 'cattle market'), and anyone sailing up the Tiber from the port of Ostia landed here. Six fluted Ionic columns grace the entrance of the temple built in honour of the god who looked after them, and other half-columns are set in the tufa walls of the sanctuary. It later became the church of Santa Maria Egiziaca.

Early in the fifth century, this future saint, after spending seventeen years as a public prostitute in Alexandria, had joined a group of pilgrims bound for the Holy Land. Kneeling before the cross on which Christ was crucified, she repented of her sins and spent the next twenty years alone in the desert, constantly resisting temptation. She was discovered by a holy man named Zosimus, who thereafter visited her each Lent with the Holy Sacrament. One day he found her dead, alongside an inscription declaring that her name was Mary. Helped by a lion, he dug a grave and buried her.

The almost contemporary, circular **TEMPLE OF HERCULES VICTOR**, was later known as the Temple of Vesta, perhaps because of its resemblance to the circular temple in the Foro Romano. This was the first temple in Rome to be built of marble, and nineteen of its twenty fluted columns have survived. Like the Temple of Portunus, the Temple of Hercules Victor survived only by serving as a Christian place of worship, rededicated in the Middle Ages as Santo Stefano delle Carrozze, and again later as Santa Maria del Sole.

Across the Piazza della Bocca della Verità beyond a baroque fountain of 1717 by Carlo Bizzaccheri, rises the church of **SANTA MARIA IN COSMEDIN** with its slender, seven-storeyed brick campanile – surely one of the finest in Rome. Set into the portico wall is an ancient drain cover in the form of a mask, into which people used to stick their hands when swearing an oath, or if they had been accused of lying. Tradition held that the Bocca della Verità (the 'mouth of truth') would bite off the fingers of any perjurer.

Santa Maria in Cosmedin was built in the late sixth or early seventh century on the site of another Temple of Hercules, built in 495 BC, and fourth-century Roman columns from the former grain market are set in its walls. In the late eighth century the church was given to orthodox Greek Christians, who had escaped from the iconoclastic Byzantine emperors, by Pope Adrian I. The tradition continues. Today you can attend Mass celebrated in Greek for Orthodox Christians in communion with the pope, and candles flicker in front of a red and gold Byzantine mosaic depicting the Virgin Mary and the infant Jesus. The name of this church probably derives from a Greek word for embellishment, and probably refers to those added by Adrian I. The portico and campanile derive from its final major restoration in the twelfth century.

Inside, eighteen ancient columns divide the basilica into three aisles. On the walls you can make out the remains of the eleventh-century frescoes. There are two apses, both frescoed with scenes from the life of Mary. In the left one Christ has just been born. This is a touchingly homely scene. One midwife pours water into a bowl, in preparation for washing the child, while two others bring his mother food and drink. The other frescoes proclaim the heavenly exaltation of the woman to whom this church is dedicated. On the right is portrayed Mary's death, above which she sits in a mandorla, carrying her son and supported by angels. Another fresco shows her once more enthroned with her divine child, this time flanked by saints.

The Cosmati, a twelfth- and thirteenth-century family of mosaicists, created for the church a breathtaking ensemble of furniture: the superb inlaid floor, two *ambones* (early Christian pulpits, one for reading the Epistle, the other, the Gospel), an episcopal throne, a curly paschal candlestick guarded by two little lions, and the ciborium on the high altar, signed and dated 'Deodatus Me Fecit 1294'. The sacristy houses an early eighth-century mosaic of the Adoration of the Magi; and the eighth-century crypt follows the pattern of the church by being divided into three tiny aisles.

Cross the Tiber by the iron **PONTE PALATINO**, which is far younger than most other Roman bridges, dating only from 1891. Upstream in the river stands a single arch of the once seven-arched **PONTE EMILIO**, built between 181 and 179 BC by Marcus Aemilius Lepidus and Marcus Fulvius Nobilior. This bridge, which provided a convenient crossing for the carts carrying tufa from the quarries at Monteverde, survived for fifteen centuries, until a flood partially demolished it. Three popes rebuilt it, but in 1598 it finally collapsed. Since then it has been known as the Ponte Rotto. Beyond it appear the three graceful round arches of the **PONTE CESTIO**, flung across the

Convoluted detailing of the fountain in Piazza Santa Maria in Trastevere. Carlo Fontana restored a far older fountain in 1692.

Behind one of the popes on Carlo Fontana's portico of Santa Maria in Trastevere are twelfth-century mosaics of the Madonna. The first church in Rome dedicated to the Virgin was built here by Julius I in the middle of the fourth century, possibly on the site of an even earlier Christian foundation. Innocent II rebuilt it in the 1140s.

Tiber in the first century BC by Lucius Cestius. His name does not appear on it, the inscriptions only recording that the emperors Valens and Gratianus rebuilt it in around AD 365, plundering travertine from the Teatro di Marcello to do so.

From the other end of Ponte Palatino, Via della Lungaretta takes us to the part of Rome where Christianity first gained a foothold, the Trastevere (literally 'across the Tiber'). The people of the Trastevere still distinguish themselves from other Romans with the term 'Noantri' – we others – not surprisingly, for the district has its own ambience and its own unity. The Trastevere was occupied before Rome itself was founded. Today its ancient streets, little squares, piquant trattorie and entrancing churches make it one of the most seductive parts of the city.

Walking along these narrow, cobbled streets you can see ahead the trees and open country of the Janiculum Hill, or Gianicolo, named after the god Janus. The route to the ancient church of Santa Maria in Trastevere passes through Piazza Sidney Sonnino, where to the right is a thirteenth-century house with a battlemented tower containing little windows. This was the home of the poet Dante Alighieri (1265–1321), and has been transformed into a library devoted to the *Divine Comedy*. At the opposite corner of the square is the church of **SAN CRISOGONO**, its romanesque tower with a fifteenth-century pointed cap quite at odds with the church's classical façade. The latter is inscribed with the name of Cardinal Scipio Borghese, who commissioned Giambattista Soria to renovate the building in 1623. This church was originally built in the twelfth century on the site of a fifth-century sanctuary, and you can discover parts of the primitive building through the sacristy. The ancient church is decorated with eighth- and tenth-century frescoes.

SANTA MARIA IN TRASTEVERE, in the lovely piazza of the same name, further on, was founded almost certainly in the third century by Pope Calixtus I. The pope's devotion to Christ led him to accept the tradition that a spring of olive-oil gushed from this spot on the very day of Christ's birth. This was the first church in Rome to be officially recognised by the state and the first to be dedicated to the Virgin Mary. Pope Innocent II rebuilt it in 1140. Over its façade is a twelfth-century mosaic of the Madonna. Ten women surround her carrying lamps, two of them extinguished. Once, it is thought, there were more of these improvident virgins who forgot to buy oil for their lamps, as in the parable, but when the mosaic was restored three lamps were relit.

Four popes appear on the portico, which was added in 1702 by Carlo Fontana, who also restored the ancient fountain in the square. Alongside the church rises the twelfth-century romanesque campanile. Inside the portico are tombstones and slabs of stone with fascinating graffiti depicting, for example, ancient ships and birds. Through it you enter the church with its Cosmatesque pavement and paschal candlestick, the whole divided by 22 ancient columns (brought from the Baths of Caracalla) which support a gilded and coffered ceiling designed by Domenichino in 1617. Its triumphal arch is decorated with a mosaic of 1140 depicting the Cross, with the letters alpha and omega, set between seven candlesticks (which might refer to the seven churches of Asia Minor) and the symbols of the evangelists. Other contemporary mosaics depict Isaiah and Jeremiah, as well as a caged bird – a symbol of Christ enchained for the sins of mankind. Pope Innocent II appears with a model of his church. Mosaics covering the apse show Mary and her divine son, enthroned beneath the hand of God, bearing a wreath and the monogram of Constantine the Great. Six other mosaics, created by Pietro Cavallini in 1291, represent the life of Mary. Saints Peter and Paul are depicted presenting the donor of these mosaics, Bertoldo Stefaneschi, to the Blessed Virgin.

Too little is known about Pietro Cavallini. Undoubtedly the greatest artist working in Rome at the time, he also left masterpieces in Naples. His works draw on the hieratic styles of Byzantium, but also imbue them with realism. Cavallini was as skilled at painting frescoes as he was brilliant with

The elegant Palazzo Corsini provides a fitting home for neo-classical sculpture as well as seventeenth- and eighteenth-century paintings.

mosaic, as is evident from his powerful, though fragmentary, fresco cycle of the Last Judgement, in Santa Cecilia in Trastevere. Faced with such a plethora of art, it is easy to neglect the fifth chapel in the north aisle, which was decorated by Borromini's follower Antonio Gherardi from 1680.

Next to the church of Santa Maria in Trastevere is the seventeenth-century **PALAZZO DI SAN CALLISTO**, built by Orazio Turiani and now a museum of folklore and poetry, devoted to Rome's carnival, rustic traditions, nineteenth-century firework displays and mannequins.

From Piazza Sant'Egidio, beyond Santa Maria in Trastevere, runs Via della Scala, passing the church of **SANTA MARIA DELLA SCALA**, which was built in 1592 with a façade by Ottavio Mascherino. The baroque interior shelters one of St Teresa of Avila's feet, brought here in 1614 when she was beatified by Pope Paul V. The road leads up to the **PORTA SETTIMIANA**, the defensive gateway in the Aurelian Wall which was strengthened in around 1500. Beside it (as a plaque declares) Raphael's mistress, La Fornaria, lived in what is now the Ristorante Romolo.

This is a suburb of tree-shaded gardens. Beyond the defensive gate stretches Via della Lungara, which Pope Julius II opened up as a suitably grand route to the Vatican. On the left appears the **PALAZZO CORSINI**, built in the fifteenth century and rebuilt by Ferdinando Fuga in 1730. Queen Christina of Sweden lived here after her conversion to Catholicism in 1654 until her death in 1689. It was also the home of General L. Duphot, the fiancé of Napoleon Bonaparte's sister, Pauline. In 1797 a Roman mob slaughtered him outside the palace, at which the French invaded Rome and deposed the pope. The palace now forms part of the Galleria Nazionale d'Arte Antica, the main part of which is at the Palazzo Barberini; this part of the collection covers mainly seventeenth- and eighteenth-century European paintings.

Opposite is the **FARNESINA**, a renaissance villa built between 1509 and 1512 by Baldassare Peruzzi for Agostino Chigi, the banker who made his money in Siena and so much enriched Rome. Cardinal Alessandro Farnese coveted this house and managed to buy it in 1579. Figs overhang its walls, which enclose a formal garden of box hedges and an arbour of bay trees. The villa was decorated by Raphael and his colleagues Giulio Romano, Giovanni da Udine and Francesco Penni. They painted the vault of the loggia with the legend of Psyche and Cupid. Other frescoes include garlands of the fruit and flowers grown in the gardens in the sixteenth century. To the right is the Loggia of the Galatea, which contains another superb fresco, *The Triumph of Galatea*, this one by Raphael. On the upper floor Peruzzi painted *trompe-l'oeil* views of Rome.

Walk back through the Porta Settimiana and take Via Garibaldi to the right, beginning the climb up to the Janiculum. Ancient walls rise to the right, while Rome unfolds below on the left. On the right a little opening in the walls reveals a flight of steps twisting to the church and convent of

The Tempietto of San Pietro in Montorio was built by Bramante between 1499 and 1502 where St Peter is said to have met his death. Martyria were traditionally circular, and Bramante used the opportunities granted by this form to create one of the first high renaissance buildings.

SAN PIETRO IN MONTORIO, which was rebuilt at the end of the fifteenth century at the expense of Ferdinand I of Aragon and Isabella of Castile.

The renaissance façade of the church is pierced with a rose window, and in the first chapel of the right aisle is a splendid painting of 1518 by Sebastiano del Piombo, savagely depicting the flagellation of Christ (based on drawings by Michelangelo). Baldassare Peruzzi painted the next chapel with a *Coronation of the Virgin*. Two baroque tombs by Bartolomeo Ammanati are enclosed in the fourth chapel on the right which was designed by Giorgio Vasari. On the other side of the church, the fifth chapel, designed by Daniele da Volterra, shelters his painting of the *Baptism of Christ*, and Bernini designed the second chapel on the left in 1640. The church also contains the tombs of Hugh O'Neill, Earl of Tyrone and his brother-in-law Roe O'Donnell, who fled to Rome after the failure of their rebellion against Elizabeth I and the subsequent clamp-down by James I.

Today the church buildings are the home of Franciscan monks. The most fascinating feature is the Tempietto, ringed by sixteen Doric columns, which was added to the complex by Bramante in 1502 and stands on the alleged site of St Peter's martyrdom. The proportions of this little building are remarkably harmonious – the diameter of the colonnade equals the height of the sanctuary, while the height of the cupola equals the radius. Inspired by antiquity and the first-century treatise on architecture by Vitruvius, its high renaissance austerity is nevertheless entirely original. The upper and lower chapels are supposed to symbolize the crucifixions of Christ and St Peter respectively.

Further up the Janiculum is the magnificent ACQUA PAOLA, a fountain built in 1612 for Pope Paul V by Giovanni Fontana and Carlo Maderno out of six columns from Old St Peter's and fragments of the Temple of Minerva which stood in the Foro di Nerva. Decorated with the dragons and eagles of the Borghese coat of arms, this is the prelude to a park of magnificent cascades and fountains, the whole strewn with statues (including those of Garibaldi, sculpted in 1895, and his Brazilian wife Anita, done in 1932).

The pine- and cypress-clad JANICULUM was not one of the original seven hills of Rome. It was incorporated into the city only when Pope Urban VIII built new walls in 1642. Yet its panoramas have been lauded by countless visitors to Rome. On the left you can see the dome of St Peter's, then the Castel Sant'Angelo, San Giovanni dei Fiorentini, the Palazzo del Justità and beyond the slopes of Villa Borghese, the Pincio and the Villa Medici. To their right rise the Trinità dei Monti and the Palazzo di Montecitorio, followed by the campanile of the Palazzo della Sapienza, the Pantheon and the Quirinal. Further to the right are the churches of Sant'Andrea della Valle and Santa Maria Maggiore. The Palazzo Farnese is a prelude to the monument to Vittorio Emanuele II, and in the distance rise the statues on San Giovanni in Laterano. The whole view is surrounded by the distant amphitheatre of the Alban, Tiburtine and Praenestine hills.

4
Piazzas and Palaces

....

PALAZZO BARBERINI *to* SAN PIETRO IN VINCOLI

aving walked from the Upper Moselle valley to Rome, Hilaire Belloc entered a café beside a long, straight street, called for bread, coffee and brandy and spent the next few moments contemplating his boots and worshipping his staff, friends of his for so long and, as he put it, 'like all true friends inanimate'. More than on any other of these tours a stout pair of shoes and if possible a sturdy staff are essential, for a walk around monumental Rome painfully reminds one that the city is built on seven hills. Monumental Rome often nestles in enchantingly narrow streets. Close by a celebrated crossroads, whose four ornate fountains represent two rivers and two Roman deities and from which the roads run steeply, we shall discover the church of San Carlo alle Quattro Fontane which Borromini began with enormous brio in 1638. Nearby is another superb church, Sant'Andrea al Quirinale, built by Bernini for Cardinal Pamphilj in the 1660s. Barberini Rome also adds its flavour to this tour. Borromini and Bernini collaborated on the Palazzo Barberini, paid for by the flamboyantly extravagant pope Urban VIII. At the centre of Piazza Barberini we shall spy the bees from the Barberini coat of arms on the celebrated Triton fountain, and in Piazza di Trevi we shall also admire the most famous fountain in Rome, which was commissioned from Nicolà Salvi in 1732 by the Corsini pope Clement XII.

To match the ancient monuments of the city, modern Rome has contributed its quota of imposing buildings, piazzas and streets. Our tour takes in Piazza della Repubblica, whose contours are shaped by the massive baths of Diocletian, and Via Nazionale which was cut through the city in the mid nineteenth century. Via Nazionale is shaded by some splendid nineteenth-century buildings, including theatres and the huge Albergo Quirinale. From here our walk takes in the Teatro dell'Opera and the fabulous church of Santa Maria Maggiore, before continuing downhill to end at San Pietro in Vincoli, which houses Michelangelo's monumental statue of Moses.

OPPOSITE *Mario Rutelli's fanciful sculptures for the fountain of the Piazza della Rebubblica were carved between 1901 and 1911.*

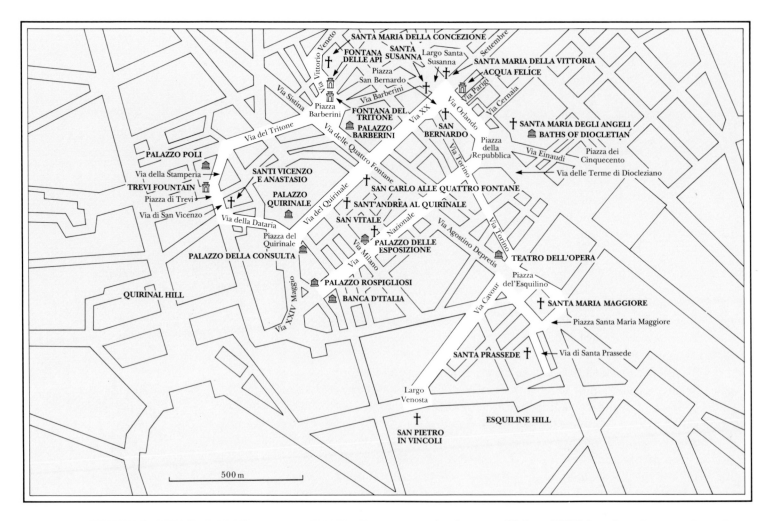

PIAZZAS AND PALACES

Maffeo Barberini, who became Urban VIII in 1623, has much to be forgiven. He flagrantly used the wealth of the church to enrich members of his own family, making no fewer than three of them cardinals and promoting others within the church. It is said that the citizens of Rome spontaneously cheered when it was announced that he was dead. Yet he was a cultivated man, a religious poet and a patron of the arts. This was the pope who consecrated the new St Peter's in 1626. And a year earlier he had commissioned Carlo Maderno to begin building the magnificent **PALAZZO BARBERINI**, the finest built in this city throughout the seventeenth century. When Maderno died six years later, the work was taken over by Gianlorenzo Bernini, of whom Urban remarked generously that if Bernini was fortunate in having Maffeo Barberini as pope, Barberini was even more fortunate in being pope during the lifetime of Bernini.

Bernini co-operated with Francesco Borromini in finishing the palace. It constituted the latter's first commission in Rome, and as yet the two greatest

Italian baroque architects were not at odds. Given their completely different characters, it is intriguing to see their work literally side by side. It can best be distinguished in the staircases of the palace, the broad rectangular left-hand flight by Bernini, and the other, curving up on the right, by Borromini.

Maderno, however, deserves due credit, not least for setting the palace back from the road, arousing your sense of expectation, as you enter through gates supported by caryatids, of the quite exceptional building beyond the palm trees. Bernini transformed the mighty façade which Maderno started, particularly by creating the central portico. This main façade, classically superimposing three orders of architecture, Doric, Ionic and Corinthian, is decked with the bees of the Barberini coat of arms and bears the papal escutcheon over the balcony. Monumental friezes run under its cornices. Borromini designed the windows of the upper storey.

Bernini also designed the magnificent salon which runs through the palace from the portico to the garden front. An illusion of greater length is created by the device of reducing the number of arches from seven to five and then to three, as far as the oval vestibule at the centre of the palace. The garden rises towards a fountain of Apollo, and from here you look back to see the basic structure of the building, this time marvelling at its elegance rather than its monumentality.

The main hall and the oval room next to it are also Bernini's work, but the dazzling decoration of the hall is the work of Pietro da Cortona. Urban VIII had already employed him to fresco the church of Santa Bibiana, near the Porta San Lorenzo. Now he produced a masterpiece, the massive *trompe-l'oeil* ceiling fresco on the theme of Divine Providence. This was its ostensible theme, but its real aim was to glorify the various members of the Barberini family. It is easy enough, though, to ignore such arrogance and simply to admire Pietro's brilliant illusion of the open sky, with its swirl of ascending and descending figures.

One wing of the Palazzo Barberini officially serves as the Galleria Nazionale d'Arte Antica (National Gallery of Paintings). The collection includes a bust of Urban VIII by Bernini, some exceptional paintings by Fra Angelico (including a triptych of the Last Judgement), two little tortured works by El Greco, Piero di Cosimo's subtle portrait of St Mary Magdalene and a *Madonna and Child* by Filippo Lippi. Tintoretto is represented here by a glowing painting of Jesus with the woman taken in adultery, and Caravaggio of a *Narcissus* and a splendid painting of Judith slicing off the head of Holofernes.

Of more than passing interest are the two other portraits which speak from the past of the bizarre relations between men and women. One is the portrait which Holbein painted of Henry VIII dressed for his wedding in 1540 with Anne of Cleves. The robes are splendid, and the puffy king strikes a comical attitude of belligerence. Henry has not yet become quite the gross figure of his final years, but his once splendid physique is gone and the little

The Barberini coat of arms, with its trio of bees, identifies the Palazzo Barberini, seen from its luxuriant garden. The palace was begun for Urban VIII by Carlo Maderno in 1624 and completed, after the latter's death, by Bernini and Borromini.

piggy eyes look out miserably, a further reminder of the good fortune experienced by his bride-to-be (in that he divorced her after a few months). More touching is a portrait of Raphael's beloved Margherita, the baker's daughter known from her father's profession as La Fornarina. Raphael apparently painted it in the last year of his life, adding his name to the ribbon on her left arm. He has not flattered his mistress, presumably not considering it necessary to lie in paint about her ragged-looking face.

The narrow Via delle Quattro Fontane in front of the palace leads down to Bernini's famous **FONTANA DEL TRITONE** in the Piazza Barberini, commissioned by Urban VIII in 1642. He topped the basin with a lavish sculpted group in which four dolphins support a massive cockle shell on their tails, while their wide-open mouths gulp in the water in the basin below. A jet of water shoots into the air, blown from a conch by the triton who kneels in the shell. The coats of arms of the Barberini and the papal insignia only serve to add to the fountain's baroque fantasy, which is somehow counterpointed by the sober architecture of the eighteenth- and nineteenth-century buildings surrounding the piazza. Opposite this fountain, at the entrance to Via Vittorio Veneto (which winds north from here to the Porta Pinciana) is Bernini's **FONTANA DELLE API**, created for Urban VIII in 1644. The original inscription declared the fountain was finished in the twenty-second year of his reign, whereas, in fact, he had occupied the throne of St Peter for fewer than 21 years. The superstitious believed that this might portend ill to Maffeo Barberini. So did he, and the inscription was effaced – to no avail, for he died shortly afterwards. So the Barberini bees, after which the fountain is called, drink from the monument which commemorates the moment when Urban VIII drank his last earthly goblet of wine.

A little way up Via Vittorio Veneto is the church of **SANTA MARIA DELLA CONCEZIONE DEI CAPPUCCINI**. Austere, as Franciscan churches were meant to be, it was built in 1626 for Antonio Francesco Barberini, who was elevated to the rank of cardinal by his twin brother Urban VIII. This austerity is belied by its five underground chapels, which contain the skeletons of some 4000 Capuchin monks, dug up from the slopes of the Quirinal Hill and brought here in 300 cartloads in 1631. The floor of these chapels is sprinkled with earth brought from Jerusalem. In the church is a painting by Guido Reni of St Michael the archangel killing the dragon (whose features were said to be those of Barberini's rival Giovanni Battista Pamphilj, elected as Pope Innocent X after the death of Urban VIII); and no one should leave the church before finding in the third chapel on the right Domenichino's painting of St Francis of Assisi, first in ecstasy and then on his deathbed. The founder himself lies in a tomb before the high altar. Its inscription speaks of the vanity of earthly wishes: HIC JACET PULVIS, CINIS ET NIHIL (Here lie dust, ashes and nothing).

Return to the Piazza Barberini and walk down Via del Tritone until you reach Via della Stamperia, which winds its way towards the celebrated Trevi Fountain (Fontana di Trevi). Across the street is the home since 1932 of the **ACCADEMIA DI SAN LUCA**. This confraternity of artists, founded in 1577, has its headquarters and own art gallery in a palace partly built by Borromini, whose courtyard is decked with a little fountain and statues. Another curiosity in Via della Stamperia is the state copperplate printing works, founded by Pope Clement XII in 1738 and housing an unrivalled collection of engravings, including those of Piranesi and Luigi Rossi. Just around the corner, in a surprisingly tiny square, is the **TREVI FOUNTAIN**. The original, small fountain was, like the present one, fed by the waters brought to Rome in 19 BC by Agrippa along an aqueduct running through the Villa Giulia. In 1732 Clement commissioned Nicolà Salvi to transform this simple fountain into a monumental waterfall, set against the south façade of the sixteenth-century Palazzo Poli. It was completed through the bounty of Clement's successor, Pope Benedict XIV, whose name is boastfully inscribed in far larger letters than those of the man who conceived the whole project.

Urban VIII, commissioned the Fontana delle Api from Bernini in what was to be the final year of his reign.

ABOVE *The papal tiara, the keys of St Peter and the coat of arms of Clement XII top the Trevi fountain.*

OPPOSITE *Beyond the huge granite basin rescued from the Foro Romano, where it had been used as a cattle trough, by Pius VII in 1818 is the façade of the Palazzo del Quirinale. This palace had been designed as a papal residence for the hot summer months when the Vatican harboured typhoid.*

The sculptures of this dramatic fountain may well derive from a sketch by Bernini. Rococo rocks plunge down to the sea. A pair of huge tritons, one of which blows into a conch shell, lead the sea-horses pulling the chariot of Neptune. The niches on either side harbour statues of Health and Abundance. Above is represented the young girl reputed to have pointed out the source of the waters to thirsty soldiers (the aqueduct was thus known as the Acqua Vergine), and Agrippa appears among his troops approving the aqueduct's design. Above are four statues representing Spring, Summer, Autumn and Winter, each bringing their unique gifts. Since Clement XII was born Lorenzo Corsini, the coat of arms atop the fountain is that of the Corsini family.

Intent on throwing coins into the fountain, visitors unjustly neglect the baroque façade of 1650 created by Martino Longhi the Younger for the church of **SANTI VICENZO E ANASTASIO** opposite. The French cardinal Mazarin paid for it, and over its doorway is the papal coat of arms. Inside, in an underground chapel, are preserved the embalmed hearts of 22 popes from Sixtus V to Pius VII (who died in 1830), for this church belonged to the Palazzo Quirinale, their former residence.

These baroque indulgences cannot smother medieval Rome. Narrow Via di San Vicenzo, running south from the church, is filled with bars, souvenir shops, wine merchants and tabacchi. A left turn takes us along Via della Dataria and up to the Piazza del Quirinale. As you climb the flight of steps which leads to the piazza, you pass a pair of ancient statues set into the wall that shores up the historic hill.

At 61 metres, the **QUIRINAL** (the name is derived from one of those given to Romulus after he had been deified) is the highest of Rome's seven hills. At its summit, the Piazza del Quirinale constitutes one of the most elegant legacies of papal Rome. Around it, between the sixteenth and the eighteenth centuries, cardinals and popes built some of the finest palaces in the city. The greatest of these is the **PALAZZO DEL QUIRINALE**.

This palace has a complex history. In the early sixteenth century the celebrated humanist, Cardinal Ippolito d'Este, built for himself a *casino* (small town residence) here, which Ottavio Mascherino and Flaminio Ponzio began transforming in 1574 into a summer residence for Pope Gregory XIII. Initially all the pope desired was a villa modelled on the Farnesina, and Mascherino accordingly provided him with a refined loggia of five arcades, flanked by two short wings. An imposing staircase was decorated by Melozzo da Forli with a fresco of Christ in Glory among his angels.

Successive architects included Domenico Fontana and Carlo Maderno. In 1617, a wing of the palace on Via del Quirinale was added by the latter, decorated inside with paintings of Indians, Japanese, Turks and Chinese to illustrate Pope Paul V's passion for sending out Christian missions. By the time of Pope Urban VIII the *casino* had become a palace. During his papacy the brick tower on the left of the main entrance was completed – a rather

squat affair, despite its marble balconies, at odds with the ostensibly sophisticated aura of its surroundings. Another century was to pass before Ferdinando Fuga completed the palace for Pope Clement XII.

The façade fronting the Piazza del Quirinale is the work of Domenico Fontana, and the monumental entrance, surmounted with statues of saints Peter and Paul, is by Carlo Maderno or Bernini. The saints recline over a broken pediment, apparently half-asleep; in the pediment above them, among the sculpted clouds of heaven, the Virgin and her son sit on top of a cherub, the infant Jesus conferring his blessing. Maderno also built one of the chapels of the palace, its vault decorated with stucco; and later another chapel (of the Annunciation) was painted by Guido Reni.

Rome was not in those days a particularly healthy spot for a summer residence. Gregory XIII's successor, Sixtus V, who erected in the centre of the piazza the two colossal statues of the Dioscuri, died in the palace, struck down by the heatwave of 1590. The Quirinal was, however, high enough to escape the malaria which continually plagued the Vatican in the summer, and popes continued to live here until 1870. It then became the residence of the kings of Italy, and since 1946 has been the home of the presidents of the republic. Twice a day there is a ceremonial changing of the guard, complete with military band and sentries in smart crimson and blue uniforms, their helmets adorned with huge green and black cockatoo feathers.

The piazza continued, meanwhile, to be enriched. In 1787, one of the obelisks which stood in front of the Mausoleum of Augustus was erected here. A massive granite basin was brought to the piazza from the Foro Romano in 1818, to create a fountain beside the magnificent statues of Castor and Pollux, taming two horses, which Sixtus V had brought from the Baths of Constantine. They are Roman copies of two Greek equestrian groups dating from the fifth century BC.

The triangular Piazza del Quirinale, sloping downhill, affords a spectacular view of much of the city. In 1739, on the opposite side from the Palazzo del Quirinale, Ferdinando Fuga created the rococo, three-storeyed **PALAZZO DELLA CONSULTA**, to house the papal courts. At the corner of the Via Dataria, begun for Innocent XIII and finished by Alessandro Specchi for Clement XII, are the papal stables. In 1866, Pope Pius IX stretched another wing in exactly the same style along the third side of the piazza. Rampant lions appear in his coat of arms over this building.

The nearby Quirinal public garden, with its equestrian statue of a cockaded, wax-moustached King Carlo Alberto, is not that of the palace itself. For security reasons, few are allowed into the Giardini del Quirinale proper, a pity, since they were laid out by Ottavio Mascherino in the first half of the sixteenth century.

Walk along Via del Quirinale, passing on the right two hideous caryatids bearing suits of armour and carrying huge dogs. The splendid little church of **SANT'ANDREA AL QUIRINALE** was commissioned from Bernini by

When Pope Sixtus V brought these statues from the Baths of Constantine to the Piazza del Quirinale he mistakenly named them as the work of the fifth-century BC Athenian sculptors Phidias and Praxiteles. They are in fact Roman copies of Greek originals from that era. The obelisk was brought here from the Mausoleum of Augustus in 1786 by Pope Pius VI.

Cardinal Camillo Pamphilj, nephew of Pope Innocent X, for Jesuit novices. Cardinal Odescalchi laid the cornerstone in 1658, and the building took twelve years to complete. The master produced a dynamic façade, hinting at the exuberant curves inside by its entrancing cornice, serpentine walls and semicircular Ionic portico, surmounted by the Pamphilj coat of arms.

Inside the elliptical church, white Sicilian jasper and red marble add sumptuousness to the pilasters, walls and chased columns. The high altar painting of the *Martyrdom of St Andrew* is (by an artistic device) apparently supported by angels and subtly lit by natural light. No figure on this altar-piece (or in the church as a whole) seems to be at rest. Saints lean over, heavenly limbs protrude, and cherubim (stuccoed by Antonio Raggi) seem to slither down from, and clamber around, the gilded cupola and the dome. The pavement by Giovanni Battista de'Rossi was carried out in 1671 under the supervision of Bernini himself, who declared that it was the only one of his churches which truly satisfied him.

A young Polish novice who died here in 1568 at the age of eighteen, shortly after coming to Rome, is celebrated at Sant'Andrea al Quirinale. Stanislas Kostka was the son of a nobleman who strongly opposed his desire to become a monk. The boy walked 350 miles to Dillingen in Upper Germany, and was eventually sent to Rome. Here, in almost continual ecstasy, the young man prayed that he would celebrate the Feast of the Assumption in Heaven, and died four days later. His body refused to sink into corruption, and was eventually transferred to this church. St Stanislas Kostka was canonized by Pope Benedict XIII in 1726. Pierre Legros designed his early eighteenth-century statue in the sacristy here, which shows Stanislas on his death bed.

A little further along Via del Quirinale, where it crosses Via delle Quattro Fontane, Bernini's rival Borromini produced in **SAN CARLO ALLE QUATTRO FONTANE** (San Carlino) not only his own masterpiece but also a church of major significance as a model for the European Baroque. His commission came in 1634, when he was scarcely known, from a Spanish order of Trinitarian monks. The tiny cloister, with its double row of arcades, was finished first, the concave pediment a hint of what was to come. Borromini then turned to the church, almost finishing it by 1641, when the monks ran out of funds. As a result, the façade was completed only in 1668 – with the odd result that the interior is one of the architect's earliest works in Rome, and the façade virtually his last, for he died a year before it was finished.

The undulating storeys of the façade are separated by a decorative entablature, so that Borromini could set concave against convex movement. Little balustrades, cherubim and elaborate capitals add a touch of refined fantasy; there is also a statue of St Charles Borromeo, to whom the church is dedicated. Inside, the minuscule incurving three-aisled church astonishingly exploits three shapes: ellipse, octagon and cross. Above the whole rises a delicate oval dome, beneath which stuccoed foliage surrounds the windows that light the interior. As the dome rises, its complex coffers diminish in size, conveying the illusion of greater height. The blue and red crosses are the symbol of the Spanish Discalced Trinitarian order, and the whole is full of symbolic references to the Trinity. Borromini added an exquisite crypt (reached from the cloister), with an octagonal chapel where he planned to be buried (although he was not).

The crossroads where this church stands is a perfect example of papal town planning. Created at the end of the sixteenth century, it offers vistas of the Piazza del Quirinale, the Porta Pia, which Michelangelo built when he was 87, the Piazza del Esquilino and the obelisk of the Trinità dei Monti. The four small fountains which lend their name to the street and the church, were set at each corner of the crossroads during the pontificate of Sixtus V. They represent the gods of the Nile and the Tiber, and the goddesses Diana and Juno. The deities recline, Juno with her swan, Diana in the shade of a tree, the Nile beside bullrushes, a lion peeping over his shoulder, and the Tiber, sheltered by willows and accompanied by his perennial symbols – the she-wolf, Romulus and Remus. Water pours from four overturned jars into the basins below.

The god of the Tiber stares moodily from the fountain at the corner of the Via delle Quattro Fontane.

Via del Quirinale merges into Via XX Settembre, flanked by grandiose palaces, which takes us on to the Largo Santa Susanna. Susanna was half-cousin to the Emperor Diocletian, who, nevertheless, beheaded her after she became a Christian, vowing herself to perpetual viginity and refusing to marry his heir and adopted son Maximianus Galerius. Her home was transformed into a church, and the crypt of this present building, where her bones now lie, has revealed traces of a third-century Roman house.

Over the centuries **SANTA SUSANNA** was rebuilt and extended. In 1585 Sixtus V added a chapel dedicated to St Lawrence, and the church was finally restored at the expense of Cardinal Rusticucci between 1592 and 1605. Unfortunately this restoration destroyed some valuable eighth-century mosaics. Still intact, however, are Carlo Maderno's façade of 1603, an early baroque delicacy of Corinthian columns and pilasters, with statues of saints Caius, Gabinius, Felicitas and Susanna, the frescoes by Baldassare Croce inside the church which depict their lives, and the lovely carved ceiling of 1595.

Across the Largo Santa Susanna lies the baroque church of **SANTA MARIA DELLA VITTORIA**, built by Pope Paul V in 1605. The architect was again Maderno, although Giovanni Battista Soria designed the façade between 1625 and 1638 at the expense of Cardinal Scipione Borghese. Originally dedicated to St Paul, this church took its present name in 1620 after Ferdinand II of Bavaria had led an army of 25,000 Catholics to victory over 100,000 Protestants at the Battle of the White Mountain near Prague. An image of the Madonna, which had rallied the dispirited Catholics, was brought in triumph to the church by Pope Gregory XV. Since that time, Santa Maria della Vittoria has been the repository of standards taken by Catholics in battle. Philip V donated a flag which he captured from the Moslems at Ceuta, and the Knights of Malta contributed a standard from the Sultan's own galley. The standards are no longer displayed, but there is still a nineteenth-century fresco in the apse depicting the victorious Catholics entering Prague. The miraculous statue of the Virgin Mary perished in a fire in 1833.

Despite Carlo Maderno's magnificent baroque interior, crammed with cherubim and gleaming with marble, Domenichino's frescoes of the Life of St Francis in the second chapel on the left, and Guercino's Trinity in the third chapel on the left, the crowning attraction of this church is Bernini's remarkable statue of St Teresa in Ecstasy in the Cornaro Chapel, depicting St Teresa of Avila, who founded the reformed order of Carmelite nuns in 1562. Bernini has portrayed a vision of 1537 which the saint herself described. By her side she saw a small, very beautiful angel, holding in his hand a long golden spear tipped with flames. Several times he seemed to plunge it into her heart. Each time he drew it out she was left aflame with the love of God, even though the pain was so sharp that she groaned aloud. Pierced by this spear of divine love, she underwent a profound experience of

Bernini's altarpiece in the Cornaro Chapel in Santa Maria della Vittoria seemed shocking to contemporaries and still has the power to shock today. As at his altar in Sant'Andrea al Quirinale, he used natural lighting from above to create the maximum visual impact.

The delicacy of the fifth-century BC *Ludovisi Throne shows the standard of work which inspired the sculptors of the Renaissance.*

insupportable sadness combined with exquisite joy. Members of the Cornaro family, who commissioned the sculpture, gaze wonderingly, as if from theatre-boxes, at the smiling angel and the swooning saint. With *trompe-l'oeil* brilliance Bernini has transformed the small chapel into an entire church.

In the Piazza San Bernardo is the fountain of **ACQUA FELICE**, set up by Sixtus V (his proper name was Felice) and designed by Domenico Fontana. The massive Moses was created by Prospero Bresciano, who was much mocked for its clumsiness and died of a broken heart. Giovanni Battista della Porta sculpted Aaron, and Gideon (in an utterly different style) was added by Flamino Vacca. Four lions, copies of ancient Egyptian ones and hence lacking in naturalism, spew water into a basin which, when the sun goes down is superbly lighted from underneath.

The church of **SAN BERNARDO**, on the southern side of the piazza, is of ancient origin; it was probably one of the four round towers which once stood at the corners of the Baths of Diocletian. In 1598, Contessa Caterina Nobili Sforza conceived the idea of transforming this tower into a church. Like a mini-Pantheon, its dome is coffered and it has niches in its circular

walls, each housing a saint. Giovanni Odazzi created its two altars in the
early eighteenth century, one dedicated to the Madonna, the other to St
Bernard. The contessa lies buried here.

Via Orlando leads past the Acqua Felice into the Piazza della
Repubblica, created in the late nineteenth century by a little-known but
deserving architect named Gaetano Koch. In the middle, Alessandro
Guerrieri and Mario Rutelli designed a mighty fountain of water nymphs
grappling with sea-monsters. On the left-hand side of the square is the
basilica of **SANTA MARIA DEGLI ANGELI** and, behind it, the **MUSEO NAZIONALE
ROMANO**, which contains an indescribably rich and varied collection of
treasures from ancient Rome and Greece (as well as a miniature model of the
Parthenon). One of its most famous sculptures, carved in the fifth century
BC, is the Ludovisi Throne, the low relief on the back of which depicts Venus
rising from the sea.

The church and museum comprise the major part of the remains of the
colossal **BATHS OF DIOCLETIAN** (the grandest of the ancient world). This
monumental construction comprised libraries, an open-air swimming pool
and concert halls, as well as the dressing rooms and differently heated pools
of the traditional Roman baths. About 3,500 people could bathe here simul-
taneously. Michelangelo was commissioned to convert the great frigidarium
of the baths into a basilica, but he died a year after building began. In 1749
the Carthusians to whom the church belonged commissioned Luigi
Vanvitelli to make alterations, and he changed the orientation of the
church. Nevertheless the main entrance and the façade are what
Michelangelo intended. Vanvitelli's entrance to the south-west is, however,
the one normally used.

*Part of the ancient brickwork of the
Baths of Diocletian in the church of
Santa Maria degli Angeli.*

ABOVE *A detail of Gaetano Koch's neo-classical Banca d'Italia.*

OPPOSITE *The Virgin holds the infant Christ beside the romanesque campanile of Santa Maria Maggiore, the tallest in Rome, which was given its final form by Gregory XI in 1377.*

We enter the church not, as is usual, by way of the nave but into what has become one of its transepts. In Vanvitelli's vestibule (the calidarium of the baths) stands a statue of St Bruno (founder of the Carthusian order), done by the French sculptor Jean-Antoine Houdon in 1766 and so realistic that Pope Clement XIV joked that it would speak if the rules of the order did not enjoin silence. Nearby are buried the painters Carlo Maratta and Salvator Rosa. Through this vestibule with its *trompe-l'oeil* coffered dome we enter the transept, stretching for 91 metres and flanked by seventeeth- and eighteenth-century paintings. At the crossing point of the nave and the transept, the red Corinthian columns of Egyptian granite formerly belonged to the baths. Their bases are sunk into the floor, which Michelangelo had to raise because the foundations were so damp. Vanvitelli added the other pillars of the church, which are in a sense fakes, made of brick stuccoed to resemble marble. The high altar is Michelangelo's, and above it is a painting by Perugino. The richly marbled tomb of Pius IV in the apse dates from 1867. Look out in the choir for the seventeenth-century frescoes, by Domenichino, of the *Martyrdom of St Sebastian.*

This is a moment to orientate ourselves. Around the corner, Via Parigi is the home of the city's tourist office. Lined with open-air stalls selling second-hand books, Via delle Terme di Diocleziano leads off Piazza della Repubblica to the main railway station and the Piazza dei Cinquecento. The railway station is a monumental work, its wings designed by Angiolo Mazzoni in the inter-war years and the nondescript façade finished in 1950. The piazza is named after 500 Italian soldiers who died in Ethiopia in 1887, and a monument to them incorporates an Egyptian obelisk with hieroglyphs proclaiming the achievements of Rameses the Great.

Still in Piazza della Repubblica, beneath the nineteenth-century colonnades opposite the church of Sant Maria degli Angeli, are tour operators, galleries selling modern art, and cinemas. The colonnades part for the entrance to Via Nazionale, created in around 1850 through the initiative of Monsignor Francesco Saverio de Merode who recognised the need to connect the central railway station with Piazza Venezia. Today the steep street is lined with shops selling leather goods, clothing and jewellery. At the end, the old street level is revealed by the 37 steps which take you down to the ancient granite pillars and the round brick arches of the portico of **SAN VITALE.** Founded over a holy well in 416, this basilica was rebuilt (save for its portico) and reduced to a single nave in 1475. The interior was frescoed in the seventeenth century by Gaspard Poussin and Andrea Pozzo. Beyond it is the pompous **PALAZZO DELLE ESPOSIZIONE,** with its grandiose Corinthian columns, its swags and its statues. As its inscription declares, this palace was built by the commune of Rome in 1882 during the reign of Umberto I.

Another, more successful building is Gaetano Koch's late nineteenth-century **BANCA D'ITALIA.** Opposite is the **PALAZZO ROSPIGLIOSI.** Built by Giovanni Vasanzio for Cardinal Scipione Borghese in 1603 and later enlarged

by Carlo Maderno, this palace (the entrance is in Via XXIV Maggio) has a fascinating collection of art which is rarely open to the public. The collection centres on thirteen paintings by Peter Paul Rubens of Christ with his twelve apostles. Here too is a portrait of Rubens's wife Hélène Fourment in her wedding dress. Another masterpiece is *A Quarrel*, painted by Diego Velazquez. And the hall of the Casino dell'Aurora is famous for its ceiling fresco in which Guido Reni in 1614 depicted Aurora scattering flowers in front of the chariot of the Sun, around which dance pretty young women.

An enterprising architect named Domenico Costanzi spotted the importance of the Via Nazionale and built its most majestic building, the Albergo Quirinale, taking as his model the renaissance masters. Finished in around 1865, it boasts round-arched doorways and windows on the ground floor. The two lower storeys, faced with rusticated stone, are topped by four others, their windows variously embellished, rising to a decorated cornice.

Albergo Quirinale became the rendezvous of the élite of late nineteenth-century Europe, welcoming the Grand Duchess Catherine of Russia, the Odaleschis, the Duke of Cambridge and the Grand Duke of Sachsen-Weimar. Celebrated musicians such as Mascagni and Puccini sat beside its fountain and trod its beautifully proportioned and monumental staircase along with the nobility. The same architect, in 1880, built the Teatro Costanzi (now the TEATRO DELL'OPERA) just behind the hotel, cleverly connecting the two buildings with a covered passage. Not surprisingly, then, a plaque on the wall of the hotel is set underneath the window from which in 1893 Giuseppe Verdi acknowledged the cheering crowds on the first performance in Rome of his opera *Falstaff*.

Take Via Torino which flanks the hotel, to reach this opera house, which was rather brutally enlarged in 1927 by Marcello Piacentini. Palm trees grow in the square in front of the building, now appositely known as Piazza Beniamini Gigli. Walk on across Via Cavour and ahead rise the steps leading up the ESQUILINE HILL to the baroque apse which architect Carlo Rainaldi gave to the church of SANTA MARIA MAGGIORE in 1673.

The main façade of Santa Maria Maggiore faces onto the Piazza del'Esquilino. On this spot the blessed Virgin Mary is said to have appeared in AD 352 to Pope Liberius and a Roman patrician named Giovanni, ordering them to build a church over an area which would the following day be exactly marked out by a patch of snow – a miracle all the more remarkable since the vision occurred early in August. Santa Maria Maggiore was therefore first known as Santa Maria della Neve (St Mary of the Snows).

In front of Santa Maria Maggiore stands a 14.5 metres high Egyptian obelisk, brought here by Sixtus V in 1587 from the Mausoleum of Maxentius. Today it supports a statue of the Virgin Mary. The romanesque campanile of the church, dating from the late fourteenth century, is, at 75 metres, the tallest in Rome. Steps mount to the façade which Ferdinando Fuga added to the basilica in 1743. He replaced an earlier façade depicting the legend of the snow with a portico, over which he built a three-arched loggia. Five doorways lead into the superb interior. (As at St Peter's, San Giovanni in Laterano and other papal churches, one of them is opened only once every 25 years.) The huge gilded nave is substantially that rebuilt by Pope Sixtus III between 432 and 440. There are 36 Ionic columns, four of granite, the rest of marble, supporting an architrave adorned with 26 fifth-century mosaics, illustrating scenes from the Old Testament. Above these is a coffered ceiling, added by Giuliano da Sangallo in the sixteenth century and gilded with part of the first cargo of gold brought back by Christopher Columbus from America and presented to Pope Alexander VI by Ferdinand of Aragon and Isabella of Castile. You are standing on a Cosmatesque pavement dating from the eleventh century. When the church is packed with worshippers on Saturday evenings, High Mass here is an especially moving experience.

On the triumphal arch are mosaics of a slightly later date from those of the nave. The blessed Virgin Mary appears in the guise of an empress.

The baroque apse of Santa Maria Maggiore seen from the Piazza del'Esquilino. This façade, completed in the 1670s, is the combined work of Flamini Ponzio, Carlo Rainaldi and Domenico Fontana.

Instead of sitting as an infant on her knee, her son, already a young man, is enthroned in glory. A theological reason lay behind this iconography, for the Council of Ephesus had just declared that Jesus was the eternal son of God and not, as the Nestorians taught, born a mere human being who later assumed divinity.

The apse of Santa Maria Maggiore dates from the thirteenth century, and its mosaics, created by the Franciscan monk Jacopo Torritti in 1295, incorporate some of those from the original fifth-century apse. They depict the coronation of the Virgin – another nod towards the Council of Ephesus which declared her the *Theotokos* or Mother of God. Surrounded by groups of angels and saints, she is worshipped by the two kneeling figures of Pope Nicholas IV and Cardinal Colonna.

Other ages added their own particular forms of architecture to Santa Maria Maggiore. The second chapel on the right, the Capella Sforza, was added by Giacomo della Porta in the 1560s and 1570s, but the plans were those of the aged Michelangelo. The audacity of the old man is astonishing, with pillars leaning crazily and an apse almost hidden by the architect's wildly successful desire to transcend what had by then become the automatic reflex of renaissance architecture.

Two large chapels date from the late sixteenth century. The Capella Sistina (Sistine Chapel) on the right was built by Domenico Fontana for Pope Sixtus V and houses a few fragments of what is supposed to be the authentic Bethlehem cradle of the infant Jesus. Sixtus lies here in a tomb by Giovanni Antonio Paracci (who was known as Valsoldo), as does the uncorrupted corpse of Pius V, in a tomb of 1572 by Leonardo da Sarzana. An extravagant sixteenth-century gilded ciborium in the form of a temple carried by four angels was created for the altar by Sebastiano Torrignani. The depiction of the Holy Family on this altar, painted in 1480 by Ceccino da Pietrasanta, was taken from the earlier chapel. Nearby is the late thirteenth-century tomb, inlaid with marble and made by Giovanni Cosma for Cardinal Consalvo Rodriguez.

In the left aisle the Capella Paolina, or Pauline Chapel, is even more opulent and is the first sizeable chapel ever to be entirely clad in coloured marble. Flaminio Ponzio drew up the plans in 1611, sedulously and successfully obeying Paul V's insistence that the walls be covered with precious stones, gold leaf and multicoloured marble. Giovanni Baglione and Giovanni Lanfranco were responsible for its frescoes, which once more celebrate the Virgin Mary. Over the altar is a painting of the Virgin, traditionally attributed to the evangelist artist St Luke but actually dating from the thirteenth century.

A sharper note appears in the iconography of this chapel. Here the triumphalist voice of the Counter-Reformation attempts to stifle not only the virtues of paganism but also the austerity of Protestantism. One wonders whether the artists of the time took a strictly impartial view of these bitter

OPPOSITE *The complex artistic delights inside the church of Santa Prassede climax in the baroque baladcchino over the high altar, and the mosaic decoration of Pope Paschal I's arch behind it.*

and often bloody religious conflicts or whether they simply seized the opportunity where they could to produce an artistic masterpiece, whether it be for Catholic or Protestant. Lodovico Cigoli, crudely frescoing the cupola in 1612, probably thought simply of his commission. He could hardly have realized that however maladroit his work seems to later generations, his was the first ever example of such a dome entirely covered in paint.

Take Via di Santa Prassede from the south-west corner of the piazza to enjoy yet another church with gorgeous mosaics, **SANTA PRASSEDE**. Built in 822 by Pope Paschal I and many times restored, it is named after Praxedis, the woman who first offered hospitality to St Peter when he reached Rome. Sixteen granite columns and six piers support its ancient nave, in which is the cover of a well down which the patroness would pour the blood of saints she had seen martyred (the church still preserves a sponge with which, it is said, she mopped up their blood). The choir boasts eleventh-century

The notorious Salita di San Francesca di Paola, where Tullia drove her chariot over her father, leads to San Pietro in Vincoli.

mosaics, depicting Christ the Redeemer, surrounded by saints Peter and Paul and receiving into heaven Praxedis and her sister St Pudentia. Here, too, saints Zeno and Pope Paschal I (alive at the time according to his square nimbus) worship their saviour. Two palm trees symbolize the Old and New Testaments, while a phoenix alludes to the Resurrection. Other mosaics depict the 24 elders and the seven-branched candelabrum of the Apocalypse, the Lamb of God, the four archangels and four evangelists.

Paschal I also built here the Chapel of St Zeno as a mausoleum for his mother. You enter it between two formerly pagan columns, made of black granite. The golden ninth-century mosaics of this chapel cover the whole vault and the walls. Rome has nothing to compare with them, and as you admire these Byzantine masterpieces you suddenly perceive that you are standing on an ancient, multi-coloured marble pavement. In the chapel next door is an even greater wonder, half of the pillar to which Christ was tied to be scourged. Made of oriental Jasper, it was brought from the Holy Land by the papal legate Cardinal Giovanni Colonna in 1223. The other half is still in Jerusalem.

From the north-western end of Piazza del'Esquilino the Via Cavour runs downhill to reach a palace which once belonged to the Borgias. From here a romantic flight of steps – today called the **SALITA DE SAN FRANCESCO DI PAOLA** but once known as the Via Scelerata in reference to the impious Tullia who recklessly drove her chariot over the dead body of her father Servius Tullius – passes through a vaulted passage and takes us to the final masterpiece of this walk. The house at the top of this passage was once inhabited by Vannozza dei Catanei, mistress of a pope and mother of his illegitimate children, Cesare and Lucrezia Borgia.

Our goal, the church of **SAN PIETRO IN VINCOLI**, was first built here by a pious woman named Theodora in 109 as a shrine to the chains with which St Peter was bound by the Romans in the Mamertime prison. They had allegedly been discovered by the daughter of Peter's goaler. Greatly altered over the centuries, the church was rebuilt in the 1480s during the pontificate of Sixtus IV, and then restored in 1503 by the architect Baccio Pontelli. The chains are displayed beneath the high altar of this basilica, whose three aisles are separated by 22 massive Doric columns. In the chapel of the confessio lie the reputed earthly remains of seven Jews tortured by King Antiochus Epiphanes, who tried to force them to eat pork.

The second chapel in the north aisle is adorned with a fine seventh-century mosaic which depicts an ageing, white-bearded St Sebastian, an image completely at odds with the usual swooning youth portrayed by most artists. And inside this renaissance church are three masterpieces by Michelangelo. His gigantic statue of Moses, designed for a never-to-be-finished tomb of Pope Julius II, is a horned and frightening fanatic, angry because, having just received the tablets of the law from the Lord he sees the children of Israel worshipping a golden calf. Michelangelo fell into a rage as

Michelangelo's monumental, horned figure of Moses in San Pietro in Vincoli carries the tables of the law. This statue was to form part of Julius II's tomb in St Peter's, but this was never finished, and this was the only one of over 40 projected statues to be realized. Two half-completed slaves are in the Louvre in Paris.

he stood before his statue, wildly knocking off a bit of one of its knees with his hammer. As he gazed on the statue four and a half centuries later, the psychiatrist Sigmund Freud expressed his belief that this tormented Moses reflected all the inner conflicts of Michelangelo himself. Michelangelo's contemporary, the painter and historian Giorgio Vasari, took a different view. 'Seated in a serious pose,' he wrote, 'Moses rests one arm on the tablets of the Law and with the other holds his long, glossy beard, whose hairs – so difficult to render in sculpture – are so soft and downy that it seems as if the iron chisel had become a brush.' Beside Moses are Leah and Rachel, wives of the Jewish patriarch Jacob, which the sculptor began and his pupils finished. For Dante, Leah and Rachel symbolized respectively the active and the contemplative life. Michelangelo has caught these attitudes perfectly.

5
Cathedral
and port

....

SAN GIOVANNI IN LATERANO *to* OSTIA ANTICA

As the French historian Jules Michelet put it on his visit to Rome in 1830, 'Beneath papal Rome is feudal Rome; beneath feudal Rome, Christian; beneath Christian Rome lies imperial Rome; and even deeper lies the Roman republic. Don't stop: keep on digging.' This walk metaphorically does that. Beginning with the Scala Santa and the church of San Giovanni in Laterano, it takes us backwards in history.

San Giovanni in Laterano was founded by Constantine, and although overlaid by the riches of later centuries, retains its ancient form. Its baptistry is the oldest in Christendom. From it our tour visits San Clemente, an even older church with ravishing mosaics which rises from what was a private Roman house, and Santo Stefano Rotondo is an exquisite building which stands on the site of a temple dedicated to Mithras. From here we linger for a while in the Baths of Caracalla, before making our way to the sepulchre of one of the most distinguished of Roman families. Not far away is Rome's celebrated Protestant cemetery, but our route pushes its way back through time by way of the walls with which Aurelian ringed the city. These walls ooze antiquity, as do the sites dotted along the Via Appia Antica, including the catacombs where early Christians were buried. Finally, this route ends even earlier in time, in Ostia Antica, the excavated city of the strange, exceedingly talented Etruscans, from whose tribes sprang the early Roman kings.

Rome's cathedral is not, as one might think, St Peter's but San Giovanni in Laterano (St John Lateran), the official seat of the Bishop of Rome (i.e., the pope). It is built on the spot where a Roman patrician named Plautinius Lateranus was executed for his part in a plot against the emperor Nero. The emperor Constantine, who founded it, endowed the basilica with more than eight thousand lamps. It is said that the Ark of the Covenant, brought by Titus from Jerusalem, resided here, while other treasures included the seamless coat of Jesus, for which the Roman soldiers had diced at his

OPPOSITE *The Circus of Maxentius on the Via Appia Antica is the best preserved of the ancient circuses and could hold some 10,000 spectators. The obelisk which Domitian placed here now graces Bernini's Fontana dei Fiumi in the Piazza Navona.*

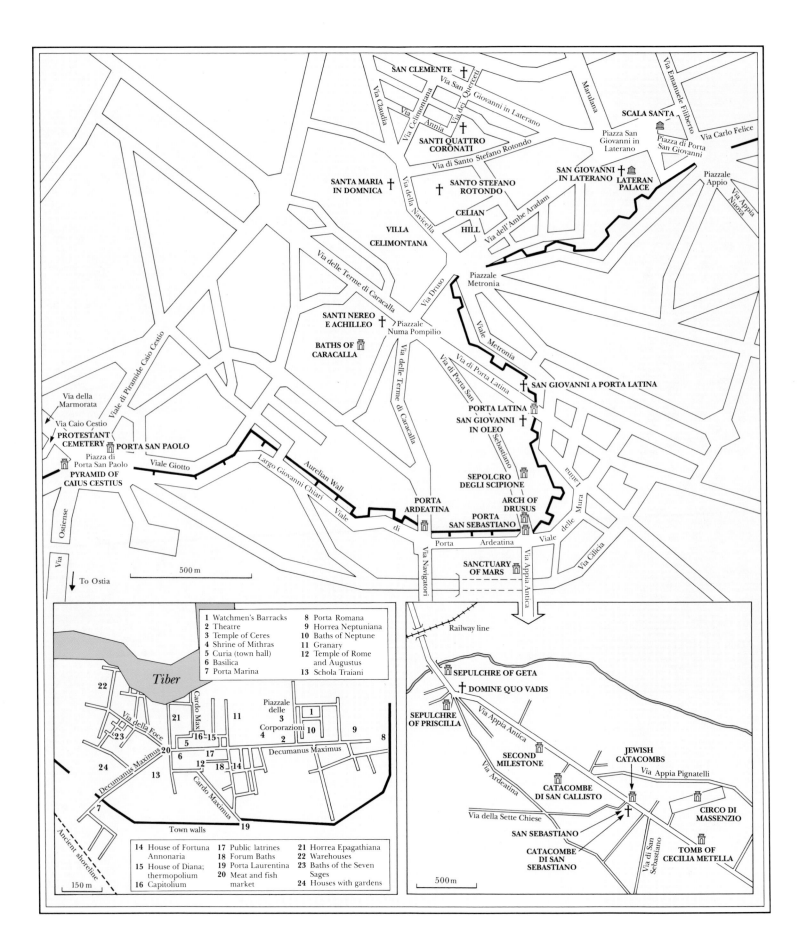

SAN CLEMENTE

Via San Quereti

SCALA SANTA

Via Claudia

Via Celimontana

Via Annia

Via dei Giovanni in Laterano

Via Emanuele Filiberto

Marulana

Piazza San Giovanni in Laterano

Via Carlo Felice

SANTI QUATTRO CORONATI

Via di Santo Stefano Rotondo

SAN GIOVANNI IN LATERANO

LATERAN PALACE

Piazza di Porta San Giovanni

SANTA MARIA IN DOMNICA

SANTO STEFANO ROTONDO

Via della Navicella

CELIAN HILL

Piazzale Appio

Via Appia Nuova

VILLA CELIMONTANA

Via dell'Ambe Aradam

Via delle Terme di Caracalla

Via Druso

Piazzale Metronia

SANTI NEREO E ACHILLEO

Piazzale Numa Pompilio

Viale Metronia

Via di Porta Latina

BATHS OF CARACALLA

Via delle Terme di Caracalla

Via di Porta San Sebastiano

SAN GIOVANNI A PORTA LATINA

PORTA LATINA

SAN GIOVANNI IN OLEO

Via della Marmorata

Via di Piramide Caio Cestio

Via Caio Cestio

SEPOLCRO DEGLI SCIPIONE

Viale delle Mura

PROTESTANT CEMETERY

PORTA SAN PAOLO

Viale Giotto

Aurelian Wall

Largo Giovanni Chiari

Via di Porta Latina

ARCH OF DRUSUS

Via Cilicia

Piazza di Porta San Paolo

PORTA ARDEATINA

PORTA SAN SEBASTIANO

Viale

PYRAMID OF CAIUS CESTIUS

Via Ostiense

Via di

Porta

Ardeatina

Via Navigatori

Via Appia Antica

500 m

To Ostia

SANCTUARY OF MARS

---

1 Watchmen's Barracks
2 Theatre
3 Temple of Ceres
4 Shrine of Mithras
5 Curia (town hall)
6 Basilica
7 Porta Marina

8 Porta Romana
9 Horrea Neptuniana
10 Baths of Neptune
11 Granary
12 Temple of Rome and Augustus
13 Schola Traiani

Railway line

SEPULCHRE OF GETA

DOMINE QUO VADIS

Tiber

22

Via della Foce

Cardo Max

21

11

Piazzale delle Corporazioni

3

1

23

16 15

5

10

24

20

6

17

9

8

13

12

18 14

Decumanus Maximus

SEPULCHRE OF PRISCILLA

Via Appia Antica

SECOND MILESTONE

JEWISH CATACOMBS

Via Appia Pignatelli

CATACOMBE DI SAN CALLISTO

CIRCO DI MASSENZIO

Cardo Maximus

Via Ardeatina

Decumanus Maximus

7

Town walls

19

Ancient shoreline

Via della Sette Chiese

SAN SEBASTIANO

TOMB OF CECILIA METELLA

Via di San Sebastiano

150 m

14 House of Fortuna Annonaria
15 House of Diana; thermopolium
16 Capitolium

17 Public latrines
18 Forum Baths
19 Porta Laurentina
20 Meat and fish market

21 Horrea Epagathiana
22 Warehouses
23 Baths of the Seven Sages
24 Houses with gardens

CATACOMBE DI SAN SEBASTIANO

500 m

crucifixion, and the reed and hairy coat of St John the Baptist. In front of the altar was a figure of Christ surrounded by figures of his apostles; and over the altar was an embossed silver baldacchino. None of these remain, for when Genseric the Vandal sacked Rome in 455 he carried them all away to Carthage. Totila the Ostrogoth pillaged the place. Earthquakes, the most severe of them in 904, wrecked it. When a fire destroyed most of the basilica in 1308, one of its relics, the skull of the child martyr St Pancras, dripped blood. Yet despite the natural disasters and the bloody events, San Giovanni in Laterano was regularly rebuilt, always preserving its ancient basilican form and its importance.

At the heart of Piazza San Giovanni in Laterano is a pinkish-white granite obelisk. Dating from the fifth century BC, it is the oldest and, at 37 metres, the tallest in Rome. Once an ornament of a temple in Thebes, it was brought from Egypt in AD 357 by Constantine, and set up in the Circo Massimo. In 1587 the obelisk was rediscovered there, broken into three pieces. Sixtus V had it raised here the following year. The obelisk today stands in front of the **LATERAN PALACE**, home of the popes until they began their exile in Avignon in 1305. Three years later the palace was ravaged by fire, and when Pope Gregory XI returned to Rome after another 69 years, he took up residence in the Vatican. Not until the reign of that great builder Sixtus V did the palace recover its former glory, re-created by Domenico Fontana in 1586. Sixtus had intended to use it as his summer palace but found the Quirinal more congenial.

To the left is one of Rome's most famous holy curiosities, the **SCALA SANTA** (Holy Steps). These 28 marble steps, today covered in wood, are said to have come from the palace of Pontius Pilate in Jerusalem, brought to Rome by St Helena, the mother of Constantine. If the legend is true, then Christ himself climbed to the house of Pilate and descended these stairs on the day of his trial. Today they lead not to a praetor's house but to the private chapel of the former Lateran Palace. This Cosmatesque work dating from 1278, houses a rare sixth- or seventh-century painting of Christ, attributed to St Luke (who sketched it out) and to artistic angels who finished it. In consequence the work is dubbed 'the painting not made by human hands'.

The staircase was enclosed in a building designed by Domenico Fontana in the 1580s. A statue in the vestibule depicts the aged Pope Pius IX on his knees, having climbed the steps in September in 1870 as a penance to avoid the Vatican being incorporated into a united Italy. An *Ecce Homo* and a statue of Judas betraying Christ with a kiss are both by the nineteenth-century sculptor Ignazio Iacometti. Other statues depict Jesus waiting to be scourged, and lying dead on his mother's lap while St John looks on. Pilgrims still climb the Scala Santa on their knees, kissing with particularly fervent devotion those parts of the steps which are said to be stained with the blood of Christ, then descending by one of the side staircases. The memory lingers of Martin Luther, ascending these steps on his knees in 1510,

OPPOSITE
CATHEDRAL AND PORT

ABOVE *The Triclinium of Pope Leo III was built in about 800 as the dining hall of the Lateran Palace, where popes traditionally entertained emperors after their coronation.*

OPPOSITE *The mighty two-storeyed portico of San Giovanni in Laterano by Alessandro Galilei. The bronze central doors come from the Curia – Sant'Adriano – in the Foro Romano.*

repeating a paternoster on each of them in the hope of releasing the soul of his grandfather from Purgatory, and at the top exclaiming, 'Who knows whether this is true?'

East of the Scala Santa is another precious relic of the old Lateran Palace, the apse of its banqueting hall. Known as the **TRICLINIUM OF POPE LEO III** (who reigned from 795 to 816), it was restored in 1743, as was its ancient mosaic. This depicts, in the centre, Christ sending out his apostles to convert the world, while on the left he gives the keys of the kingdom to St Sylvester and the standard of the Cross to the emperor Constantine. In the scene on the right, St Peter is portrayed giving to the emperor Charlemagne the banner of Christianity and to Pope Leo III the papal stole. The medieval symbolism is clear. Legend had it that Pope Sylvester I, who died in 335, had cured Constantine of leprosy when he baptized him, in return receiving grants of vast territories (the spurious 'Donation of Constantine', which conferred on Sylvester primacy over Antioch, Jerusalem, Constantinople and Alexandria, as well as dominion over the whole of Italy). As church and state had thus formed an alliance, so, the mosaic proclaimed, once again the spiritual descendant of St Peter would confer legitimacy on the Holy Roman Empire while the emperor, in his turn, protected the papal throne.

All this is an entrancing prelude to the great church founded by Constantine. It was built on land given to him as part of the dowry of his wife Fausta, land he proceeded to give to Pope Melchiades. The church which rose here was destroyed by the Vandals, restored, wrecked by earthquake, rebuilt a second time, devastated by the fire of 1308 which also took the Lateran Palace, rebuilt by Pope Clement V, and shortly afterwards burned down again. In 1369 Giovanni di Stefano began the present basilica, which since then has been enlarged, restored (almost completely by Borromini in the mid seventeenth century) and so much embellished that to explore it today is a complex as well as a rewarding experience.

Sixtus V's obelisk stands outside the north façade. Here Domenico Fontana, in 1586, created a double-tiered portico, beneath which on the left is a statue of King Henri IV of France, a great benefactor of this church, sculpted by Nicola Cordier in the first decade of the seventeenth century. Henri was made honorary canon of San Giovanni in Laterano, and to this day the basilica includes a Frenchman among its canons.

Behind Fontana's façade rise two towers of 1360, and five more doors lead from here to the nave. Undoubtedly, however, the most impressive way of entering the church is from the east end (for Rome's great basilica is orientated in the exact opposite fashion from the demands of Christian tradition, its high altar – as in St Peter's, and other Roman churches – to the west).

In 1731 Alessandro Galilei won a competition, entered by 23 leading architects of the day, to rebuild this majestic entrance to **SAN GIOVANNI IN LATERANO** for Pope Clement XII. Inspired by St Peter's, he used gigantic Corinthian columns and flat pilasters to create a portico over which rises an

arcaded loggia. A triangular pediment shelters the balcony from which the pope blesses the people. Above the balustrade seventeen baroque statues, each 7 metres high, proclaim the faith: Jesus at the centre, flanked by his apostles and the four doctors of the Church. As the inscription on this façade roundly declares, this is the mother and chief church of Rome and of the whole world ('*omnium urbis et orbis Ecclesiarum Mater et Caput*').

Five doorways give entrance to the atrium, save that the one on the extreme right is blocked up, to be opened only during jubilee years (which are declared four times a century). The central bronze doors came from the Curia, the meeting place of the Roman senate which Diocletian built in 283. To their left is a statue of Constantine, discovered when his baths on the Quirinal were being excavated in 1621. The atrium itself, as well as its chapels, is decorated with fifth-century mosaics.

From this entrance, ancient green marble columns, which survive from the fourth-century basilica, separate twin side aisles from the nave – thus reproducing the five aisles of the earlier basilica. Although San Giovanni in Laterano is full of treasures from widely differing eras of Christian art, the majestic sweep of its design overwhelms everything, giving an impression of unity which centres on the papal altar ahead. The subtle colours used here by Borromini help to confer an air of tranquillity to this massive building.

Shortened in the seventeenth century, the venerable columns of the nave were incorporated into new piers by Borromini. They flank niches in which stand twelve baroque sculptures of the apostles. Designed by Carlo Maratta, these huge statues were executed by craftsmen working under the direction of Carlo Fontana. Behind the first pier of the twin aisle to the right is a fragmentary painting, said to be by Giotto, of Pope Boniface VIII proclaiming in 1300 the first-ever papal jubilee year.

The friezes above the apostles were stuccoed by Algardi with (on the left) scenes from the Old Testament and (on the right) scenes from the New. Above are Old Testament prophets, painted in the eighteenth century, beneath a wooden ceiling decorated by Giacomo della Porta. The pavement is Cosmatesque, and in 1287 the Cosmati also created the tomb of Cardinal Casati in the far right aisle.

Beside it is the Corsini Chapel which Galilei created in 1732. As Pope Clement XII Lorenzo Corsini proved no great success, although hardly assisted by the financial crisis he had inherited from his predecessor, Benedict XIII. He did, however, win public approval by reintroducing the state lotteries, which Benedict had condemned, and he was also the first pope to issue paper money in Rome. From the proceeds Clement was able to finance the rebuilding of the west façade of this church – an equally lasting achievement. He died in 1740 and lies in his chapel in an urn which came from the Pantheon. The saint depicted in a mosaic over the altar is Lorenzo's ancestor Andrea Corsini, a Carmelite monk who became Bishop of Fiesole in 1349 and was adept at settling quarrels. If the classical design of

Perhaps by Giotto, this fresco on one of the piers of San Giovanni in Laterano shows Boniface VIII proclaiming the first-ever papal jubilee year of 1300.

this mosaic sits oddly in a late baroque chapel, this is because it was copied from a painting by the early seventeenth-century genius Guido Reni.

Under the crossing is the papal altar, where the pope alone celebrates High Mass unless as a special honour he grants the right to another. The present altar, rebuilt by Pius IX in the nineteenth century, protects a wooden one on which both St Peter and his successor St Sylvester are said to have celebrated. Beneath this altar, steps lead down to a fifteenth-century statue of St John the Baptist, carved out of wood, and the superb early renaissance tomb of Pope Martin V, created by Simone Ghini in 1431. It describes Pope Martin as *temporum suorum felicitas* ('the joy of his time'). Today visitors toss coins on it.

Pride of place here goes to a gothic baldacchino of 1367, designed by Giovanni di Stefano and frescoed by Barna da Siena. It houses silver reliquaries with the heads of St Peter and St Paul. The fourteenth-century originals were stolen by the French in the late eighteenth century: these are approximate copies. Statues of the two saints sit under this canopy in what looks like a huge cage. Their reputed skulls are powerful relics. When the troops of the Holy Roman Emperor Frederick II were menacing Rome in 1241, Pope Gregory IX brought them out in procession to rally the people.

Two nineteenth-century tombs are set against the arches on either side of the apse behind the papal altar. The one on the right, created by Giuseppe Lucchetti in 1891, holds the earthly remains of Pope Innocent III, who died in 1216 at Perugia and was buried there. His bones were brought here by his distant successor on the throne of Peter, Leo XIII, who died in 1903 and lies in the left-hand tomb, the work of Giulio Tadolino. Innocent was a brilliant statesman, who popularized the papal title Vicar of Christ, defined as a person set halfway between God and man, a prelate 'above man but below God'.

Behind this impressive ensemble of high altar and tombs, the mosaics in the apse, made by the same Franciscan monk who decorated the apse of Santa Maria Maggiore, were ill-restored in the nineteenth century when Leo XIII ordered the apse to be lengthened. Originally created in around 1291 their motifs include the head of Jesus and the Holy Spirit in the form of a dove, descending on to a cross which is a jewelled symbol of triumph. Again the artist has depicted rivers flowing from this cross to quench the thirst of believers. Beside them on the left are later mosaics, depicting the Virgin Mary with saints John, Andrew, John the Baptist, Peter and Paul. The little kneeling figure is the donor, Nicholas IV, suitably humble in the presence of these holy ones. Beside him stand two saints dear to his heart, St Francis of Assisi and St Anthony of Padua, both depicted in miniature. Below them amidst palm trees are the nine remaining apostles; and the two other minuscule figures are the mosaicists, Jacopo Torriti and Jacopo da Camerino. The transepts which stretch on either side of the papal altar were commissioned by Pope Clement VIII from Giacomo della Porta and their swaggering curves were completed around the end of the sixteenth century. Giacomo frescoed his transepts with mannerist paintings of the conversion of Constantine and his notorious donation to the pope.

It is time, however, to take two steps back into the past, first into the cloisters and then into the baptistry. The cloisters are reached through a door in front of the steps leading to the Chapel of the Blessed Sacrament. On the way notice the tomb of Cardinal Ranuccio Farnese (near the last central pillar of the nave), which is by Vignola. The Chapel of the Blessed Sacrament, built around 1600 by the architect Pier Paolo Olivieri on behalf of Pope Clement VIII, is also worth noting, since it accommodates what is reputed to be half of the table on which Jesus celebrated the first Holy Communion. (The other half is in the church of Santa Pudenziana.) The metal lintel and the bronze columns of this chapel came from the prows of the ships which once adorned the rostra in the Foro Romano.

The exquisite cloisters of San Giovanni in Laterano were created by Jacopo and Pietro Vassaletto between 1215 and 1232. Their little twin columns are deliciously varied, as are the capitals and the frieze of mosaic which adorns the entablature, by the Cosmati. Among the fragments of the former basilica placed here are some bas-reliefs from the tomb which Arnolfo di Cambio made for Cardinal Annibaldi.

You reach the other ancient gem of this church, the baptistry, from Piazza San Giovanni in Laterano. This is the oldest in the Christian world, built here by Constantine in 324, and is the prototype of every later octagonal baptistry. Eight columns of white marble rising from eight columns of porphyry were set up in the next century and support the cupola. A bronze bath of the seventeenth century covers the fifth-century font. Mosaics dating from the fifth to the seventh centuries embellish the spot, some of them in the chapels which later extended the building. The bronze doors of the Chapel of St John the Baptist were made for the Baths of Caracalla and those of the Chapel of St John the Evangelist in 1196. The vault of the latter chapel is decorated with a mosaic depicting the Lamb of God amidst flowers and birds. An equally pastoral note is struck by the fifth-century mosaics of the Chapel of St Rufina, where acanthus leaves are set against a blue sky. Equally fascinating are the seventh-century mosaics of the Chapel of St Venantius. Here the Madonna, surrounded by Dalmatian saints, is depicted beside the two cities of Bethlehem and Jerusalem. Pope John IV, who built this chapel in 640, was himself a Dalmatian who spent much of his wealth ransoming Christian slaves in his homeland from their Avar and Slav captors. He also sent an abbot to rescue the relics of saints from these invaders, including the martyr Venantius. The charm of these mosaics is set off by Andrea Sacchi's high baroque scenes from the life of St John the Baptist, painted around the cupola, and by the work of more flamboyant painters who decorated its walls when Pope Urban VIII had the baptistry restored in the seventeenth century. This gentle baptistry

OPPOSITE *The exquisite cloister of San Giovanni in Laterano. In typical romanesque fashion, the entrances are emphasized by more ornate columns – here they have barley-sugar twists and are supported on the backs of lions.*

stands on the site of the home of Constantine's wife, Fausta, whom he had smothered to death in a warm bath because she murdered his son by a previous marriage.

A yet more grisly tale connected with this church concerns the trial of Pope Formosus in 897, nine months after his death. His successor, Pope Stephen VI, had the corpse of Formosus exhumed, dressed in his papal vestments, accusing him of perjury, covetousness and numerous other ecclesiastical sins. A deacon was assigned the task of defending Formosus, and (needless to say) failed to gain the acquittal of the mute corpse. Formosus was judged guilty. The three fingers of his right hand, formerly used to bless the faithful, were cut off. The rest of his body was placed in a common grave, later dug up again and thrown into the Tiber. No subsequently elected pope took the name Formosus.

Half-way along Via di San Giovanni in Laterano stands the church of **SAN CLEMENTE**, the origins of which go back to the very beginnings of Christianity, built on one of the private houses in which the early Christians would clandestinely gather to worship their proscribed god. Its whitewashed walls and the dusty, homely streets surrounding it are unremarkable. Nor, in the piazza, does the equally plain twelfth-century portico, supported on four granite Corinthian and Ionic columns, give any hint of the glories within. Entrance, in fact, is usually by the side door.

San Clemente is the best preserved of the medieval basilicas of Rome, a fascinatingly complex structure comprising two churches, one set above the other. Two rows of eight ancient columns divide the upper church into three aisles. The building is set out almost perfectly according to the structure of the earliest Christian churches; and although the choir was rearranged in the twelfth century, the screen which separates it from the nave bears the monogram of Pope John II, who occupied the chair of St Peter for a mere three years in the early sixth century. The central area, unusually preserving much of its original layout, is where the laity would stand and worship, with the schola cantorum reserved for the clergy and a pair of ambones for reading the Epistle and Gospels. Here, too, are the mosaics of the Cosmati, in the pavements, paschal candle, tabernacle, bishop's throne and baldacchino. On the episcopal throne is engraved the name of Cardinal Anastasius, who sat on it in the early twelfth century, while the baldacchino is decorated with an anchor, in memory of the one supposedly tied around the neck of St Clement when he was drowned in the Black Sea.

In the first half of the twelfth century, the apse and the triumphal arch were covered with a beautiful series of mosaics. Byzantine in style, they portray Christ, against a background of stars, blessing his followers, supported by saints Paul and Lawrence as well as the four evangelists, St Peter and Pope Clement (with a boat). The twelve apostles are piquantly represented as doves. The Old Testament figures represented are Isaiah and Jeremiah, while the cities of Jerusalem and Bethlehem signify the Old and

New Testaments. More complex in its symbolism is the mosaic depicting the Triumph of the Cross. The crucifix has become the tree of life. A vine grows from the foot of the cross. The symbol of death has become the symbol of life. The vine encircles saints who include the four doctors of the church and John the Baptist. And in case this symbolism has been lost, the rivers of Paradise also flow from Christ's cross, from which the faithful, portrayed as stags, are drinking. One of them is tempted by a serpent. Underneath these is the Lamb of God, with his apostles, now depicted as sheep, coming from the cities of Bethlehem and Jerusalem to revere him. So the Old Testament and the New are both witness to the divinity of Christ. And the tabernacle in this apse matches the mosaics in the skill of its execution, as one would expect from the hand of Arnolfo di Cambio.

The Chapel of St Catherine of Alexandria, on the left of the entrance, is worth looking for, in part because its decorations so completely contrast with the rest of the building. Here in 1431, the Florentine artist Masolino da Panicale painted an Annunciation, several saints (including Christopher and Ambrose) and scenes from the life of St Catherine of Alexandria herself.

The lower church, which you reach from the right-hand side of the nave, was sacked in 1084 by the troops of the Norman invader Robert Guiscard, rebuilt, but properly excavated only in 1861, when an astonishing, multi-layered history was revealed. In the crypt lie the bones of St Clement, by tradition the third or fourth pope, after whom the church is named. His corpse was allegedly brought here by the missionaries, saints Cyril and Methodius after he was drowned in the Black Sea. This saint's life is of genuine historical significance, for he wrote a still-surviving letter (calling for peace in the church of Corinth) which constitutes the most important first-century Christian document outside the Bible.

Ninth- to eleventh-century frescoes decorate the walls of this three-aisled lower church, which, judging from the square nimbus of Pope Leo IV who appears in the mid ninth-century fresco of the Ascension, may have been financed by him. Other frescoes show scenes related to St Clement, including the chapel which angels built over his corpse at the bottom of the Black Sea. (Annually the sea would retreat so that pilgrims might visit his shrine.) We see a widow, whose son was lost in the crowd on one such occasion, returning a year later to find that the dead Clement had miraculously kept him alive. Other frescoes of the period contain some amusing Christian tales. St Alexis works as a servant in his father's house and, unrecognized, sleeps under a staircase for seventeen years. The pagan Sisinnus, struck blind to stop him kidnapping the pope, orders his servants to do so. They suffer the same fate and kidnap a column instead. This series of frescoes incorporates the oldest surviving inscriptions in Italian.

Under the apse are the remains of the cavernous Mithraeum (Temple of Mithras), one of its tufa-walled rooms with a cippus depicting this god (who wears a Phrygian cap) sacrificing a bull to the sun. An ill-supported tale

The cloister of the often-neglected but exceedingly rewarding church of San Clemente, dedicated to the fourth pope. The medieval upper church sits on top of a lower church mentioned by St Jerome in 392. This in its turn lies above a first-century building which includes a third-century temple of Mithras.

declares that this was a house taken from Clement and handed over to the priests of Mithras. There is still more to be excavated here.

This part of the city is laid out in the ancient manner like a chess board, and there are many fascinating churches in the area which are worth exploring. Retrace your steps a little way on the Via di San Giovanni in Laterano, and take Via dei Querceti to one of them, **SANTI QUATTRO CORONATI**. First built in the ninth century, this church was sacked by the Normans and rebuilt in 1116. The thirteenth-century pavement is Cosmatesque. Santi Quattro Coronati has a late sixteenth-century ceiling, and the apse frescoes are the baroque work of Giovanni di San Giovanni, painted around 1630; but its cloister remains almost as it was in the early twelfth century, with a fountain of the same date cooling its garden. Among the chapels leading off this cloister, do not miss that dedicated to St Sylvester, its mid twelfth-century frescoes depicting the saint curing Constantine of leprosy and receiving from the grateful emperor the forged donation. The date of these frescoes (1246) is significant, for precisely at this moment Pope Innocent IV was resisting the arrogance of the excommunicated Hohenstaufen emperor Frederick II, the pope maintaining that his authority was supreme in temporal as well as spiritual matters. In such conflicts, it seemed wise to reinforce the papal position with some judicious iconography. Innocent also attempted to reinforce his position by attempting to have the emperor assassinated.

The four crowned saints to whom this church is dedicated are either four Roman soldiers who were scourged to death under Diocletian for refusing to offer sacrifices to the pagan god Aesculapius (and appear in Giovanni di San Giovanni's fresco) or four Pannonian sculptors who laid down their tools when commanded to create a heathen idol. Whoever they were, their bodies lie in sarcophagi in the crypt under the high altar.

A little further south along Via dei Querceti, turn right alongside the Celian hospital and then left again to reach Via della Navicella and two more entrancing churches. **SANTA MARIA IN DOMNICA** is one of the sweetest in Rome. The piazza in front of the church is graced by a marble fountain of

The sixteenth-century sculpture of a ship gives its name to Via della Navicella and stands outside the church of Santa Maria in Domnica.

1513 in the form of a ship (hence the name of the street, which means 'little boat'), a sixteenth-century copy of an antique ex-voto. The classical subtleties of the Doric portico of Santa Maria in Domnica indicate that its entrance was restored in the early sixteenth century by Andrea Sansovino and his pupils, but the interior of the basilica retains its ancient form, sympathetically restored to designs by Raphael. (The cartoons for these are now housed in Windsor Castle, as are those for his tapestries in the Vatican.)

The three aisles inside this church are separated by eighteen ancient granite columns. The splendid mosaic at the end of the nave derives from the period of the church's foundation by Pope Paschal I in the early ninth century. It depicts the glorification of the Virgin. Dressed in blue and heavy with child, she is surrounded by angels in white robes. Paschal, with his square nimbus, kneels humbly at her feet. To the right of the apse are saints Peter and Paul, dressed in white, their nimbuses gold, while those of the angels are blue. Flowers made of glittering stones transform this mosaic into a garden, wherein sits Our Lady, for the first time in Rome depicted in Majesty, occupying the central place of honour. This new iconography is probably due to Greek monks, who had fled to Rome to escape the wrath of the Byzantine emperors, bringing with them their own exalted notions of the honour due to the Blessed Virgin Mary. Although the Medici pope Leo X helped to restore this church, the Medici passion for allegory fortunately means that his laudable work is not proclaimed from the rooftops but alluded to gently, in the heraldic devices of the triple ostrich plumes, the yoke and the lion incorporated in the frieze (created to patterns of Giulio Romano) above the windows.

To the left of the church is the **VILLA CELIMONTANA**, built amidst luxurious public parklands which were laid out in 1582 on the slopes of the Celian Hill. And across the road, Via Santo Stefano Rotondo takes you to what is arguably the most memorable (San Giovanni in Laterano included) of all the churches in this area of the city. It certainly made an impact on Charles Dickens. 'To single out details from the great dream of Roman churches would be the wildest occupation in the world,' he wrote. 'But St Stefano Rotondo, a damp, mildewed vault of an old church in the outskirts of Rome, will always struggle uppermost in my mind, by reason of the hideous paintings with which its walls are covered. These represent the martyrdoms of saints and early Christians; and such a panorama of horror and butchery no man could imagine in his sleep.' But it has other claims to fame.

Standing on the **CELIAN HILL**, **SANTO STEFANO ROTONDO** is ancient, built a few years after the sack of Rome by the Vandals in 455, and modelled on the church of the Holy Sepulchre in Jerusalem. It is also massive – the largest circular church in the world – although its proportions are so exquisite that its size never overwhelms the worshipper. Plundering pagan columns, its builders left later generations a severe and bare house of God. Over the centuries it was covered with marble and mother of pearl, but today, all this has vanished. A mosaic in the apse remains from the seventh century, and 56 marble and granite Corinthian columns still surround the interior. They encompass a smaller (although still vast) circle of 22 Ionic columns at the centre which forms the heart of the building. The 34 frescoes which so terrified Dickens are the late sixteenth-century work of Cristoforo Roncalli da Pomarance (Pomarancio) and Antonio Tempesta. Pope Gregory XII commissioned them, in a bid to prepare Jesuit missionaries for martyrdom. This church is built on a curious site – almost certainly the meat market set up here at the time of the emperor Nero. (Some indeed have argued that the church itself was a market-hall, later transformed into a religious building.) **NERO'S MITHRAEUM** has been excavated nearby, the best preserved temple to Mithras in Rome. Beyond the church stretch the remains of an aqueduct built at the time of the emperor Claudius.

Leaving Santo Stefano Rotondo, walk down the steep, tree-shaded Via della Navicella to reach the Piazza Metronia. Here a gateway pierces an evocative stretch of the pink walls which Aurelian built around Rome in AD 271. Occasional ferns grow from the arched walkways of these walls, in what is a curiously isolated, almost desolate part of Rome.

Via Druso runs south-west from the piazza as far as the Piazzale Numa Pompilio, named after Romulus's successor Numa Pompilius. To the right is

The numerous tortures to which Christian saints and martyrs where subjected grace the walls of Santo Stefano Rotondo. These frescoes were commissioned by Pope Gregory XIII to prepare missionaries for the hardships to come.

the ancient little church of **SANTI NEREO ED ACHILLEO**, sumptuously rebuilt by Pope Leo III in around 800. The church is dedicated to two eunuchs who served the family of the Roman emperor in the first century AD. Converted to Christianity (it is said) by St Peter himself, they were banished with their Christian patroness, Flavia Domitilla, niece of Domitian, to an island on the coast of Terracina. Flavia herself refused to sacrifice to idols and was therefore burned to death. The relics of this royal virgin, brought from the catacombs in the eighth century, also lie here.

Allowed to fall into ruin during the Avignon captivity of the papal Curia, the church of these martyrs was restored in 1597 by Cardinal Cesare Baronio, a man fortunately with an eye for ancient beauty, whose express aim was to preserve what he could of the older building. In consequence, the lovely Cosmatesque baldacchino still rises on four columns of African marble over the high altar, as it first did in the thirteenth century; and in the apse are mosaics of 795 with slender Byzantine figures depicting the transfiguration of Christ and the annunciation. In the apse, two lions support the ancient marble episcopal throne. Cardinal Baronio, supposing that St Gregory the Great read his twenty-eighth homily from this throne, had part of the text inscribed on it. Referring to the patrons of this church, Gregory declared, 'These saints before whose tomb we are assembled despised the world. They trampled it under their feet when peace, plenty, wealth and health gave it charms.'

To the right of the church is the entrance to the **BATHS OF CARACALLA**. In their relative isolation from the city they still exude an air of imperial grandeur. Building was begun by Antoninus Caracalla in AD 212, but the baths were not finished until 235, by which time they were the largest in Rome, covering an area of more than 11 hectares (27 acres). The emperor Aurelian restored them and these luxurious baths continued in use until 597, when the Vandals wrecked the aqueduct that supplied the 80,000 litres of water needed to fill the cisterns feeding the pools and fountains.

The baths were surrounded by gardens. The ancient, tree-lined walks are replaced by parks and modern garden centres, while parasol pines and laurels deck the ancient ruins. The baked bricks used for building the baths were formerly covered in marble, seductive frescoes, rich mosaics and precious stones.

On entering the baths today, you come first to a rectangular frigidarium (the cold water bath) with dressing rooms on either side which are still paved with mosaics. From the frigidarium you move on along what was once a vast central hall with vaults supported on granite pillars, to the tepidarium (filled with lukewarm water), on either side of which were gymnasiums. Next comes the massive circular hot water pool, the calidarium, which had a diameter of 34 metres and, finally, the sudatorium or perspiring room. In fact the rooms were used in the opposite order to this. Beneath the baths there was an underground chapel for the worshippers of Mithras.

OPPOSITE *The glory that was ancient Rome in the Baths of Caracalla. Begun by the emperor in AD 212, they could accommodate up to 6000 bathers. They fell out of use in the sixth century after invaders damaged the aqueducts supplying the vast amounts of water needed.*

Shops, libraries and an art gallery fostered the cultural tastes of the bathers, so it is fitting that nowadays, on summer evenings, despite the problems of acoustics, the Baths of Caracalla are the venue of some of Rome's most exuberant and spectacular concerts and operas. Excavations in the sixteenth and seventeenth centuries uncovered a profusion of treasures in these baths. The mosaics are now displayed in the Vatican Museum, while other finds are in the Museo Nazionale of Naples, and (as mentioned) a couple of basins from here grace the Piazza Farnese.

Running south-east from the Piazzale Numa Pompilio, Via di Porta Latina soon reaches the crenellated **PORTA LATINA**. In the sixth century, Belisarius fortified this gate, as well as the rest of the Aurelian wall, with blocks of travertine, after he had driven the Goths from Rome. He also probably constructed the two round towers that flank the gate, which is today also defended by a portcullis.

To the left, just before you reach the gateway, the five storeys of a twelfth-century campanile, increasingly delicate as they rise, accommodate the bells of **SAN GIOVANNI A PORTA LATINA**. A church has stood here since the fifth century, and although several times restored, San Giovanni a Porta Latina has preserved fourteen ancient Ionic columns. Four of them, two marble, two granite, grace the romanesque portico with its five arcades and thirteenth-century Cosmatesque mosaics. The other ten columns, all Ionic, but all different, divide the church into a nave and two aisles. Two fluted marble columns almost certainly came from a pagan building, and the other eight gleam with marble, porphyry and granite. They support a baroque roof added in 1678. A magnificent cycle of twelfth-century frescoes, in three tiers, portraying 46 scenes from the Old and New Testaments, adorns the nave, and the hexagonal apse is decorated with more frescoes. These depict the throne of God, surrounded by angels and the symbols of the evangelists, flanked by the 24 elders of the Apocalypse. The apse's lovely coloured marble pavement dates from the tenth century.

Nearby on the right is the tiny octagonal church of **SAN GIOVANNI IN OLEO** (St John in the Oil). It marks the spot where St John the Evangelist is reputed to have been plunged into a cauldron of boiling oil and escaped unhurt, indeed refreshed. The earlier church which stood here was rebuilt in 1509, perhaps by Bramante, whose hand can be detected in the lively terra-cotta frieze. The inscription on this church ('At God's pleasure') does not refer to St John's ordeal but was the family motto of the French Franciscan monk Benoit Adam, who financed its building in 1509.

A short stroll south-west from San Giovanni in Oleo leads to the **SEPOLCRO DEGLI SCIPIONE** – the tomb hewn into the rock, which the Scipio family built for themselves in the third century BC. In the nearby public gardens is another burial place – a perfectly preserved columbarium decorated with mosaics. This chamber was built in the first century AD by Pomponius Hylas to contain the ashes of himself and his wife. In a small

The twelfth-century campanile of San Giovanni a Porta Latina, the slender white columns contrasting with the red brick.

stuccoed and painted underground room, archaeologists have discovered urns in which were deposited the remains of slaves freed under Augustus and Tiberius Caesar.

From the Porta Latina, Viale di Mura Latina winds its way alongside the **AURELIAN WALL** as far as the **PORTA SAN SEBASTIANO**, the most impressive of its gates, like the Porta Latina, strengthened by Belisarius with crenellated round towers linked by a gallery above the gateway. Beside it is a small museum devoted to the history of the Aurelian Wall. Close by is the third-century Arch of Drusus, part of the aqueduct that brought water to the Baths of Caracalla.

From this gate, **VIA APPIA ANTICA** (the Appian Way), much of it still paved in basalt from the Alban Hills as it was in Roman times and displaying the ancient pavements at either side, leads from the old city towards the catacombs. This 'Queen of Roads' was begun more than a mile inside the present line of the walls by the censor Appius Claudius in 312 BC. He succeeded in fulfilling a bold conception: an absolutely straight carriageway which would run for about 90 kilometres as far as Terracina. The problems of building such a road through the Pontine Marshes were brilliantly overcome. Measuring 4.15 metres in width, the Appian Way allowed two carriages to pass with ease, and it was bordered by wide, hard shoulders of packed earth, supported by a stone kerb. The final 28 kilometres offered a further innovation, being flanked by a specially dug canal, enabling travellers to proceed at a more leisurely pace by boat.

From the Porta San Sebastiano, you can walk to the little church of Domine Quo Vadis, less than a kilometre along the Via Appia Antica. If you want to go further take the 118 bus (which starts at the Colosseum and has a stop just inside the Porta San Sebastiano) as far as the Catacombe di San Callisto (Catacombs of St Calixtus) from where you can walk to the Tomb of Cecilia Metella, just over a kilometre away.

Leaving Porta San Sebastiano, Via Appia Antica runs gently downhill beside a recently excavated sanctuary dedicated to Mars. Scarcely 100 metres from the gate you spot the Roman milestone with inscriptions by the Emperors Vespasian and Nerva. (This is in fact a copy, the original now sits on the balustrade of the Capitol.) The road passes under the railway bridge to cross a tributary of the Tiber, now called the Marrana delle Caffarelle but known to the ancients as the Almone. Regarding it as a sacred river, the priests of Cybele would annually wash the statue of their goddess in its waters. Beyond this river, on the left, is the first of the sepulchres outside the present walls of Rome: the so-called **SEPULCHRE OF GETA**.

The ancient Romans insisted that cemeteries and tombs be built outside the sacred precincts of the city, and the environs of Via Appia Antica thus became prime sites for burial grounds and tombs. Geta and his brother Caracalla were sons of Septimus Severus by his second wife, Julia, a woman of outstanding learning and a diligent patroness of the arts. According to

Gibbon, these vain and vicious sons 'discovered, almost from their infancy, a fixed and implacable antipathy for each other.' After the death of Septimus Severus, his sons were proclaimed joint emperors. Utterly unable to agree on their mutual responsibilities, they agreed to discuss their problems in their mother's apartments. Caracalla hired centurions to kill Geta and eventually more than 20,000 men and women were put to death to protect Caracalla from any possible revenge.

Just beyond the Sepulchre of Geta, at the junction with the Via Ardeatina, the little seventeenth-century church of **DOMINE QUO VADIS** lies to the left. The name derives from the legend that St Peter, fleeing persecution, met his Lord here and asked where he was going (*Domine quo vadis?*) Jesus replied *Venio iterum crucifigi*, indicating that he was on his way to Rome, to be crucified again. At this the mortified Peter abandoned his flight, returned to Rome and was himself crucified. The church houses a copy of a stone with what are said to be the footprints of Christ. The original is in the church of San Sebastiano.

St Peter almost certainly lies buried under the high altar of the basilica of St Peter's but the bodies of countless other Christians were consigned to the catacombs ahead. Across the road from Domine Quo Vadis is a pagan burial place – a circular tomb, topped by a small medieval tower. The tomb was built as the **SEPULCHRE OF PRISCILLA**, wife of Flavius Abascatus who was one of the chief ministers of Domitian, and has lavish early Christian frescoes. We then pass a replica of the second milestone of the Via Appia Antica, just beyond which is the entrance to the **CATACOMBE DI SAN CALLISTO**.

The area so far excavated of this underground burial place consists of four floors of galleries stretching for over 400 by 300 metres. This was the first legal Christian cemetery of Rome, and Calixtus was the deacon who laid it out at the beginning of the third century. Becoming pope in 217, Calixtus continued to extend the catacombs, where he himself was to be buried along with most of his successors for the next hundred years.

In 1855 the papal crypt was discovered. Some of those lying here – who include Sixtus II, Anteros, Pontianus, Fabian, Lucius and Eutychianus – met their death by martyrdom, as the great letters MTP inscribed beside the tombs of Pontianus and Fabian indicate. Once the body of St Cecilia lay in the neighbouring crypt, but when her body was found to be uncorrupted in 1599, she was removed from the sarcophagus and taken to the church of Santa Cecilia in Trastevere. Stefano Maderna sculpted her likeness and a copy of this work (the original is in the church) is on display here. The walls of this crypt were first frescoed in the fourth century, and traces of these paintings remain. Finer and earlier frescoes, dating from the early third century, decorate the walls of other parts of the crypt, some of them depicting baptism and the eucharist. Finally, in the crypt of a deacon named Severus, there is an inscription of 298, in which, for the first known time, the Bishop of Rome is called the pope.

ABOVE *Urns and a broken pediment adorn the seventeenth-century church of Domine Quo Vadis. It was commissioned by Urban VIII and is remarkably restrained considering its date and the religious significance of the site.*

OPPOSITE *The tree-shaded Via Appia was begun in 312 BC by the censor Appius Claudius and later extended as far as Brindisi.*

Christians were not the only ones to bury their dead in underground cemeteries. Just beyond Via Appia Pignatelli, which runs off to the left, are the huge Jewish catacombs of Vigna Rondini which even embody a massive, vaulted synagogue for funerals, and which you can visit only with special permission. A little further along the Via Appia Antica a column of 1852 celebrates the repairs carried out to the road at the expense of Pope Pius IX, to the right of which rises the basilica of **SAN SEBASTIANO**. It was founded as the Basilica Apostolorum in the fourth century on the spot where the bodies of Saints Peter and Paul were buried in 158 to keep them out of the clutches of the persecuting emperor Valerian. When the body of St Sebastian was brought here, after suffering martyrdom during the reign of Diocletian, the church was rededicated to St Sebastian.

When Cardinal Scipione Borghese commissioned Flaminio Ponzio and Giovanni Vasanzio to rebuild the church in 1612, Vasanzio incorporated into his façade six ancient granite columns from the earlier church, setting them to support a portico of three graceful classical arches. Above it rises an equally elegant second storey with a low, triangular pediment. In the first chapel on the right is one of those legendary stones bearing the imprint of Christ's own foot, while the last chapel on the right is the work of Carlo Maratta. Innocenzo Tacconi, one of the pupils of Annibale Carracci, was responsible for the painting over the high altar. And the most impressive work of art is a statue of St Sebastian by Bernini's pupil Antonio Giorgetti.

This is where the word 'catacomb' was first used. From the church itself you climb down into the crypt, for a guided tour of the **CATACOMBE DI SAN SEBASTIANO**. These catacombs date back to the first century BC, for they were used by pagans before the Christians took over. The very first crypt on the left displays a relief of a peacock, one of the pagan symbols of immortality. Late third-century graffiti honour saints Peter and Paul, as a strong confirmation of the legend that their bodies once did lie here.

Some 200 metres beyond the church, on the other side of the Via Appia Antica, are the ruins of the **CIRCO DI MASSENZIO** (Circus of Maxentius). In front of it in AD 309 the emperor Maxentius built a mausoleum for his son Romulus. It was part of a much larger complex. Behind the mausoleum is an arena some 520 metres long and 92 metres wide designed for chariot racing. A pair of semi-cylindrical towers (once flanking twelve gates) indicate where the races began. At the far end is a triumphal arch. Next to this arena stood an imperial palace.

Via Appia Antica now runs uphill to reach a still majestic tomb, the massive circular tower built as **THE TOMB OF CECILIA METELLA**. She was the daughter-in-law of an Augustan soldier and statesman named Marcus Licinus Crassus, and her father, Quintus Metellus Creticus, was a magistrate and soldier who helped to conquer Crete. Crassus was a fellow consul with Pompey and a friend of Julius Caesar. The three men formed the first Roman triumvirate in around 60 BC. Crassus's military and political

The massive stone sepulchre of Cecilia Metella is 29.5 metres in diameter and, like the Castel Sant'Angelo, served as a stronghold: in the thirteenth century it was used as the keep of the Caetani's castle.

triumphs made him rich. His lands, Pliny records, were worth more than 8000 talents (a colossal sum), while his personal wealth, according to Plutarch, amounted to another 7000 talents. His death was miserable. Lured into a parley with the Parthian general Surenas in 53 BC, Crassus was murdered. Another enemy, pouring molten gold into the mouth of his severed head, allegedly remarked, 'Guzzle now what in life you were so greedy for'.

Crassus' wealth passed to Cecilia's husband, and when she died he built for her this remarkable mausoleum. The diameter of her tomb, which is clad in travertine, is 29.5 metres. Its frieze of ox heads led to this neighbourhood being called the Capo di Bove. Eleven metres high and once topped with a cone, it was given its present crenellations in the late thirteenth century, when the Caetani family turned the tomb into the keep of their neighbouring fortress, the ruins of which can be seen beyond it. And across the road is another charming ruin. The roofless church of San Nicolo is one of the few ancient Gothic churches of Rome, and its humble belfry looks as if it could still hang a couple of not-too-heavy bells.

Take the bus back to Porta San Sebastiano. Viale di Porta Ardeatina takes you westward from here alongside the Aurelian Wall by way of the **PORTA ARDEATINA** and then more circuitously along the walls to the **PORTA SAN PAOLO**, which used to be called the Porta Ostiensis. Its south-facing wall was rebuilt by Honorius in 402, while the double arch facing the city is contemporary with the wall. Belisarius added its towers. In the Piazza Ostiense is the marble-faced **PYRAMID OF CAIUS CESTIUS** which the praetor erected in 12 BC, intending it to serve as his tomb. Clearly a taste for the Egyptian suffused Rome during the Augustan age. An inscription records that this pyramid, which is 27 metres high, was built in 330 days.

Inside the gate, follow Via Caio Cestio as far as Rome's **PROTESTANT CEMETERY** (officially the *Cimitero degli straneri acattolici*). Here under pines and cypresses, amid the scent of oleanders and wild strawberries, cats scrabble about marble tombs depicting weeping angels. Buried in the cemetery is Keats (his epitaph, written by himself, runs 'Here lies one whose name was writ in water') and the heart of Shelley (the rest of his body was cremated on the shore near Viareggio), who observed that 'It might make one in love with death to know that one should be buried in so sweet a place.' On his gravestone is inscribed Leigh Hunt's laconic epitaph for his friend, 'Cor cordium'. Another of Shelley's friends, Edward Trelawny (who supervised the cremation), is also buried here, as well as the novelist R. M. Ballantyne.

If you take the metro line B from the Pyramid of Cestius to Magliana, a train from there will plunge you even deeper into the past. The remarkable Etruscan village of **OSTIA ANTICA** was founded in around 338 BC, to supervise the traffic along the Tiber and also to protect the river from Tyrrhenian pirates. For this reason the settlement closely resembles a military camp, protected by a series of walls and gates.

Keats and his friend Joseph Severn lie side-by-side in the Protestant Cemetery, while through the trees appears the pyramid which Caius Cestius built in 12 BC to serve as his own tomb.

Its strategic position soon brought great wealth to Ostia Antica, and the settlement flourished and public buildings were added; a theatre in the time of Augustus, a forum during Tiberius's reign, as well as a temple dedicated both to Augustus and to the goddess of Rome (Rome is still to be seen, depicted as an Amazon). A harbour, created under Claudius and officially opened by Nero in AD 54, was important enough to appear minted on some of the latter's coins. Trajan then enlarged the port (naturally rededicating it to himself).

In the third century the citizens enthusiastically took to Mithraism, building several sanctuaries to the sun-god. The main one shelters a statue in which the bust of the god is surrounded by flames and flanked by torch-bearers. Ostia Antica even set up its own fire brigade, and its second-century barracks are visible today. Moreover, the Jews of the settlement were catered for by a synagogue, in the ruins of which you can still see the oven in which they baked unleavened bread. Only in the fourth century, when Constantine deprived the settlement of many of its privileges and made it into a suburb of Rome with the title *Portus Romae*, did Ostia Antica begin to decline. Meticulously excavated, baths, warehouses (*horrea*), four storeyed brick buildings (*insulae*), a food market and theatres have again been laid open.

Ostia Antica shows to advantage the regular street plans common to Etruscan and Roman settlements.

The way in leads past the sepulchres of the Via delle Tombe to the Porta Romana, one of the three gates to Ostia Antica. From here the main street, the Decumanus Maximus, crosses the entire town, passing baths still decorated with black and white mosaics, temples and theatres. The Baths of Neptune have a mosaic pavement depicting the god, surrounded by tritons, naiads and dolphins, driving four horses. Another mosaic in the next hall depicts a goddess, again surrounded by tritons and led by Hymen. Streets lead off to corn mills, other temples and a forum, and an excellent museum contains much more that has been recovered from the ruins. The semicircular theatre is exquisite, and behind it is a square which once comprised 70 offices, each connected with one of Rome's major trading partners. Mosaics still depict not only the region but also the chief produce of these centres, so that Sabrata in North Africa, for example, is shown with an elephant. A Mithraeum of the seven spheres is decorated with a mosaic that depicts the signs of the zodiac and the seven circles of the planets. Juno, Minerva and Jupiter share a great temple. Other temples are dedicated to Cupid and Psyche and to unconquered Hercules.

Modern Ostia, to the east of the ancient settlement, is also quite old. The Tiber still afforded the spot an important strategic function; tolls brought in a goodly revenue; and in the first half of the ninth century Pope Gregory IV decided to fortify the village. Six hundred years later Pope Martin VI defended it with a new tower, around which was built a renaissance fortress commissioned by Cardinal Giuliano della Rovere (later Julius II) from Baccio Pontelli in 1485. The cardinal also commissioned the little church of Sant'Aurea, which houses what is probably the gravestone of St Augustine's mother, who died in 387. Ostia looked set for a revival of its fortunes, but the Tiber flooded in 1557, perversely changed it course and left the place stranded. The village, though it still retains its walls and has utilized its fortress as an archaeological museum, lost all hope of commercial prosperity when it was bypassed by the Fiumicino canal in 1613.

Season and weather permitting, this may be an opportune moment to take the train onwards for a swim at Rome's seaside resort, the Lido di Ostia, where you will find an ample range of hotels and eating places, and easy connections back to the city.

Three charioteers enjoy a ride beside a mer-man in the mosaics of Ostia Antica. The abandonment of the settlement after the silting-up of the harbour explains the excellent state of preservation of the floors in many of Ostia's buildings.

6
Papal city

....

CASTEL SANT'ANGELO *to* THE VATICAN

Our final tour is of the trapezoidal enclave which is today the heart of the Catholic church and the personal fief of the pope. Our tour of the area begins beside the Tiber, at Castel Sant'Angelo, the mausoleum built by the emperor Hadrian, and since used as a fort, a prison and a museum. Then we walk into the smallest state in the world, climbing into Bernini's superb Piazza San Pietro. The great basilica is the heir of that begun by Constantine and completed by his son Constantius. In exploring it we shall discover astonishing survivals from Old St Peter's, such as Giotto's mosaic of Jesus walking on the water, which now embellishes the ceiling of the portico.

New St Peter's is a complex building in which several of the greatest sixteenth and seventeenth-century architects had a hand. Inside we shall walk around its superb treasures, beginning with the Pietà, the only statue which Michelangelo signed, admiring Bernini's famous baldacchino, and ending with monuments which startle the British by celebrating some of our exiled Stuarts. After ascending to the dome and visiting the crypt, we walk to the Vatican museums with their unrivalled collections of antique statues, renaissance paintings and frescoes and religious art of nearly two millennia.

CASTEL SANT'ANGELO on the right bank of the River Tiber – a massive building, 64 metres in diameter – was begun in AD 130 by the emperor Hadrian to serve as his own tomb and that of his successors. Antoninus Pius finished it in 139. A cylinder rose above a huge square base, clad in travertine, filled with earth to support cypress trees and statues, and crowned by a mound that bore the emperor's tomb. The mausoleum is dubbed 'the castle of the holy angel' because in 590 Pope Gregory the Great, crossing the river to pray for an end to the pestilence which was afflicting the city, had a vision of an angel, on top of the building, sheathing a sword to symbolize the cessation of the plague. The castle, like papal Rome itself, was repeatedly

OPPOSITE *The dome of St Peter's rises above the Ponte Sant'Angelo. The Via della Conciliazione was driven through the old streets of the Borgo to provide a grand vista of the basilica.*

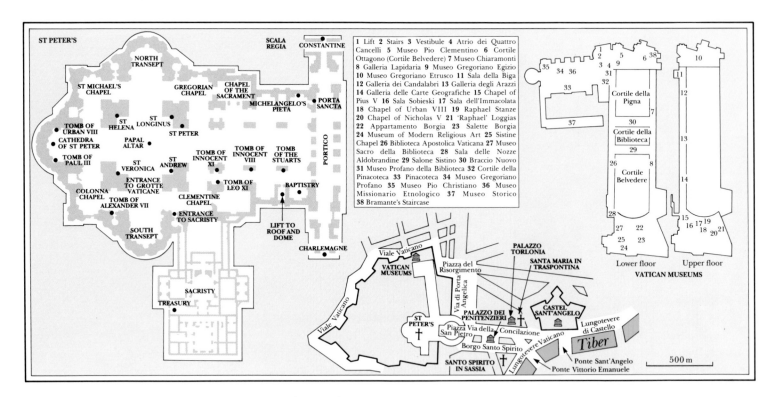

PAPAL CITY

besieged and restored. From Castel Sant'Angelo a covered passageway (the Passetto) leads directly to the Vatican, enabling popes to take refuge here in time of trouble. The octagonal towers at the angles of the building (the work of Antonio da Sangallo the Elder) modified its structure without destroying its defensive look. Outer ramparts were added in the mid sixteenth century during the pontificate of Pius IV, and a marble statue of an angel (since 1752 put inside and replaced by a more durable bronze one) was added to crown the whole building.

In view of its formidable past, the castle rightly houses today a museum of arms and armour, entered by the original doorway of the mausoleum. Passageways lead through the ancient structure to the hall which houses the marble angel. In a courtyard is a well, placed here (as the coat of arms reveals) by the Borgia pope Alexander VI. The castle progressively loses its martial aspect as a staircase climbs to the bathroom of Pope Clement VII, prettily frescoed by Giulio Romano. Frescoes of scenes from the Old Testament and from the life of Alexander the Great by Perino del Vaga and Pellegrino Tibaldi decorate the Pauline rooms. In the next room Perseus appears, amongst maidens and unicorns, by del Vaga. The finest part of Castel Sant'Angelo must be the Chapel of Leo X, simply because of its façade by Michelangelo. The topmost terrace offers a fine panorama of the neighbouring city, as well as a frisson of musical delight, since from here the vengeful Tosca in Puccini's opera leaped to her death.

The balustrades of the five-arched **PONTE SANT'ANGELO**, built by the emperor Hadrian in 136, are graced by twelve statues – saints Peter and Paul, and ten angels done by Bernini's pupils. The first two angels carry respectively the spear which pierced the side of the crucified Christ and the sponge which was filled with vinegar to slake his thirst. The fifteenth-century statues of saints Peter and Paul, carrying the keys of the Kingdom of Heaven and a sword, were set up here in the mid sixteenth century.

Walk west alongside the river to the far end of Lungotevere Vaticano to reach **PONTE VITTORIO EMANUELE**, a graceful early twentieth-century bridge of three arches, built of brick and stone, from which you can admire the even greater elegance of Ponte Sant'Angelo. Another ruined bridge, less famous than the Ponte Rotto, can also be spotted in the Tiber, known for some reason as the Ponte Neroniano. Julius II planned to rebuild it in the early sixteenth century, but died before his plans were realized.

At the west end of Lungotevere Vaticano, the Borgo Santo Spirito leads to the church of **SANTO SPIRITO IN SASSIA**. From its façade, added by Ottavio Mascherino in 1585 and from the rebuilding by Antonio da Sangallo the Younger 45 years earlier, it would be difficult to guess that this church was founded for Anglo-Saxon pilgrims by the warrior King Ine of Wessex, who had abdicated in 726 to die in Rome shortly after. Sassia, in the title of the church, derives from Saxony. Another king of Wessex, Aethelwulf, the father of Alfred the Great, re-endowed the church and a nearby hospice with money known as Peter's Pence, a tax which proved a bone of contention between the English clergy and the papacy until King Henry VIII abolished it in 1534. Baccio Pontelli built the campanile of this church, and beside it still stands the hospital founded by Innocent III in about 1198 and beautifully rebuilt in the second half of the sixteenth century for Pope Sixtus V.

Cross Borgo Santo Spirito and take the narrow street alongside the **PALAZZO DEI PENITENZIERI**, the home of the Penitentiaries who hear confessions in St Peter's, to reach Via della Conciliazione. This handsome street was conceived by Benito Mussolini as a noble approach to St Peter's. Its name – the 'Street of Conciliation' – marks the end of the strife that had existed between the papacy and the Italian state since Pope Pius IX had forbidden Catholics to participate in the political life of the Italian kingdom and shut himself up as a prisoner in the Vatican. His successor-but-one, Pius X, discreetly opened up channels of communication with the political authorities, and in 1929 Pius XI negotiated a treaty with Mussolini, then prime minister, which for the first time recognized Italy as a kingdom. In return, Mussolini agreed to accept Catholicism as the official religion of the country, and the papacy was indemnified for the loss of its former states.

By this Lateran Treaty, the Vatican City was recognized as a new, independent state, governed under the absolute power of the pope. The Vatican then issued six basic laws, proclaiming the rights of its citizens. Thus was set up the smallest independent state in the world, just under 45 hectares in area. Today a few other parts of Rome, although belonging to the republic of Italy, are also regarded as extra-territorial. These include the papal palace at Castel Gandolfo, the Vatican radio station at Santa Maria di Galeria, and the basilicas of San Paolo fuori le Mura, Santa Maria Maggiore and San Giovanni in Laterano. Like the Vatican City, they are not required to pay taxes to the republic and their freedom from expropriation is guaranteed by law.

This is the legal basis for this trapezoidal enclave in the city of Rome on the right bank of the Tiber. It is bounded by massive medieval and renaissance walls, except the opening of Piazza San Pietro (St Peter's Square) ahead, parts of which can be glimpsed along the streets leading off to the right of Via della Conciliazione. The main thoroughfare incorporates several fine buildings from the past. **SANTA MARIA IN TRASPONTINA**, the headquarters of the Carmelite nuns, stands a little way back towards Castel Sant'Angelo, on the opposite side of the road. Founded in 1566 by a Lombard cardinal who was later elected Pope Pius V (and canonized after

One of the twin fountains and part of the massive colonnade of Piazza San Pietro, on which the coat of arms incorporates the escutcheon of Pope Alexander VII Chigi.

his death), this is a sumptuous building. Its chief treasure is the pillar to which St Peter is said to have been tied for scourging, as a prelude to his crucifixion. Next to the church, the **PALAZZO TORLONIA**, built by Antonio Montecavallo for Cardinal Adriano da Corneto between 1496 and 1504, is a Palazzo della Cancelleria in miniature.

The **PIAZZA SAN PIETRO** centres on an obelisk with four lions surrounded by luxurious lamps and flanked by two fountains. The obelisk came originally from Heliopolis, and its first resting place in Rome was in Caligula's circus. In 1586, 800 workmen toiled to raise it in its present position. Around this obelisk, Gianlorenzo Bernini constructed (between 1657 and 1663) two semicircular sets of colonnades. Enhancing their grandeur are four rows of travertine columns on the balustrade, topped with 140 statues of saints and martyrs. Pope Alexander VII, who commissioned the work, made sure that posterity remembered this by having his name inscribed six times on the colonnades, and his coat of arms repeated on the balustrade.

Holding the key of the kingdom of heaven, Giuseppi de Fabris's St Peter guards the entrance to his church, Pius IX commissioned it, and the statue of St Paul opposite by Adamo Tadolini, as replacements for older statues.

As an approach to the great church this piazza is magnificent. It is also uncluttered, since it must cater for the crowds who throng here for the papal blessing. The church itself is designed for the same purpose. Hilaire Belloc, who attended the coronation of Pope Pius XII in 1939, could be pardoned afterwards for the hyperbole of describing **ST PETER'S** as 'the only architectural work of Man which has exactly fulfilled its object'. The predecessor of this remarkable building was a basilica begun by Constantine in the second decade of the fourth century and constantly embellished since then. A new St Peter's was first mooted when Leon Battista Alberti discovered that the south wall was listing by some 2 metres.

Many of the greatest architects and artists of the Italian Renaissance were, at various stages, employed on the new church. Donato Bramante planned the building as a Greek cross with four great piers to support a cupola. After his death in 1514, three architects, Raphael, Giuliano da Sangallo and Fra Giovanni Giocondo, were assigned the work, and they changed Bramante's Greek cross into a Latin one. Baldassare Peruzzi reverted to Bramante's design in 1520, and very little work was done until the reign of Pope Paul III, when Antonio da Sangallo the Younger became chief architect of the new building and reverted to the Latin cross plan.

After Peruzzi's death in 1546, Paul appointed Michelangelo as architect in chief, and he continued in charge under two successive popes. The drum of his dome was finished by the time of his death in 1564, and the great dome was completed by Giacomo Barozzi da Vignola. Throughout this time, worship continued in the apse of Old St Peter's, which was not demolished until the papacy of Clement VIII (1592–1605). Finally, Carlo Maderno built a new apse, which emphasized the Latin cross design by extending the nave further to the east, demolishing the incomplete façade.

Paul V, the reigning pontiff when the church was finished in 1612, had his name inscribed on the pediment of the façade. Today we climb a triple flight of steps (flanked by statues of saints Peter and Paul) to Maderno's portico, its entablature supported on eight columns and four pilasters. Statues of Jesus and eleven of his apostles stand on the balustrade. The missing apostle is St Peter himself, who is buried inside the church. Maderno made up for him on the balustrade with a statue of St John the Baptist.

At either end of the portico is an equestrian statue: on the left, Charlemagne by Agostino Cornacchini; and on the right, the magnificent Constantine, by Bernini. This statue is at the foot of the Scala Regia, Bernini's last great work, which narrows as it rises making it appear far longer than it really is.

Of the five bronze doors giving access to the church, the centre one is from Old St Peter's. Its mid fifteenth-century reliefs, finished by Antonio Filarete, depict Pope Eugenius IV kneeling to receive the keys of the Kingdom of Heaven from St Peter, who is then shown crucified amidst a crowd of Romans and Jews. Other reliefs depict visitors to the Council of Florence over which he presided. Did Filarete or the pope decide that those honoured here should be Africans, Greeks and Ethiopians? Jesus and Mary are also portrayed; and above this door is a much restored mosaic supposedly by Giotto, which was also rescued from the older church. As is customary in papal churches, the bronze door at the extreme right (the Porta Santa) is opened only every 25 years. On it is Christ crucified, his bronze knee polished with the touch of many hands. Pope John XXIII appears on the next door. The door to the left of the central one depicts martyrdom, with an unpleasant degree of sadism, and the reliefs on the fifth door seem only to reveal how poor that technique has become since the days of Filarete.

Inside, your eyes are first drawn to Bramante's gilded and coffered ceiling, then to the bronze baldacchino which Bernini created over the tomb of St Peter. Invariably, however, there is a crowd before the chapel on the right where, sheltered behind bullet-proof glass, is Michelangelo's marble Pietà. Michelangelo was 25 when he created this statue of the Virgin Mary, – the only one that he signed, on the ribbon falling from her left shoulder.

Beside the pier to the right of the dome, is Arnolfo di Cambio's seated bronze statue of St Peter, his foot completely smoothed by the kisses and touches of the faithful. In a roundel above is a portrait of Pope Pius IX, since he paid for the costly red and gold ornament around the throne and the canopy above it. Of the four huge statues in the niches of the piers which support the dome, only one, St Longinus, in the niche near the enthroned Peter, is by Bernini, and his exuberance shames the three other inferior sculptures of saints Helena, Veronica and Andrew.

Pope Urban VIII unveiled Bernini's baldacchino in 1633, and the Barberini bees of his family coat of arms swarm over the foliage of the barley-sugar columns which spin up to the angels who support its canopy. Steps lead down to the most sacred spot in the church, Maderno's marbled confessio, above which burn oil lamps.

Bernini's equestrian statue of Constantine at the foot of the Scala Regia matches that of Charlemagne at the far left of the portico of St Peter's.

At the end of the second century a priest named Gaius claimed that the triumphal tomb of St Peter was situated on the Vatican Hill (while St Paul, he asserted, had a similar tomb on the Via Ostia). Constantine levelled the top of the hill because he believed that its mausoleum contained Peter's grave, and over it he built his basilica. Excavations intended to determine whether this could really be the burial-place of St Peter were authorized in 1939 by Pope Pius XII. Among the bones the archaeologists discovered were those of a large-framed man who lived in the first century AD. Following this work the pope's response was admirably judicious. Asked whether the tomb of St Peter had been found, he answered, 'Beyond all doubt, yes.' To the question whether the bones were those of the saint, he replied, 'It is impossible to prove with certainty that they belong to the body of the apostle.'

Michelangelo's great dome rises above, its pendentives filled with mosaics of the four evangelists, the frieze below the dome inscribed in Latin with Christ's words 'You are Peter, and on this rock shall I build my church, and I shall give you the keys of the kingdom.'

The entrance to the crypt (*Grotte Vaticane*) is in the south-east pier near the statue of St Andrew. These lie between the levels of the old and new churches, and contain the sarcophagi of renaissance and twentieth-century popes and artefacts saved from Old St Peter's. Save this visit until you have explored the rest of the church, because the exit is outside the main door.

At the west end of the church, beyond the baldacchino, is the Cathédra, the ancient wooden papal throne, encased in bronze and admired by the statues of the four doctors of the church – the whole another glamorous conception by Bernini. Above the throne he created a riot of gilded angels, surrounding a window in which is depicted the Holy Spirit in the form of a dove. Of the two statues of the popes whose tombs flank it all, Paul III, sculpted on the left by Guglielmo della Porta, looks much humbler than the Urban VIII sculpted by Bernini on the right.

At this point, St Peter's might seem as much a house of stupendous religious art as a house of God. Left of the apse, in the Colonna Chapel is a relief by Alessandro Algardi of St Leo driving Attila the Hun from Rome. Then, against the wall of this aisle, Bernini surpassed himself in his monument to Pope Alexander VII. The pope, who sports a little moustache and neatly trimmed beard, has laid aside his tiara and prays bareheaded. Below him a huge red and white marble drapery is being lifted by a skeleton, whose bony claws hold up an hourglass. The doorway beneath the statue has become Alexander's symbolic tomb. To the right of the pope is a lady with her foot on a globe representing the Mediterranean, and on his left another woman presents her baby to him.

More splendid tombs are situated in the south aisle, two of them between the third set of pillars from the west end of the church. On one side Algardi's statue of the Medici pope Leo XI sits blessing us, while a woman on his right pours out money and a relief below depicts scenes from his life.

OPPOSITE *Bernini's baldacchino over the burial place of St Peter, and the interior of the dome. The inscription 'You are Peter and on this rock I shall build my church', is legible round the dome and in the roundel St John the Evangelist composes his gospel.*

On the other side, Innocent XI, in a statue designed by Carlo Maratta, sits regally above a scene of slaughter, showing Jan Sobieski – King Jan of Poland – relieving Vienna in 1683.

Between the next set of pillars is a rare survival from Old St Peter's: Antonio Pollaiuolo's tomb of Pope Innocent VIII. The pope is carrying the head of a spear, representing the lance with which St Longinus pierced the side of crucified Christ, given to him by the Ottoman Sultan in gratitude for the pope's keeping his rival hostage in Rome.

There is a special British interest in the fascinating monuments between the last pair of pillars in this aisle. One was sculpted by Canova for the classical tomb of Cardinal Henry of York, last of the Stuarts. He was Bishop of Frascati, and when the French Revolution plundered his fortune and forced him into exile in Venice, King George II gave him a pension of £4000. His bust is here flanked with those of James and Charles Edward Stuart, respectively the Old and Young Pretenders to the British throne. Opposite is the tomb and portrait of the Old Pretender's wife, Maria Clementina Sobieski, although she was never Queen of England, Scotland and Ireland, as the inscription claims.

The baptistry, at the very end of the aisle, has a porphyry font with a curious history, for once it was the sarcophagus of the emperor Otto II. He was later ejected from it and lies buried in the Vatican grottoes. The painting of the baptism of Jesus behind this font is by Carlo Maratta. An archway beside the baptistry allows you to take the lift up to the dome of St Peter's. From the terrace you can look out over the smaller domes and the Sistine Chapel, admire Michelangelo's splendid dome and see across to the Alban Hills. Then you climb the steps within the dome as far as the first gallery, which affords a vertiginous view to the floor of the basilica 53 metres below. From here a yet more taxing curving staircase rises to the spiral one which takes you on between the inner and outer shells of the dome to the terrace under the lantern. The view here is superb particularly of the Vatican palaces with their courtyards and over the high walls of the Vatican gardens. On a clear day you can see virtually all of Rome and as far as the Tyrhennian coast.

To visit the **VATICAN MUSEUMS** and the **SISTINE CHAPEL**, walk back into the Piazza San Pietro, past the Swiss Guards with their halberds and bee-striped pantaloons, past the papal post office and the shops selling religious mementoes. Along the colonnades on the left you reach Via di Porta Angelica, with its tea room, snack bars, trinket shops and stalls. Follow the massive walls of the Vatican, signposted to direct visitors to the museums.

An impressive modern staircase, built in 1932 by Giuseppe Momo and Antonio Maraini, coils from the museum entrance to a courtyard which looks out on to the dome of St Peter's. The Vatican authorities have provided different itineraries for visitors according to their interest of the museum. These are confusing enough, though all take you through the

ABOVE *The entrance to the Vatican museums is by way of the mighty helicoidal staircase designed in 1932 by Giuseppe Momo with bronze balustrades showing all the papal escutcheons, by Antonio Maraini.*

OPPOSITE *Looking down from the dome of St Peter's to the Piazza San Pietro, which centres on an obelisk set up in Alexandria by Augustus, brought to Rome by Caligula and re-erected here by Domenico Fontana in 1586.*

The Laocoön group. The priest of Apollo and his sons are being crushed and bitten by serpents after they had tried to warn the Trojans against admitting the Greeks' wooden horse.

Sistine Chapel and Raphael's Stanze. I am simply going to describe some of the best-known and well-loved areas and artefacts, and the map on page 158 will help you to pin-point them.

The Vatican Museums and Galleries are formed from a number of different collections, covering an enormous variety of media and periods, among which are: the Museo Profano and the Museo Gregoriano Profano containing the pagan antiquities; the Museo Sacro (early Christian artefacts, including many from the catacombs); the Museo Pio-Christiano; the Appartamento Borgia and the galleries of modern religious art; the Pinacoteca (picture gallery), the Museo Gregoriano Egizio and the Museo Gregoriano Etrusco; the galleries containing maps and Raphael's tapestries; the Museo Pio-Clementino and Museo Chiaramonti (Greek and Roman sculpture); the Biblioteca Apostolica Vaticana (library exhibition rooms); the Museo Storico telling the history of the papacy; the chapels of Nicholas V and Urban VIII, the Raphael Stanze and the Sistine Chapel.

One of the most celebrated statues is that of Laocoön and his two sons, grappling with serpents, a group sculpted in Rome in the first century AD by artists from Rhodes. Today this statue, discovered on the Esquiline Hill in 1506, is displayed in the Cortile Ottagono (Octagonal Courtyard) of the Museo Pio-Clementino (also called the Cortile Belvedere, not to be confused with the main Cortile Belvedere, the large courtyard at the southern end of the Vatican Palace), as are the celebrated Apollo Belvedere, the willowy god copied in the second century AD from a bronze original made six centuries earlier by Leochares. A Roman copy of a fourth-century BC Venus by Praxiteles is in the Gabinetto delle Maschere (Cabinet of Masks).

On the second floor, the sumptuous Galleria dei Candalabri is divided into six sections by ancient Roman marble candelabra; the Galleria degli Arazzi has such delights as tapestries woven in Brussels from cartoons by Raphael's pupils; and the Galleria delle Carte Geografiche was decorated in the sixteenth century with such entrancing maps of Italy that you almost fail to notice the magical stuccoes and frescoes of its barrel-vaulted ceiling.

Raphael's Stanze (rooms), like the Sistine Chapel, have been restored and their colours glow again. They were built for Pope Julius II, who asked the young Raphael to decorate them in 1508, and their frescoes are filled with contemporary allusions. Because of the one-way system, they cannot be visited in chronological order. The first room we see (the *Stanza dell'Incendio di Borgo*) was frescoed for Pope Leo X, who succeeded Julius II in 1513. Consequently this room's paintings glorify previous popes of the same name. It shows Raphael at his fiery best, depicting the *Coronation of Charlemagne by Leo III in St Peter's*, the same pope defending himself against charges of perjury and adultery, the naval battle of Ostia when Pope Leo IV was magnanimous to the vanquished, and a fire which raged in the Borgo in 847. The panic caused by the Borgo fire is vividly conveyed, as naked men leap over walls, a baby in swaddling clothes is let down and an aged man is carried to safety by his son. But help is at hand. Leaning from a window, Pope Leo IV is about to put out the fire with the sign of the cross.

Still more famous are the frescoes in the next of Raphael's rooms, the *Stanza delle Segnatura*, the first room of the group to be frescoed. The first fresco he painted in this room shows the Holy Spirit, the Blessed Virgin Mary and St John the Baptist worshipped by a company of laymen and clerics who include Dante, Fra Angelico and Pope Sixtus IV (the uncle of Julius II). Above a window in this room poets and writers are shown on Parnassus. Raphael's love of antiquity has led him to give a place here to the blind Homer, as well as to Virgil, Dante and Boccaccio. Opposite this scene are depicted the emperor Justinian and Pope Gregory IX among the cardinal virtues. But the most famous work in this room is painted on the remaining wall, where Raphael has depicted the *School of Athens*. A black-haired man, seated by a block and writing, is almost certainly a portrait of Michelangelo, shown as Heraclitus of Ephesus, while the greybeard representing Plato is a portrait of Leonardo da Vinci. One man, in a black hat to the right of the fresco looks out at us – a self portrait of Raphael himself, whose companion in a white hat is the artist Sodoma. In front of them, drawing on a tablet on the floor, Bramante impersonates Euclid.

Raphael had half-finished the *Stanza di Eliodoro* when Julius II died, so he is the hero of the *Mass at Bolsena*, and the *Expulsion of Heliodorus*, whereas Leo features prominently in *Leo I repulsing Attila*. Raphael frescoed for this room the celebrated Mass at Bolsena, when real blood from the sacred host is said to have stained the altar linen. Oddly enough, no blood appears in the fresco, and Julius II is depicted watching the miracle. In another famous scene a dejected St Peter is depicted about to be liberated from prison by the angel. In the 'Attila' scene, Raphael has painted the horses of the Huns as wilder even than their riders, whereas the pope and two cardinals sit meekly on white mules. The room is named after the scene of Heliodorus attempting to steal the treasures of the temple at Jerusalem and being expelled by an angel on horseback. The contemporary relevance of the scene is indicated by the presence of the pope, ever ready in his own time to assert the temporal rights of the papacy over their secular usurpers.

The *Sala di Constantino* was painted to Raphael's designs after his death, for the most part by Giulio Romano. It shows the stirring events of the life of Constantine, including his fake donation, the Battle of Milvian Bridge, the appearance of the cross and his baptism in the baptistry of San Giovanni in Laterano. Amid the frenzy of the battle is painted a dwarf (perhaps one of those unfortunate men whose growth was deliberately stunted from birth by means of drugs usually derived from knotweed, in order to entertain great households), who grins maniacally as he puts on a helmet.

Raphael lived long enough to paint some of the arcades of the loggia of this palace, which Bramante had begun building and the painter completed. While you are in this part of the museum, take care not to miss the nearby

Chapel of Nicholas V, frescoed by Fra Angelico. The frescoes, some of them faded, show clearly the stoning of St Stephen (with the still-to-be-converted Saul holding the cloaks of the tormentors) and, underneath this scene, St Lawrence roasting to death on a griddle.

Directly below the Raphael Stanze is the Appartamento Borgia, the frescoes, by Pinturicchio, having a massively plastic quality. In the Sala dei Santi an elaborate fresco shows the disputation between St Catherine of Alexandria and the emperor Maximian. In the background is the arch of Constantine. The face of Catherine is said to be that of the pope's daughter, Lucrezia, while Pinturicchio himself peeps out from behind the emperor's throne and Antonio da Sangallo is depicted holding a T-square.

Pinturicchio's Annunciation, in the Sala dei Misteri della Fede (Room of the Mysteries of the Faith), is set beneath a classical arch beyond which God the Father launches the dove from heaven. The nativity takes place not in the depth of winter but in springtime, Jesus lying on a rug on the grass, his hand on his chest, as if his parent have brought him out for a picnic. The Borgia pope Alexander VI, tiara on the floor, kneels in front of a dazzling Resurrection. The swarthy pope is much bigger than the sleeping soldier who was meant to be guarding Jesus's tomb. His risen Lord has burst open the coffin lid and is set above it in a mandorla of gold, a theme which must have comforted the pope as he lay dying in this room in 1503. Another soldier, holding a lance and still awake, is a portrait of Alexander's son Cesare Borgia, a great friend of Pinturicchio. Whereas the Sistine Chapel is always packed, often these rooms, whose frescoes I far prefer to Michelangelo's Last Judgment, are quiet and sometimes even empty.

Before you reach the Sistine Chapel you have to pass through some of the Borgia apartments which in 1973 pope Paul VI decided to fill with a horrible collection of modern religious art. Would that some latter-day Napoleon Bonaparte could arise and loot it. A greater problem with the Sistine Chapel is that you have to enter from the wrong end as far as the painting goes, so that you see Michelangelo's frescoes the wrong way round. Nine restorers worked through the 1980s on this chapel. The restoration has proved controversial, with some experts declaring that much of Michelangelo's work has been ruined. Undoubtedly it has been vigorously renewed, and Michelangelo's colours are astonishingly luminous. The famous finger of God which charges Adam with life has been completely repainted, but this boldness may be defended by the fact that this was not the original work of Michelangelo but of his admirer Daniele Carnevali. In addition it must be said that the great work would scarcely be visible at all by now, save for such restorations over the centuries. Even in Michelangelo's own lifetime, mould was alarmingly appearing on the painting.

What the newly restored luminosity cannot conceal is the essential pessimism of this vast project. From the shame of Noah's nakedness to the Last Judgment there is scarcely a hint of the drama of man's salvation.

OPPOSITE *Raphael's celebrated* School of Athens *is the epitome of high renaissance painting and thought, propounding the example of ancient Greek philosophers and adapting, in a masterly fashion, the laws of linear perspective so that the fresco could be seen coherently from more than one viewpoint.*

Michelangelo believed that the older one grew, the less chance one had of escaping hell. Tortured by unrequited love, in part homosexual – 'tormented by the body's fierce demands', as one of his poems has it – his mood from beginning the work till the completion of the Last Judgment in 1541 grew increasingly black. The Christ who judges on the wall of this chapel is an angry and not a merciful God. Do not forget to look at the frescoes on the walls: they are masterpieces in their own right by Perugino, Pinturrichio and Botticelli, among others.

Until 1587, there were no buildings between the two long ranges running down the hill, but the Salone Sistina was built between then and 1589 by Domenico Fontana, and the Braccio Nuovo (New Wing) in 1817–22 by Raffaele Stern for Pius II. The Salone Sistina is used to display the Vatican Treasure – gifts to the papacy – which is changed annually, The Braccio Nuovo teems with busts and statues of emperors and their gods. A huge personification of the Nile reclines on a sphinx, while his little ones clamber about him. One of the most famous items in this wing is the *Augustus of Prima Porta*, found in 1863 in the Villa of Livia, 12 kilometres away from Rome on the Via Flaminia.

The way to the Pinacoteca is reached across the courtyard where the entrance to the museums is situated. Each room is filled with masterpieces, many of them looted by Napoleon and returned by the Congress of Vienna in 1815, with the happy stipulation that the general public was allowed to see them. As a result works of art hang here outside their natural context, in particular three masterpieces by Raphael (his *Transfiguration*, from the church of San Pietro in Montorio, his *Coronation of the Virgin*, from the church of San Francesco in Perugia, and his *Madonna of Foligno*, which served as the altarpiece of Santa Maria in Aracoeli). Whatever the loss to the churches, to be able to see these pictures hanging together is a total delight.

In the earlier rooms among the paintings of the Umbrian school, there is an attractive picture of St Jerome accompanied by a sad looking lion, the work of Raphael's father, Giovanni Santi. Another altarpiece intended for no less an exalted position as the high altar of St Peter's, is the Stefaneschi Triptych by Giotto, one of its six panels with a background in which the Tuscan landscape is mingled with the topography of Rome. Fra Angelico's series of episodes from the life of St Nicholas of Bari depicts the original Santa Claus handing out gifts and looking after sailors.

Ten superb tapestries designed by Raphael for the Sistine Chapel are familiar to British art lovers since their cartoons (reversed, as in all such works) are in London's Victoria and Albert Museum. The three altarpieces by Raphael already mentioned are stunning, and on analysis turn out to be surprisingly alike in their composition. Intended to carry the worshipper in spirit to Heaven, each depicts onlookers looking up at some miraculous act of grace. That said, the tone of each is quite different. The most animated is undoubtedly the *Transfiguration*, its vivacity enhanced by the use of a multi-

plicity of colours: greens, blues, pinks, yellows and the white, billowing garments and cloak of the transfigured Christ, who with Moses and Elijah floats in the sky. In the Bible story only his three closest disciples were present at the transfiguration, but Raphael, painting in the last year of his life, has included an extraordinarily vivid assembly of onlookers. Then you spot that only one of them, a boy who is almost fainting with ecstasy, is actually observing the transfiguration, while everyone else looks at him and his family. On the left of the *Transfiguration* Raphael's *Madonna of Foligno* exudes calm. Two saints and a naked cherub look up at her, as does the man who commissioned the painting, while St John the Baptist, with a shaggy coat and even more dishevelled hair, gazes out at us and points up to the Virgin and Child. In the pastoral scene behind the cherub is a rainbow. In contrast to the other two paintings, the design of the *Coronation of the Virgin*, which hangs on the right of the *Transfiguration*, contrives to cut the painting into two almost completely separate halves. The onlookers stand around her empty tomb, now filled with lilies. Above the clouds, musicians play as Christ raises the diadem over the head of his mother and little winged heads softly whirr in the ether above.

Giotto's Stefaneschi triptych in the Pinacotheca was commissioned by Cardinal Stefaneschi for the high altar of Old St Peter's. He can be seen kneeling in the foreground of the central panel.

Leonardo da Vinci's *St Jerome* dominates the next room, squatting among the rocks, his head almost skull-like in its emaciation, the lion curled at his feet far fiercer than that of Giovanni Santi. Then the masters of drama put in their appearance: Caravaggio, with a foreshortened *Deposition*; a ghastly *Martyrdom of St Erasmus* by Nicolas Poussin, in which the saint's tormentors are rolling out his intestines; and Domenichino's *Last Communion of St Jerome*, in which the dying and half-naked desert saint is fed the viaticum by richly dressed ecclesiastics. It is good to avert one's eyes from both of these paintings for a glimpse through the windows of the lawns and fountains of the Vatican Gardens. By contrast with these paintings, Titian's *Madonna of the Frari* (painted in 1528 for the Venetian church of that name), although it included a semi-nude and punctured St Sebastian, seems tame.

Michelangelo's remarkable model for the dome of St Peter's (or rather a copy of it), its sections numbered and lettered, occupies a whole room. And the last room of all contains, unexpectedly, Sir Thomas Lawrence's portrait of King George IV in his garter robes. Painted when the artist was at the height of his powers, it was commissioned by Pius VII when Lawrence visited Rome in 1819 to paint both the pope and his secretary of state, Cardinal Ercole Consalvi. Lawrence's portrait of Pius VII hangs in Windsor Castle.

Our glimpse through the window of the Pinacoteca is a reminder that the Vatican is set in gardens which three days a week are open for guided tours. Parterres, a rock garden, woodlands and arched pathways are still set out as they were in the seventeenth century. Carlo Maderno designed one of his celebrated fountains for these gardens, today known as the Fountain of the Galley after the model galley, made of lead and placed in its basin by Pope Clement VI. Giovanni Vasanzio designed an apparently natural rock fountain, above which rises a gigantic stone eagle. Once the gardens were decorated with ancient statues, such as the *Laocoön* and the *Apollo Belvedere*. And Villa Pia is a casino designed for Pope Pius IV by Piero Ligorio in the 1560s in the form of an oval courtyard, graced with sculptures and a fountain, and inspired by the ruins of the temple of Praeneste at Palestrina.

Because the museums are so vast and are filled with so many outstanding paintings and sculptures, each time you visit you will discover new delights. It is here above all that the importance to this city of the artistic and cultural patronage of the popes can be seen, in the sheer volume of works they commissioned and collected for the glory of God, themselves and Rome.

OPPOSITE *Sixtus V appoints Platinus as librarian of the Vatican in this charming painting by Melozzo da Forli.*

TEMPLA DOMVM EXPOSITIS VICOS FORA MOENIA PONTES
VIRGINEAM TRIVII QVOD REPARARIS AQVAM
PRISCA LICET NAVTIS STATVAS DARE COMMODA PORTVS
ET VATICANVM CINGERE SIXTE IVGVM
PLVS TAMEN VRBS DEBET NAM QVAE SQVALORE LATEBAT
CERNITVR IN CELEBRI BIBLIOTHECA LOCO

Appendices

....

CHRONOLOGY OF EVENTS • POPES • EMPERORS
ARTISTS AND PATRONS • OPENING TIMES

CHRONOLOGY OF EVENTS

BC

753	Legendary foundation of Rome by Romulus
750	Roman abduction of Sabine women
616	Accession of Lucius Tarquinius Priscus; Capitol founded
534	Accession of Lucius Tarquinius Superbus, last king of Rome
509	Dedication of Temple of Jupiter Optimus Maximus
507	Junius Brutus and Tarquinius Collatinus first consuls
498	Temple of Saturn founded in the Foro Romano
484	Temple of Castor and Pollux built in the Foro Romano
450	*Lex Publilia* (laws of state) published
390	Gauls sack Rome
366	Temple of Concord built
312	Appian Way begun
264–241	First Punic war
241	Rome gains control of Sicily
220	Circus Flaminius built
218–201	Second Punic war
217	Hannibal victorious at Lake Trasimene
202	Hannibal defeated at Zarna
179	Basilica Aemilia built
164	Basilica Aemilia restored
149–146	Third Punic war
144	Aqua Marcia, first high-level aqueduct, built
73	Revolt of Spartacus and slaves
63	Catiline conspiracy suppressed by Cicero
60	First triumvirate of Caesar, Pompey and Crassus
58	Caesar's campaigns in Gaul
55	Caesar's invasion of Britain
50	Augustus's House of Livia built
48	Caesar defeats Pompey at Pharsalia
44	Caesar becomes dictator for life and is assassinated in the Foro Romano on 15 March
42	Battle of Philippi between Imperialists and Republicans
31	Octavian's forces defeat those of Anthony and Cleopatra at Battle of Actium
27	Octavian first emperor as Augustus
27–25	Agrippa builds original Pantheon
13	Work commences on Ara Pacis Augustae
2	Foro di Augusto built

AD

64	Rome burned in fire lasting six days and reconstructed by Nero
72	Vespasian begins building of Colosseum
80	Colosseum finished by Titus
81	Arch of Titus raised
81–96	Domitian's palace on Palatine constructed
96–8	Foro di Nerva built
113	Trajan's column erected
118	Work commences on Hadrian's villa at Tivoli
118–28	Hadrian rebuilds Pantheon
130	Work starts on Hadrian's Mausoeum
176–80	Column of Marcus Aurelius erected
203	Arch of Septimus Severus built in the Foro Romano
217	Caracalla inaugurates the baths begun by his father

270	Aurelian Wall begun	508	Colosseum and San Giovanni in Laterano damaged by earthquake	1527	Rome sacked by French army
284	Curia (Senate House) rebuilt by Diocletian; Diocletian overhauls the administration of the Empire	536	Belisarius recaptures Rome from Goths	1537	Capitol restored
		546	Totila the Ostrogoth occupies Rome; Belisarius recaptures the city	1626	St Peter's consecrated
306	Basilica of Maxentius begun			1642	Construction begins of new city walls
309	Temple of Romulus Maxentius dedicated; Circus of Maxentius begun	549	Totila retakes Rome	1796	Napoleon invades Rome
		552	Totila defeated in a battle in the Apennines and Rome once more comes under Byzantine control	1798	French occupy Rome and proclaim republic
312	Accession of Constantine the Great after the Battle of the Milvian Bridge; Basilica of Maxentius completed			1809	Napoleon annexes Rome and papal states
		608	Column of Phocas erected	1815	Congress of Vienna returns Rome to pope
		609	Pantheon rededicated as a church	1848	Popular insurrection and free constitution
313	Christians granted freedom of worship under Edict of Milan	800	Charlemagne crowned Emperor by Pope Leo III	1849	Garibaldi enters Rome and repels French troops (April); city besieged (June) and falls (July)
314	San Giovanni in Laterano begun	846	Rome sacked by Saracens		
315	Arch of Constantine built	1300	Pope Boniface VIII proclaims first Holy Year	1861	Kingdom of Italy established; Vittorio Emanuele II
320–9	Basilica built on supposed site of St Peter's burial on Vatican Hill, dedicated to saints Peter and Paul, then St Sebastian and finally St Peter	1308	Clement V forced by Philip V of France to move papacy to Avignon; Lateran palace and San Giovanni in Laterano destroyed by fire	1870	Nationalists reoccupy Rome
				1871	Rome becomes capital of Italy
330	Seat of empire removed to Byzantium; original church of San Lorenzo fuori le Mura built	1347	Cola di Rienzo proclaims a new Roman Republic with himself as Tribune and instigates judicial and social reforms, but is forced to abdicate in December	1878	Death of Vittorio Emanuele; accession of Umberto I
				1900	Assassination of Umberto; accession of Vittorio Emanuele III
337	Constantine's baptism and death			1921	Mussolini's 'March on Rome'; Fascist party established
378	Visigoths defeat imperial army at Adrianople	1348	San Giovanni in Laterano severely damaged and San Paolo fuori de Mura destroyed by earthquakes		
410	Alaric the Goth pillages Rome, plundering pagan temples but sparing Christian churches			1929	Lateran Treaty recognizes Vatican City state
		1354	Cola di Rienzo reinstated, but killed by mob in October	1943	Rome declared 'Open City' after US bombing
420–38	Basilica of Santa Maria Maggiore built	1377	Gregory XI returns papal court to Rome	1944	City briefly occupied by Germans and liberated by Allied troops
452	Rome spared by Attila the Hun	1378–1415	Papal Schism, with two rival curias	1945	Mussolini executed
455	Genseric the Vandal plunders city	1413	Rome invaded by King of Naples	1946	Abdication of Vittorio Emanuele; Umberto II reigns for one month; Italy becomes a republic
468–83	Santo Stefano Rotondo built	1417	Martin V elected as pope; end of Schism		
476	Last emperor, Romulus Augustulus deposed by Odoacer; end of Western Empire	1473–81	Sistine Chapel built for Sixtus IV	1960	17th Olympic Games held in Rome
		1508–12	Michelangelo's frescoes for ceiling of Sistine Chapel	1980	Work commences on restoration of Sistine Chapel frescoes

POPES

Pope	Dates	Pope	Dates	Pope	Dates	Pope	Dates
Peter	42–67	Simplicius	468–83	Leo III	795–816	John XVIII	1004–09
Linus	67–76	Felix III	483–92	Stephen V	816–17	Sergius IV	1009–12
Anacletus I	76–88	Gelasius I	492–6	Paschal I	817–24	Benedict VIII	1012–24
Clement I	88–97	Anastasius II	496–8	Eugenius II	824–7	John XIX	1024–32
Evaristus	97–105	Symmachus	498–514	Valentine	827	Benedict IX	1032–45
Alexander I	105–15	Hormisdas	514–23		(Aug–Sept)	Sylvester III	1045
Sixtus I	115–25	John I	523–6	Gregory IV	827–44		(Jan–March)
Telesphorus	125–36	Felix IV	526–30	Sergius II	844–7	Benedict IX	1045
Hyginus	136–40	Boniface II	530–2	Leo IV	847–55		(April–May;
Pius I	140–55	John II	533–5	Benedict III	855–8		deposed)
Anicetus	155–66	Agapetus I	535–6	Nicholas I	858–67	Gregory VI	1045–6
Soter	166–75	Silverius	536–7	Adrian II	867–72	Clement II	1046–7
Eleutherius	175–89	Vigilius	537–55	John VIII	872–82	Benedict IX	1047–8
Victor I	189–99	Pelagius I	55–61	Marinus I	882–4	Damascus II	1048
Zephyrinus	199–217	John III	561–74	Adrian III	884–5		(July–Aug)
Calixtus I	217–22	Benedict I	574–9	Stephen VI	885–97	Leo IX	1049–54
Urban I	222–30	Pelagius II	579–90	Formosus	891–6	Victor II	1055–7
Pontianus	230–5	Gregory I	590–604	Boniface VI	896	Stephen X	1057–8
Anterus	235–6	Sabinian	604–6		(April)	Nicholas II	1059–61
Fabian	236–50	Boniface III	607	Stephen VII	896–7	Alexander II	1061–73
Cornelius	251–3		(Feb–Nov)	Romanus	897	Gregory VII	1073–85
Lucius I	253–4	Boniface IV	608–15		(Aug–Nov)	Victor III	1086–7
Stephen I	254–7	Deusdedit I	615–18	Theodore II	897	Urban II	1088–99
Sixtus II	257–8	Boniface V	619–25		(Nov–Dec)	Paschal II	1099–1118
Dionysius	259–68	Honorius I	625–38	John IX	898–900	Gelasius II	1118–19
Felix I	269–74	Severinus	638–40	Benedict IV	900–903	Calixtus II	1119–24
Eutychianus	275–83	John IV	640–42	Leo V	903	Honorius II	1124–30
Gaius	283–96	Theodore I	642–9		(July–Sept)	Innocent II	1130–43
Marcellinus	296–304	Martin I	649–54	Sergius III	904–11	Celestine II	1143–4
Marcellus I	308–9	Eugenius I	654–7	Anastasius III	911–13	Lucius II	1144–5
Eusebius	309–10	Vitalian	657–72	Lando	913–14	Eugenius III	1145–53
Miltiades	311–14	Deusdedit II	672–6	John X	914–28	Anastasius IV	1153–4
Sylvester I	314–35	Donus	676–8	Leo VI	928	Adrian IV	1154–9
Marcus	336	Agatho	678–81		(May–Dec)	Alexander III	1159–81
	(Jan–Oct)	Leo II	682–3	Stephen VIII	929–31	Lucius III	1181–5
Julius I	337–52	Benedict II	684–5	John XI	931–5	Urban III	1185–7
Liberius	352–55	John V	685–6	Leo VII	936–9	Gregory VIII	1187
Felix II	355–58	Conon	686–7	Stephen IX	939–42		(Oct–Dec)
Liberius	358–66	Sergius I	687–701	Marinus II	942–6	Clement III	1187–91
Damasus I	366–84	John VI	701–5	Agapetus II	946–55	Celestine III	1191–8
Siricius	384–99	John VII	705–7	John XII	955–64	Innocent III	1198–1216
Anastasius I	399–401	Sisinnius	708	Leo VIII	963–5	Honorius III	1216–27
Innocent I	401–17		(Jan–Feb)	Benedict V	964–6	Gregory IX	1227–41
Zosimus	417–18	Constantine	708–15	John XIII	965–72	Celestine IV	1241
Boniface I	418–22	Gregory II	715–31	Benedict VI	973–4		(Oct–Nov)
Celestine I	422–32	Gregory III	731–41	Benedict VII	974–83	Innocent IV	1243–54
Sixtus III	432–40	Zacharias	741–52	John XIV	983–4	Alexander IV	1254–61
Leo I	440–61	Stephen II	752 (Mar)	John XV	985–96	Urban IV	1261–4
Hilarius	461–8	Stephen III	752–7	Gregory V	996–9	Clement IV	1265–8
		Paul I	757–67	Sylvester II	999–1003	Gregory X	1271–76
		Stephen IV	768–72	John XVII	1003	Innocent V	1276
		Adrian I	772–95		(June–Dec)		(Jan–June)

Adrian V	1276 (July–Aug)
John XXI	1276–7
Nicholas III	1277–80
Martin IV	1281–5
Honorius IV	1285–7
Nicholas IV	1288–92
Celestine V	1294 (July–Dec)
Boniface VIII	1294–1303
Benedict XI	1303–04

Papal exile in Avignon
1309–77

Clement V	1305–14
John XXII	1316–34
Benedict XII	1334–42
Clement VI	1342–52
Innocent VI	1352–62
Urban V	1362–70
Gregory XI	1370–8

End of papal exile in Avignon;
Papal Schism

Urban VI	1378–89
Boniface IX	1389–1404
Innocent VII	1404–06
Gregory XII	1406–15

End of Papal Schism

Martin V	1417–31
Eugenius IV	1431–47
Nicholas V	1447–55
Calixtus III	1455–8
Pius II	1458–64
Paul II	1464–71
Sixtus IV	1471–84
Innocent VIII	1484–92
Alexander VI	1492–1503
Pius III	1503 (Sept–Oct)
Julius II	1503–13
Leo X	1513–21
Adrian VI	1522–3
Clement VII	1523–34
Paul III	1534–49
Julius III	1550–5
Marcellus II	1555 (April)
Paul IV	1555–9
Pius IV	1559–65
Pius V	1566–72
Gregory XIII	1572–85
Sixtus V	1585–90
Urban VII	1590 (Sept)
Gregory XIV	1590–1
Innocent IX	1591 (Oct–Dec)
Clement VIII	1592–1605
Leo XI	1605 (April)
Paul V	1605–21
Gregory XV	1621–3
Urban VIII	1623–44
Innocent X	1644–55
Alexander VII	1655–67
Clement IX	1667–9
Clement X	1670–6
Innocent XI	1676–89
Alexander VIII	1689–91
Innocent XII	1691–1700
Clement XI	1700–21
Innocent XIII	1721–4
Benedict XIII	1724–30
Clement XII	1730–40
Benedict XIV	1740–58
Clement XIII	1758–69
Clement XIV	1769–74
Pius VI	1775–99
Pius VII	1800–23
Leo XII	1823–9
Pius VIII	1829–30
Gregory XVI	1831–46
Pius IX	1846–78
Leo XIII	1878–1903
Pius X	1903–14
Benedict XV	1914–22
Pius XI	1922–39
Pius XII	1939–58
John XXIII	1958–63
Paul VI	1963–78
John Paul I	1978 (Aug–Sept)
John Paul II	1978–

EMPERORS

Augustus	27 BC–AD 14
Tiberius	14–37
Caligula	37–41
Claudius I	41–54
Nero	54–68
Galba	68–9
Otho	69
Vitellius	69
Vespasian	69–70
Titus	79–81
Domitian	81–96
Nerva	96–8
Trajan	98–117
Hadrian	117–38
Antoninus Pius	138–61
Marcus Aurelius and Lucius Verus	161–9
Marcus Aurelius	169–77
Marcus Aurelius and Commodus	177–80
Commodus	180–92
Pertinax	193
Didius Julianus	193
Septimius Severus	193–8
Septimius Severus and Caracalla	198–209
Septimius Severus, Caracalla and Geta	209–11
Caracalla and Geta	211–12
Caracalla	212–17
Macrinus	217–18
Elagabalus	218–22
Alexander Severus	222–35
Maximinus I	235–8
Gordian I and Gordian II	238
Balbinus and Pupienus Maximus	238
Gordian III	238–44
Philip	244–9
Decius	249–51
Gallus and Hostilianus	251
Gallus and Volusian	251–3
Valerian and Gallienus	253–60
Gallienus	260–8
Claudius II	268–70
Quintillus	270
Aurelian	270–7
Tacitus	275–6
Florian	276
Probus	276–82
Carus	282–3
Numerian	283–4
Carinus	283–5
Diocletian	284–286
Diocletian and Maximian	286–305
Constantius I	305–6
Galerius	305–10
Licinius	308–24
Flavius Severus	306–7
Maxentius	306–12
Maximinus II	309–13
Constantine I	306–37
Constantine II and Constans	337–40
Constans	340–50
Constantius II	350–61
Magnentius	350–3
Julian	361–3
Jovian	363–4
Valentinian I	364–7
Gratian and Valentinian II	375–83
Valentinian II	383–92
Theodosius I and Honorius	393–5
Honorius	395–423
Valentinian III	425–55
Petronius Maximus	455
Avitus	455–6
Majorian	457–61
Libius Severus	461–5
Anthemius	467–72
Olybrius	472
Glycerius	473
Julius Nepos	474–5
Romulus Augustulus	475–6

ARTISTS AND PATRONS

Names of churches, palaces, monuments, etc., are those in which important works are found or with which artists and patrons are particularly associated.

Alberti, Leon Battista (1404–72), architect, theorist: author of *Della pittura* (1436); designed Palazzo Venezia.

Alexander VII, Pope (1655–67): patron of Bernini, Pietro da Cortona; founder of Chigi library; his monument by Bernini is in St Peter's.

Algardi, Alessandro (1595–1654), sculptor: tomb of Leo XI; relief of *Pope Leo driving Attila from Rome* in St Peter's.

Angelico, Fra (1400–55), painter: *Last Judgement* triptych in the Palazzo Barberini; and the chapel of Nicholas V in the Vatican, with scenes from the lives of St Stephen and St Lawrence.

Arnolfo di Cambio (*c.* 1245–1302), architect, sculptor.

Bernini, Gianlorenzo (1598–1680), sculptor, architect, painter, patronized by Paul V and Urban VIII: baldacchino, apse, tomb of Urban VIII and monument to Alexander VII in St Peter's; colonnades of Piazza San Pietro; Daniel and Habbakuk in the Chigi Chapel of Santa Maria del Popolo; Cornaro Chapel in Santa Maria della Vittoria; San Pietro in Montorio; Sant'Andrea al Quirinale; Palazzo Barberini; Piazza Barberini; and Piazza Navona fountains..

Borghese, Scipione (1576–1633), cardinal, nephew of Paul V: Villa Borghese; San Sebastiano.

Borromini, Francesco (1599–1667), architect Palazzo Barberini; San Carlo alle Quattro Fontane; oratory of Chiesa Nuova; Sant Ivo alla Sapienza; and Sant'Agnese in Agone.

Botticelli, Sandro (1444/5–1510), painter: Sistine Chapel frescoes.

Bramante, Donato (1444–1514), architect: apse of Santa Maria del Popolo; cloisters of Santa Maria della Pace; and one of architects of new St Peter's.

Canova, Antonio (1757–1822), sculptor: tomb of Clement XIII in St Peter's; and tomb of Clement XIV in Santi Apostoli.

Caravaggio (Michelangelo Merisi) (1573–1610), painter: Santa Maria del Popolo; Pinacoteca Vaticana; the Contarelli Chapel in San Luigi dei Francesi; and Sant 'Agostino.

Carracci, Annibale (1560–1609), painter; Palazzo Colonna; Palazzo Farnese; and Santa Maria del Popolo.

Cavallini, Pietro (1250–1330), painter and mosaicist: San Giorgio in Velabro; Santa Maria in Aracoeli; and Santa Maria in Trastevere.

Chigi, Agostino (1465–1520), banker: commissioned Farnesina (built by Perruzzi); and Chigi Chapel in Santa Maria del Popolo.

Clement VII, Pope (1523–34): commissioned Michelangelo's *Last Judgement* in the Sistine Chapel; and rooms in Castel Sant'Angelo.

Cortona, Pietro da (1596–1669), painter and architect: frescoes Chiesa Nuova; Santa Bibiana; and Palazzo Barberini.

Domenichino (Domenico Zampieri) (1581–1641), painter: Sant'Andrea della Valle; Santa Maria in Trastevere; Santa Maria della Vittoria; Santa Maria degli Angeli; San Pietro in Vincoli; Palazzo Farnese; and Pinacoteca Vaticana.

Donatello (Donato de' Bardi) (1386–1466), sculptor: Santa Maria in Aracoeli; St Peter's Treasury.

Filarete, Antonio (Antonio Averlino) (*c.* 1400–69), sculptor and architect: door reliefs in St Peter's; and San Marco.

Fontana, Carlo (1634–1714), architect: Santa Maria dei Miracoli; San Marcello; Santa Maria del Popolo; Santa Maria in Trastevere; Santi Apostoli; and Palazzo di Montecitorio.

Fontana, Domenico (1543–1607), architect and engineer: streets; piazzas; palaces; churches; fountains; aqueducts; Column of Marcus Aurelius; Palazzo della Cancelleria; Palazzo del Quirinale; Santa Maria Maggiore; Lateran Palace; and San Giovanni in Laterano.

Fontana, Giovanni (1540–1614): Acqua Paola fountain.

Ghirlandaio, Domenico (1449–94), painter: Palazzo Colonna and Sistine Chapel.

Giambologna (Giovanni Bologna) (1529–1608), painter: Palazzo Venezia.

Giotto di Bondone (1267/77–1337), painter: San Giovanni in Laterano; and Stefaneschi triptych in Pinacoteca Vaticana; and mosaics in the portico of St Peter's.

Giulio Romano (*c.* 1492–1546), architect and painter: Farnesina; Santa Maria dell'Anima; Castel Sant'Angelo; and Raphael's Stanze in Vatican.

Gozzoli, Benozzo (*c.* 1420–97), painter: Santa Maria in Aracoeli; and Santa Maria sopra Minerva.

Innocent X, Pope (1644–55): patron of Algardi, Bernini, Borromini; commissioned rebuilding of San Giovanni in Laterano; Fontana dei Quattro Fiumi; his portrait by Velasquez and bust by Bernini are in the Palazzo Doria Pamphilj.

Julius II, Pope (1503–13), patron and intellectual; laid out Via Giulia, Via della Lungara; commissioned Bramante to rebuild St Peter's; enlarged the Vatican forming its classical sculpture collection; commissioned Raphael to decorate the Stanze; gave commissions to Michelangelo for the Sistine Chapel ceiling and his own tomb (which was never completed).

Leo X, Pope (1513–21): patron of Raphael; developed Borgo and Vatican areas; and a chapel in Castel Sant'Angelo.

Lippi, Filippino (*c.* 1457–1504), painter, son of Filippo: Carafa Chapel in Santa Maria sopra Minerva.

Lippi, Fra Filippo (*c.* 1406–69), painter: Palazzo Barberini.

Longhi, Martino the Elder (*fl.* 1570–d. 1591), architect: Palazzo Altemps; Chiesa Nuova; Santa Maria della Consolazione; and Palazzo Senatorio.

Longhi, Martino the Younger (1602–60), architect: San Bartolomeo; and Santi Vicenzo e Anastasio.

Lotti, Lorenzetto (1490–1541), sculptor: Pantheon; Santa Maria dell'Anima; and Chigi Chapel in Santa Maria del Popolo.

Lotto, Lorenzo (1480–1556), painter: Palazzo dei Conservatori; and Palazzo Barberini.

Maderna, Stefano (1576–1636), sculptor: Santa Maria Maggiore

Maderno, Carlo (1556–1629), architect: St Peter's; Sant'Andrea della Valle; Santa Maria della Pace; Santa Maria della Vittoria; Palazzo Borghese; Palazzo Barberini; Palazzo del Quirinale; Palazzo Rospigliosi; Acqua Paola; and Vatican Gardens.

Mantegna, Andrea (1431–1506), painter: Palazzo Venezia.

Martin V, Pope (1417–31): initiated city restoration; Palazzo Colonna; and San Giovanni in Laterano.

Michelangelo Buonarroti (1475–1564), sculptor, architect, painter and poet: Piazza del Campidoglio; Palazzo Senatorio; Palazzo del Museo Capitolino; Palazzo Farnese; Santa Maria degli Angeli; Santa Maria sopra Minerva; Moses in San Pietro in Vincoli; Castel Sant'Angelo; Sistine Chapel frescoes; and *Pietà* in St Peter's.

Nicholas V, Pope (1447–55): patron of Alberti, Fra Angelico, Benozzo Gozzoli, and Giuliano da Sangallo; Palazzo dei Conservatori; Castel Sant'Angelo; Vatican Museums; chapel in Vatican; and founded Vatican Library.

Paul III, Pope (1534–49): patron of Michelangelo; Antonio da Sangallo the Younger; Vasari; Palazzo Farnese; Piazza del Popolo; Piazza del Campidoglio; Palazzo della Cancelleria; Castel Sant'Angelo; St Peter's; Cappella Paolina in Vatican; and Orti Farnesiani on Palatine.

Paul V, Pope (1605–21): St Peter's; Palazzo Borghese; Santa Maria Maggiore (tomb); and Acqua Paola.

Perugino, Pietro (1446–1523), painter: Sistine Chapel.

Peruzzi, Baldassare (1481–1537), architect and painter: St Peter's; Palazzo Altemps; Santa Maria della Pace; and Farnesina.

Piero di Cosimo (1462–1521), painter: Sistine Chapel; Palazzo Barberini.

Pinturicchio (Bernardino di Betto) (1454–1513), painter: Santa Maria in Aracoeli; Santa Maria del Popolo; Appartemento Borgia in the Vatican; and Sistine Chapel.

Piranesi, Giovanni Battista (1720–80), etcher: many of his views of Rome are in the state copperplate printing works in the Via della Stamperia.

Pollaiuolo, Antonio del (1433–98), sculptor and painter: Palazzo dei Conservatori; and St Peter's (including tomb of Innocent VIII).

Porta, Giacomo della (*c.* 1537–1602), architect: Palazzo Senatorio; Gesù; Palazzo Farnese; Palazzo dei Conservatori; San Nicola in Carcere; Acqua Felice; Santa Maria Maggiore; San Giovanni in Laterano; Santa Maria sopra Minerva; San Giovanni dei Fiorentini; and Villa Borghese fountains.

Rainaldi, Carlo (1611–91), architect, son of Girolamo: Santi Apostoli; Santa Maria dei Miracoli; Chiesa Nuova; Santa Maria Maggiore; Sant'Agnese in Agone; and Orti Farnesiani.

Rainaldi, Girolamo (1570–1655), architect: Palazzo Senatorio; Sant'Agnese in Agone; Gesù e Maria; Orti Farnesiani; and Palazzo Pamphilj.

Raphael (Raffaello Sanzio) (1483–1520), painter and architect: Stanze in the Vatican; Sistine Chapel; St Peter's; Chigi Chapel in Santa Maria del Popolo; Sant'Agostino; Santa Maria della Pace; Farnesina; and Palazzo Barberini.

Reni, Guido (1575–1642), painter: Palazzo della Cancelleria; Santa Maria della Concezione dei Cappuccini; Palazzo del Quirinale; Palazzo Rospigliosi; and San Giovanni in Laterano.

Sacchi, Andrea (1559–1661), painter: San Giovanni in Laterano; and St Peter's.

Salvi, Nicolà (1697–1751), architect: Trevi Fountain.

Sangallo, Antonio da, the Elder (1455–1534), architect, brother of Giuliano: Santa Maria di Montserrato; and Castel Sant'Angelo.

Sangallo, Antonio da, the Younger (1483–1546), architect: St Peter's; Santa Maria di Loreto; Santa Maria del Popolo; the Cesi Chapel in Santa Maria della Pace; Santa Maria sopra Minerva; Palazzo Farnese; Piccola Farnesina; Palazzo Baldassini; Bastione del Sangallo; and Castel Sant'Angelo.

Sangallo, Giuliano da (*c.* 1443–1516), architect: Santa Maria Maggiore; and St Peter's.

Sansovino, Andrea (*c.* 1470–1529), sculptor and architect: Santa Maria in Aracoeli; Santa Maria del Popolo; Sant'Agostino; and Santa Maria in Domnica.

Sansovino, Jacopo (*c.* 1486–70), sculptor and architect: San Marcello; Sant'Agostino; Santa Maria di Montserrato; San Giovanni dei Fiorentini; and Santa Croce.

Sarto, Andrea del (1486–1530), painter: Palazzo Spada.

Sixtus IV, Pope (1471–84): patron of Botticelli; Sistine Chapel; Santa Maria del Popolo; Santa Maria della Pace; San Pietro in Vincoli; and Santo Spirito hospital.

Sixtus V, Pope (1585–90): improved and embellished city; patron of Domenico Fontana; San Giovanni in Laterano; Lateran Palace; re-erection of Column of Marcus Aurelius; and resiting of Vatican obelisk.

Torrigiani, Sebastiano (d. 1596), sculptor: Santa Maria Maggiore.

Urban VIII, Pope (1623–44): patron of Carlo Maderno, Bernini, and Borromini; Palazzo Barberini; St Peter's; Vatican; Castel Sant'Angelo; Fontana del Tritone; and Fontana delle Api.

Vasari, Giorgio (1512–74), painter, architect and art historian: Palazzo della Cancelleria; San Pietro in Montorio; Villa Giulia; and San Giovanni Decollato.

Verrocchio, Andrea del (1435–88), painter: Santa Maria sopra Minerva.

Vignola, Giacomo Barozzi da (1507–73), architect: St Peter's; Gesù, Palazzo Farnese; San Giovanni in Laterano; Piazza del Campidoglio; and Orti Farnesiani.

OPENING TIMES

Most churches and public buildings are closed from 12 noon or 1.00 p.m. until 3.30 or 4.00 p.m., and are also liable to be closed to visitors, without notice, during services. Some of the principal churches and those not normally open at standard hours are listed below. Many museums and collections, too, are open only in the morning and closed on Mondays and main public holidays. All hours of opening, including some of those given in the following list, are periodically liable to alteration (winter hours, too, often differ from summer), and it is always advisable, therefore, to check before planning a visit.

Accademia di San Luca, Via della Stamperia: Monday, Wednesday, Friday and last Sunday in month 10.00–1.00.

Ara Pacis, Via di Ripetta: Tuesday to Saturday 9.00–1.30; Sunday 9.00–1.00; also Tuesday and Saturday 3.30–7.00.

Baths of Caracalla, Via delle Terme di Caracalla: Tuesday to Saturday 9.00–6.00; Sunday and Monday 9.00–1.00.

Baths of Diocletian, see Museo Nazionale Romano delle Terme.

Castel Sant'Angelo, Lungotevere Castello: Tuesday to Saturday 9.00–2.00; Monday 9.00–7.30; Sunday 9.00–1.00.

Catacombs of St Calixtus, Via Appia Antica: Thursday to Tuesday 8.30–12.00, 2.30–5.00.

Catacombs of St Sebastian, Via Appia Antica: Friday to Wednesday 9.00–12.00, 2.30–5.00.

Churches, see under saint.

Colosseum, Piazza del Colosseo: daily 9.00–7.00, except Wednesday and Sunday 9.00–1.00.

Foro Romano and Palatine Hill, Via dei Fori Imperiali: daily 9.00–7.00, except Tuesday and Sunday 9.00–2.00.

Galleries:
    Colonna, Via di Pilota: Saturday 9.00–1.00.

    Doria Pamphilj, Piazza del Collegio Romano: Tuesday, Friday to Sunday 10.00–1.00.

    Nazionale d'Arte Antica (Palazzo Barberini), Via delle Quattro Fontane: Monday to Saturday 9.00–2.00; Sunday 9.00–1.00.

    Nazionale d'Arte Antica (Palazzo Corsini), Via della Lungara: Tuesday to Saturday 9.00–7.00; Sunday 9.00–1.00; Monday 9.00–2.00

    Nazionale d'Arte Moderna, Viale delle Belle Arti: Tuesday to Saturday 9.00–2.00; Sunday 9.00–1.00.

    del Palazzo Spada, Piazza Capodiferro: Tuesday to Saturday 9.00–2.00; Sunday 10.00–1.00.

Gesù, Piazza del Gesù closed 12.30–4.30.

Museums;
    Capitoline, Piazza del Campidoglio: Tuesday to Saturday 9.00–2.00; Sunday 9.00–1.30; also Tuesday 5.00–8.00 and Saturday 8.00–11.00.

    Etruscan (Villa Giulia), Viale delle Belle Arti: Tuesday to Saturday 9.00–7.00; Sunday 9.00–1.00.

    Folklore, Piazza Sant'Egidio: Tuesday to Saturday 9.00–1.30; Sunday 9.00–12.30.

    Jewish, Lungotevere Cenci: Monday to Thursday 9.30–2.00, 3.00–5.00; Friday 9.30–1.30; Sunday 9.30–12.00; closed Saturday.

    Keats–Shelley, Piazza di Spagna: Monday to Friday 9.00–1.00, 2.30–5.30.

    Nazionale Romano delle Terme (Baths of Diocletian), Piazza dei Cinquecento: Tuesday to Saturday 9.00–2.00; Sunday 9.00–1.00.

    Rome (Palazzo Braschi), Piazza San Pantaleo: Tuesday to Saturday 9.00–2.00; also Tuesday and Thursday 5.00–8.00; Sunday 9.00–1.00.

    Vatican, Viale Vaticano: Monday to Saturday 8.45–1.00; admission free last Sunday of month.

    Waxworks, Piazza dei Santi Apostoli: 9.00–8.00.

Orti Farnesiani (Farnese Gardens), Clivus Palatinus from Foro Romano: Tuesday to Saturday 9.00–6.00; Sunday 9.00–1.00.

Ostia Antica: Tuesday to Sunday 9.00–12.00, 3.00–6.00.

Palaces:

Barberini, see Galleria Nazionale d'Arte Antica.

Braschi, see Museum of Rome.

dei Conservatori, see Capitoline Museum.

Corsini, see Galleria Nazionale d'Arte Antica.

Doria Pamphilj, see under galleries.

del Museo Capitolino, see under Capitoline Museum.

Nuovo, see under Capitoline Museum.

Spada, see under galleries.

Venezia, Via del Plebiscito: Tuesday to Saturday 9.00–2.00; Sunday 9.00–1.00.

Palatine, see Foro Romano.

Pantheon, Piazza della Rotonda: Monday to Saturday 9.00–7.00; Sunday 9.00–1.00.

Sant'Agnese in Agone, Piazza Navona: 5.00–7.00 p.m. only; festivals 10.00–1.00.

Sant'Andrea al Quirinale, Via del Quirinale: closed 12.00–6.00 and on Tuesdays.

San Clemente, Via di San Giovanni in Laterano: 9.00–12.00, 3.30–6.30.

Santa Francesca Romana, Foro Romano: 9.30–12.30, 3.30–6.30.

San Giovanni in Laterano, Piazza San Giovanni in Laterano: basilica 7.00–7.00; cloisters 9.00–12.00, 3.00–6.00; baptistry 8.00–12.00, 3.00–6.00; Scala Santa 6.00–12.00, 2.30–7.00.

Santi Giovanni e Paolo, Piazza Santi Giovanni e Paolo: 8.30–11.30, 3.30–6.00, closed Sunday morning.

Sant'Ivo alla Sapienza: Via degli Staderari: Sunday 10.00–11.00, or ask porter.

Santa Maria in Cosmedin, Piazza Santa Maria in Cosmedin 9.00–12.00, 3.00–5.00.

Sepolcro degli Scipione, Via di Porta San Sebastiano: Tuesday to Saturday 9.00–1.30; also Tuesday, Thursday and Saturday 4.00–7.00.

Sistine Chapel, see Vatican Museums.

Tomb of Cecilia Metella, Via Appia Antica: Tuesday to Saturday 9.00–1.30, 2.00–7.00; Sunday and Monday 9.00–1.00.

Trajan's Market, Via Quattro Novembre: Tuesday to Saturday 9.00–1.30; also Tuesday, Thursday and Saturday 4.00–7.00; Sunday 9.00–1.00.

Villas:

Borghese, Viale dell'Uccelliera: Tuesday to Saturday 9.00–2.00; Sunday 9.00–1.00.

Farnesina, Via della Lungara: Monday to Saturday 9.00–1.00.

Giulia, see Etruscan Museum.

Glossary of Terms

....

Ambo (pl. Ambones) Pulpit or reading desk in early Christian church.

Apse Projecting part of church, usually semicircular and vaulted, at end of choir, aisles or nave.

Atlantes Male figures or half-figures used to support an ENTABLATURE.

Baldacchino Ornamental canopy on columns, projecting from wall or suspened from roof over an altar, throne or tomb.

Baroque Artistic and architectural style prevalent in the seventeenth and eighteenth centuries, characterized by exaggerated windows, columns, mouldings, etc., in a desire to break up the surface of the wall. In painting it was the style of the Counter-Reformation, and meant to appeal to the viewer's emotions.

Basilica Rectangular building with colonnades and semicircular APSE, originally for public assembly, later for Christian worship.

Caryatid Draped female figure used to support an ENTABLATURE.

Catacomb Subterranean cemetery with galleries and recesses for tombs.

Censor One of two magistrates in early Rome who drew up the census and supervised public morals and conduct, and assessed property for taxes.

Columbarium Subterranean sepulchre with compartments for urns containing the ashes of the deceased.

Column Cylindrical or tapering pillar, usually consisting of a base, shaft and capital, supporting an ENTABLATURE, or standing alone as a monument.

Composite Order Roman order of architecture, combining CORINTHIAN and IONIC features.

Confessio Open space sunk in the floor of a church representing the tomb of a martyr.

Console Wall projection, forming a bracket or corbel, used for support.

Consul One of two annually elected magistrates exercising supreme authority in the Roman republic.

Corinthian Order The lightest, most slender and most ornate of the Greek architectural orders, featuring a fluted column and an upturned bell-shaped capital adorned with acanthus leaves.

Curia Roman tribal subdivision, later applied to division of people or senate; the senate house. Also the authorities and functionaries of the papal court.

Doric Order Oldest and simplest of Greek architectural orders, with a fluted, baseless shaft and a moulded capital.

Entablature Flat architectural member supported on a colonnade, on which the roof rests.

Fresco Method of painting on plastered wall, ceiling, etc. In *fresco verro*, the paint is applied while the plaster is still wet, so that the colours are absorbed into it and do not fade. The colours are applied to dry plaster in *fresco secco*, and so are more fugitive.

Gothic Architectural style widespread in western Europe from the late twelfth to early sixteenth century, notable for the use of pointed arches, rib vaults and flying buttresses.

Greek cross   Cross with upright and transverse arms of equal length, intersecting at mid-point

Ionic Order   Light, graceful Greek architectural order with slender proportions and spiral volutes on the corners of the capitals.

Latin cross   Cross with long upright and shorter transverse arms, intersecting above mid-point.

Lictor   Roman officer, bearing fasces insignia, attending a magistrate and responsible for apprehending and punishing criminals.

Mannerism   European art style prevalent from about 1520, noted for its spatial incongruity and elongation of human forms to render them more graceful than would the correct proportions.

Pilaster   Square or rectangular pillar projecting from a wall. Like COLUMNS, pilasters are the architectural orders and carry ENTABLATURES. Because they are attached to the wall, they have little practical architectural function.

Putto (pl. putti)   Representation of child or youth, used from the Renaissance on in painting and sculpture.

Renaissance   Italian revival of classically inspired art, which took root in the fourteenth century and spread to the rest of western Europe; European style of art and architecture characteristic of this period, conventionally distinguished as Early, High and Late Renaissance.

Rococo   Ornate, often fanciful, style of decoration and architecture originating in France, prevalent in the eighteenth century.

Romanesque   Style of architecture and painting, prevalent in Italy and western Europe from the tenth to the thirteenth centuries, featuring round arches, barrel and groin vaults, decorative arcades and profuse carved ornament.

Senate   Supreme governing council of ancient Roman republic and empire, with varying membership and functions.

Stucco   Very fine plaster used for decoration of walls, ceilings, etc.

Tribune   Roman official, especially one appointed to protect the rights of the plebeians from the patricians.

Tuscan Order   Roman architectural order, simple and plain in style.

Vault   Method of spanning a larger space than might be possible with a flat ceiling, as the arch can carry more weight and spreads the downward thrust of this weight more evenly through the walls.

Further Reading

....

Bentley, James, *Italy: The Hilltowns*, George Philip, London, 1990

Cellini, Benvenuto, *The Life of Benvenuto Cellini, written by himself*, English translation, Phaidon Press, London 1949. (Penguin Classics edition, Harmondsworth, 1956)

Dudley, D. R., *Urbs Roma; a sourcebook of classical texts on the city and its monuments*, Phaidon Press, London, 1967

Fauré, Gabriel, *Rome*, English translation, The Medici Society, London 1926

Gibbon, Edward, *The History of the Decline and Fall of the Roman Empire*, six volumes 1776–88. (Penguin Classics edition, Harmonsworth, 1985)

Goethe, J. W. von, *Italian Journey*, English translation, 1900

Hartt, Frederick, *Michelangelo*, Thames and Hudson, London 1965

Hibbert, Christopher, *Rome, the Biography of a City*, Penguin Books Ltd, Harmondsworth 1985

Hobhouse, Penelope; Taylor, Patrick and Johnson, Hugh, *The Gardens of Europe*, George Philip, London 1990

James, Henry, *Italian Hours*, The Grove Press, New York 1989

Livy (Titus Livius), *The History of Rome from its Foundation*, English translation in four volumes: *The Early History of Rome, Rome and Italy, The War with Hannibal* and *Rome and the Mediterranean*, Penguin Books Limited, Harmondsworth

Marino, Laura, ed. *The Museums of Rome*, Edizioni Latium, Rome 1987

Sharp, Mary, *A Traveller's Guide to the Churches of Rome*, Hugh Evelyn, 1967

Stendhal (Marie Henri Beyle), *A Roman Journal*, English translation Orion Press, 1989

Vasari, Giorgio, *The Lives of the Painters, Sculptors, and Architects*, English translation J. M. Dent and Sons Ltd, London, 1963

Index

....

References to illustrations appear in italics, after the text references